D1556922

CHALLENGES
IN HEALTH CARE
MANAGEMENT

John D. Blair
Myron D. Fottler

with the assistance of
Grant T. Savage and Carlton J. Whitehead

CHALLENGES IN HEALTH CARE MANAGEMENT

Strategic Perspectives for Managing Key Stakeholders

 Jossey-Bass Publishers

San Francisco • Oxford • 1990

CHALLENGES IN HEALTH CARE MANAGEMENT
Strategic Perspectives for Managing Key Stakeholders
by John D. Blair and Myron D. Fottler

Copyright © 1990 by: Jossey-Bass Inc., Publishers
350 Sansome Street
San Francisco, California 94014
&
Jossey-Bass Limited
Headington Hill Hall
Oxford OX3 0BW

Library of Congress Cataloging-in-Publication Data

Blair, John D. (John David), date.
    Challenges in health care management : strategic perspectives for
managing key stakeholders / John D. Blair, Myron D. Fottler with the
assistance of Grant T. Savage and Carlton J. Whitehead.
        p.   cm.—(The Jossey-Bass health series)
    (The Jossey-Bass management series)
    Includes bibliographical references and index.
    ISBN 1-55542-288-8
    1. Health facilities—Business management.   2. Health facilities—
Administration. I. Fottler, Myron D. II. Title. III. Series.
RA971.3.B52   1990
362.1′1′0681—dc20   90-41826
                                                                                    CIP

Manufactured in the United States of America

The paper in this book meets the guidelines for
permanence and durability of the Committee on
Production Guidelines for Book Longevity of the
Council on Library Resources.

JACKET DESIGN BY WILLI BAUM

FIRST EDITION

Code 9091

A *joint publication in*
The Jossey-Bass Health Series *and*
The Jossey-Bass Management Series

Contents

Preface

In the health care industry, as in industry in general, the implementation of business strategy has been problematic. While strategy formulation has become more formalized, systematic, and sophisticated over the past decade, the resulting strategic plans often are left in file drawers. They do not drive the day-to-day activities of managers or other organizational participants. The meetings, telephone calls, and other management activities that regularly occur at the operational level are detached from any strategic considerations, and strategic goals are not reinforced. Strategic goals are either not attained or only partially attained.

The gap between strategic decisions and the operational activities found in practice is also mirrored in the management literature. The literature of strategic management and of organizational theory focuses on the relationship between the organization and its external environment, while the literature of organizational behavior and of operations management focuses on internal management behaviors and processes. Consequently, there is no literature that focuses on the *integration* of the macro and micro perspectives of management.

Our book offers the reader a way to better integrate the strategic and operational levels so that each reinforces the other. We feel that management activity at the middle (meso) level of analysis has been neglected. In particular, we believe that the management of key stakeholders is crucial to attainment of the organization's strategic objectives. *Stakeholders* are those individuals and groups who have an interest in and are influenced by the organization. Since not all stakeholders are equally important to the organization or to a particular manager, each manager needs to focus on and strategically manage *key* (rather than *marginal*) stakeholders. Which stakeholders are key depends on the nature of the decision (that is, the issue under consideration) and the value of a particular stakeholder's actual or potential contributions to the organization. Such contributions can be economic or noneconomic.

Although numerous articles and a few books have been written on various aspects of stakeholder management, no single volume has provided a foundation of knowledge regarding both the theoretical and the applied aspects of stakeholder management. None of the current literature has been applied to the health care industry. To this point, stakeholder management has been done intuitively or has been picked up in the school of hard knocks. A systematic approach concerning how to identify, assess, diagnose, and manage key stakeholders through various generic strategies and specific tactics tied to the organization's strategic objectives has not been developed in the literature.

Edward Freeman's book *Strategic Management: A Stakeholder Approach* (1984) provided many of the initial theoretical underpinnings of this book. In *Challenges in Health Care Management,* we have extended existing theory through the development of new concepts and then applied these concepts to the health care industry. We have also provided much more detail than the existing literature contributes about how health care executives might apply the stakeholder approach to integrate their day-to-day activities with their organizations' strategic objectives. The book draws on existing case studies, more than thirty in-depth interviews with senior health care executives, and a survey questionnaire to determine current practices regarding the management of stakeholders.

We present an analytical framework and detailed procedures for applying the stakeholder management concept.

Throughout the book, we integrate the theoretical and practical aspects of stakeholder management and thereby help close the gap between the macro and micro perspectives in management theory. By discussing the special techniques and specific applications of stakeholder management, our book helps readers understand and put into practice those skills necessary for the effective management of key stakeholders in a way that reinforces the strategic goals of the organization. By emphasizing the necessity of managing stakeholders ethically and of viewing stakeholder management as a dynamic process, this book also contributes to the professionalization of health care management.

Who Should Read This Book

We have written this book for several audiences. First and foremost are the health care executives in a variety of organizations who are on the "firing line," trying to manage their stakeholders effectively without much guidance from the literature. We believe that stakeholder management is what health care managers actually *do* more or less strategically and with more or less success. They try to determine which stakeholders are important on a particular issue at a particular time and then try to keep those stakeholders at least minimally satisfied with the inducements offered by the organization. In this way, managers ensure that the necessary stakeholder contributions will continue to flow to the organization.

Second, strategic management and health care management academicians should find this book of interest, since it provides a new theoretical perspective on what the strategic management of organizations is and offers new insights into what health care executives do. It also closes the gap between macro and micro theories regarding managerial behavior. The arguments in the book are intuitively compelling and buttressed by numerous case studies, anecdotes, and quotations from health care executives. Consequently, the book could be used as a basis for future academic research on stakeholder management, as some of the relationships we found through

qualitative evidence could be tested systematically and empirically. It could also be used as a supplement to a standard text
in organizational theory, strategic management, or health care
systems.

Third, the book should be of interest to board members,
physicians, and other health professionals who are interested
in better management of health care organizations. The stakeholder management process, outlined in Part Two, can be used
by anyone who works with stakeholders in any part of the health
care system.

Fourth, managers in non–health care institutions should
find the book of interest. While the cases and anecdotal evidence are drawn from health care examples, the process described in Part Two is general. Stakeholder identification, assessment, diagnosis, negotiation, and management are processes
applicable to any industry. The stakeholder management resource sections at the ends of Chapters Three, Four, and Five
provide forms to fill out that can assist managers attempting to
apply stakeholder management processes to any industry.

Overview of the Contents

The first two chapters introduce the reader to the concepts applicable to strategic stakeholder management in health
care organizations. In Chapter One, we define and illustrate
concepts such as stakeholder, key stakeholder, different levels
of strategy, inducements, contributions, disinducements, discontributions, and the strategic stakeholder management process. We also discuss the increasing number, significance, and
lack of supportiveness of health care stakeholders and present
case studies of the effects of stakeholder (mis)management.
Chapter Two further examines the theoretical underpinnings
of strategic stakeholder management by defining, assessing, and
illustrating the middle (meso) level *of analysis* (not middle management *in the organization*), where stakeholder management
integrates the strategic and operational activities of managers.
We argue in Chapter Two that strategic stakeholder management translates environmental forces into groups and organi-

zations holding stakes in the organization's decisions and actions. Managing those stakeholders (and interactions with their representatives) strategically allows the manager and the scholar to link macro and micro realities.

The next three chapters describe the generic processes involved in managing stakeholders. Chapter Three describes the process of assessing organizational stakeholders and concludes with a resource section to assist managers in implementing the assessment process described. Chapter Four describes the four generic stakeholder management strategies (involve, collaborate with, defend against, and monitor) that apply to supportive, "mixed-blessing," nonsupportive, and marginal stakeholders. It also describes an overarching strategy for moving stakeholders from less supportive to more supportive categories. In this chapter, we provide a case study and discuss assignment of managerial responsibility for various stakeholders. Chapter Five describes the generic process of negotiation with various types of stakeholders to achieve at least minimal levels of positive relations with them *and* positive outcomes. Each of these three chapters provides a resource consisting of standardized forms that helps practitioners to apply the concepts to their own organizations.

The last four chapters discuss specific strategies and tactics that illustrate how to apply the generic strategies for managing particular stakeholders. Chapter Six discusses strategies and tactics for managing physician stakeholders that require different degrees of commitment of time and resources from physicians and hospitals. We also present the physician's perspective, since we believe that a manager must understand the stakeholder's perspective to manage the stakeholder effectively. Chapter Seven explores one type of hospital-physician collaboration—the joint venture. We illustrate the subtleties of achieving both financial and collaborative success in joint ventures and provide strategies for attaining at least limited success in them. Chapter Eight discusses what health care executives can do to involve their internal stakeholders more effectively in achieving their organizations' strategic objectives. We outline and detail steps for implementing this involvement strategy. Finally, Chapter Nine summarizes the book's line of argument and provides some ethical guidelines for implementing stakeholder management strategically.

Since the book discusses both theoretical and practical concerns, different chapters will be of greater interest to some readers than to others. For the academic community, Chapters One, Two, and Nine will be of special interest. The other chapters provide more detailed concepts and strategies, with management applications and examples. For practicing health care executives, Chapters Three through Eight will be of particular interest, since they focus on *how to apply* strategic stakeholder management concepts.

Acknowledgments

Many people have contributed their energy and expertise to this book. In particular, Grant T. Savage and Carlton J. Whitehead from Texas Tech University have contributed many ideas for many chapters in this book and are listed with us on the author page for their assistance.

Grant Savage, associate professor of management at the College of Business Administration and of health organization management at the School of Medicine, significantly influenced the development of the strategic negotiation concepts in Chapter Five and the joint venture diagnosis and strategy approaches in Chapter Seven.

Carlton Whitehead is professor and coordinator of management at the College of Business Administration, professor of health organization management at the School of Medicine, and director of the Program in Organizational Design and Strategic Management at the Institute for Management and Leadership Research. His most important contributions in Chapter Four were on diagnosing key stakeholders and developing and implementing generic strategies for them; in Chapter Five they were on developing the approach to negotiation.

Other faculty who provided intellectual support are John Buesseler and Susan Stanton from the School of Medicine and Mark Peterson, Robert Phillips, and Ritch Sorenson from the

Institute for Management and Leadership Research in the College of Business Administration. Catherine Duran and Timothy Nix, doctoral students in management at Texas Tech University, Susan Dymond, a fellow in health organization management, and Charles Slaton, vice-pres. of Santa Rosa Memorial Hospital, have also made major contributions as research assistants and colleagues. Sharon Topping, a doctoral student in health services administration at the University of Alabama, Birmingham, provided helpful input and review.

Alis Valencia, former editor of the health series at Jossey-Bass, was instrumental in the development of this book. Her suggestions had an important influence in shaping the organization and style of the book to appeal to multiple audiences. Rebecca L. McGovern, the present editor of this series, helped us with the final revisions. She also found three excellent outside reviewers whose critical comments and detailed suggestions challenged our thinking and helped us refine the manuscript. Both editors worked with us very closely to ensure that we provided the very best writing we could.

Throughout the book, we quote various health care executives from the Northeast, Southeast, and Southwest who were interviewed for the project. We conducted interviews that lasted from one-half hour to four hours with approximately thirty top-level and middle-level executives and conducted multiple interviews in some cases. We greatly appreciate the willingness of these busy health care executives to give freely of their time. Without their insights and candor, this book would not have been possible.

We also appreciate the support of administrative officials at Texas Tech University and the University of Alabama, Birmingham. At Texas Tech University, we are particularly indebted to Robert Phillips, director of the Institute for Management and Leadership, Carl Stem, dean of the College of Business Administration, and Carlton J. Whitehead, coordinator of the management area. At the University of Alabama, special thanks are also due to Charles J. Austin, chair of the Department of Health Services Administration, Keith Blayney, dean of the School of Health-Related Professions, and Gene

Newport, dean of the School of Business, for providing a conducive work environment that allowed the book to be completed.

Diane Hyche, Martha Posey, and Marilyn Thompson of the University of Alabama, Birmingham, provided typing of various drafts of the chapters, administrative support, and assistance for the project. Without their help and that of the graduate students mentioned above, we could not have fulfilled our other responsibilities.

We conclude with a special note of thanks to our wives, Starr and Carol, for support of this research-and-publication endeavor. Their understanding of the time required for this activity, as well as their patience, is truly appreciated.

John D. Blair
Lubbock, Texas

August 1990

Myron D. Fottler
Birmingham, Alabama

The Authors

John D. Blair is professor of management in the College of Business Administration at Texas Tech University. He is also associate chairman of the Health Organization Management Department in the School of Medicine at the Texas Tech University Health Services Center and director of the program in health organization management at the Institute of Management and Leadership Research at Texas Tech University. He received his B.A. degree (1966) from Gustavus Adolphus College in sociology and his M.A. (1972) and Ph.D. (1975) degrees from the University of Michigan in sociology. His graduate specializations were in social organization, complex organizations, and military sociology.

Blair is currently program chair of the Health Care Administration Division of the Academy of Management and is fellow and council member of the Inter-University Seminar on Armed Forces and Society. His primary research interests have been in the effective management of health care organizations facing environmental turbulence. His specific focus has been on integrating strategic management and organizational behavior issues and research through the stakeholder approach. The work of Blair and his colleagues in this area has appeared in *Hospital and Health Services Administration, Health Care Management Review,* and *The Physician Executive Journal of Management.* Blair was formerly associate editor of the *Journal of Man-*

agement and is one of the two founding editors of the *Yearly
Review of Management.* He is currently associate editor of *Armed
Forces and Society,* is on the editorial board of the *National Journal of Sociology,* and is a frequent reviewer for other journals
such as *Hospital and Health Services Administration.*

Blair's research for a decade (1975–1984) focused on
changes in military organizations and organizational responses
to turbulent and changing environments. He has published extensively on these and related topics. His previous books include *The All-Volunteer Force* (1977, with J. Bachman and D. R.
Segal) and *Leadership on the Future Battlefield* (1985, edited with
J. G. Hunt). From 1985–1989, he was a member of the board
of governors of the Southern Management Association.

Myron D. Fottler is professor of management and director of the Ph.D. program in administration-health services with
a joint appointment in the School of Business and the Department of Health Services Administration in the School of Health-
Related Professions at the University of Alabama, Birmingham. He received his B.S. degree (1962) from Northeastern
University in industrial relations, his M.B.A. degree (1963) from
Boston University in human relations, and his Ph.D. degree
(1970) from the Graduate School of Business at Columbia University in business, with concentrations in management and industrial relations.

Fottler is a frequent presenter at academic meetings and
currently serves on the editorial review boards of *Health Care
Management Review* and *Journal of Behavioral Economics.* His main
interests in recent years have included the integration of business strategy and human resources, health care job design,
managed care, stakeholder management, and the impact of
prospective payment in hospitals. He has published extensively
in these and related areas in most of the major management
and health care journals. His books include *Manpower Substitu-
tion in the Hospital Industry* (1972), *Prospective Payment* (1985, with
H. L. Smith), *Applications in Personnel/Human Resources Management* (1988, with S. M. Nkomo and R. B. McAfee), and *Strategic
Management of Human Resources in Health Services Organizations*
(1988, with S. R. Hernandez and C. L. Joiner).

Fottler has been a visiting lecturer at several universities and has served as a reviewer for many of the major health care and management journals as well as for various book publishers, such as Jossey-Bass and Health Administration Press. He is a past program chair and past division chair of the Health Care Administration Division of the Academy of Management. He has also served as a site visitor for the Accrediting Commission for Graduate Education in Health Services Administration.

CHALLENGES IN HEALTH CARE MANAGEMENT

░░░

CHAPTER I

Managing Health Care Stakeholders

Managers of health care organizations, as well as most other types of organizations, have been plagued by an environment that is increasing in complexity and turbulence. Organizations have made many attempts to cope with this environment. Perhaps the ideal organization to manage would be one that operated as a system isolated or closed from the environment. This ideal organization would allow managers to have complete control because no uncertainty would exist. However, reality is pushing us further from this ideal, no matter how much we prefer to cling to the thought that there are ways to protect ourselves from this often hostile atmosphere. In fact, ways to buffer organizations from the environment are appealing but elusive management tools.

Since these issues of environmental complexity and turbulence are often thought of as fundamental to organizational survival, strategic management approaches have emerged that attempt to provide overarching strategies to achieve and sustain a competitive advantage in the marketplace in different industries (for example, Miles and Snow, 1978; Porter, 1980, 1985) as well as specific tactics and operational planning to implement these strategies (for example, Quinn, 1980; Hrebiniak and Joyce, 1984; Morrisey, Below, and Acomb, 1987). Strategic management has also become of great concern to health care executives and scholars who research health care organizations

1

(for example, Shortell, Morrison, and Robbins, 1985; Smith and Reid, 1986; Luke and Begun, 1988, Shortell, Morrison, and Friedman, 1990). An ever-increasing body of academic and manager-oriented literature is evidence that researchers and practitioners are continually searching for more efficient and effective strategic management theories and techniques.

In this book we develop and describe in detail what we call *strategic stakeholder management.* We will be looking at a set of concepts related to but not the same as strategic management. Our approach deals with those who hold stakes in different organizations and how they can be managed. Here we will also use the word *strategy.* In so doing, we refer to management actions that deliberately or even inadvertently impact on the nature of the relationships between the organization and its stakeholders.

The strategic management literature recognizes different types of strategy: *corporate* strategy, which focuses on what businesses, industry segments, or markets the organization should be in, and *competitive or strategic business unit strategy,* which directs organizational resources toward how to compete in that particular business, industry segment, or market.

For simplicity throughout this book, we will refer to *competitive strategy,* by which we mean the organization's overall business-oriented strategy as opposed to other types of strategy, such as stakeholder and negotiation strategies discussed in Chapter Two. Our use of *competitive strategy* will incorporate both broad corporate strategy and more specific strategic business unit strategy.

Competitive strategy may be *planned.* Planned strategy may be explicitly articulated, for example, in a formal strategic plan that resulted from a strategic management retreat by senior executives or as developed by a planning staff. Alternatively, competitive strategy may be *emergent,* that is, resulting from actions by managers and others in the organization that have the same impact operationally without an explicit strategy ever being formulated—or despite the planned and pronounced strategy and perhaps in opposition to it (see, for example, Murray, 1978; Quinn, 1980; Shortell, Morrison, and

Robbins, 1985; Mintzberg, 1988a, 1988b). This distinction between planned and emergent strategy is similar and quite parallel to the contrast used in strategic management between synoptic (preplanned, comprehensive, rational decision making) and incremental (less comprehensive and more opportunistic) (see, for example, Fredrickson, 1984; Shortell, Morrison, and Robbins, 1985).

The strategic stakeholder management process that we describe throughout this book represents a new and potentially more valid approach to the management of health care organizations than what has existed in the past. It is more consistent with what good managers actually *do* on a day-to-day basis. For them, this process is typically intuitive and learned by trial and error over time through many, often painful, experiences. In this book we articulate a systematic way to think about these processes with stakeholder strategy formulation and implementation in mind but without—we hope—all the bumps many managers have taken in learning the hard way. Based on our field research with practicing managers and the theory that we have developed, we provide a set of models, strategies, and techniques that permit other managers to approach this daily challenge proactively.

The primary purpose of strategic stakeholder management is to transform the complex relationships that exist in and between organizations and the external environment into a logical, systematical framework that can be communicated and acted on. Instead of searching for ways to close the organization away from the environment or to buffer the organization from the environment, it instead seeks to manage relationships with the environment. Thus managers seek to promote proactively the integration of the organization with the environment as a strategic management tool. Stakeholders are an integral part of this management technique because they represent those aspects or pieces of the relevant environment that are potentially beneficial or threatening to the organization.

These stakeholders may be selected by management and invited to become stakeholders. However, more often these stakeholders exist independently of managerial choice. In other words, those individuals, groups, and organizations that hold a stake in the organization are there—by definition. Whether managers like it or not, they are stakeholders.

Thus, stakeholders and their management are highly relevant to overall strategic management, and approaching stakeholder management strategically is, we argue, a key component in achieving competitive success. We will discuss the competitive impact of stakeholders and the specific linkages between stakeholder management and strategic management at length in Chapter Two.

Stakeholder management is becoming an important approach to conceptualizing and performing the management role in all organizations (see, Mason and Mitroff, 1981; Freeman, 1984; Carroll, 1989). The organizational stakeholder concept is also becoming increasingly significant to the analysis of the forces affecting health care organizations and their managers. Elsewhere, our colleagues and we have examined a variety of stakeholder management issues (Fottler, 1987; Blair and Whitehead, 1988; Blair, Savage, and Whitehead, 1989; Whitehead and others, 1989; Fottler and others, 1989; Blair, Slaton, and Savage, 1990). *Health care stakeholders have a vested interest in the organization. More specifically, they are the individuals, groups, and organizations who (1) have a stake in the decisions and actions of the organization and (2) may attempt to influence those decisions and actions* (Fottler, 1987; Blair and Whitehead, 1988).

Here we integrate and elaborate on the existing pieces of the stakeholder management process—from a strategic perspective. Strategic stakeholder management integrates in a systematic way what managers often deal with separately: strategic management, marketing, human resource management, public relations, organizational politics, and social responsibility. It focuses attention on managing stakeholders both internal and external to the organization. To illustrate, a hospital might manage patient or physician relationships to increase utilization or collaborate with competing hospitals to minimize costly technology duplication.

Strategic stakeholder management involves the management of all stakeholders (internal or external to the organization) who can or may impact the formulation, implementation, or success of the organization's competitive strategy. In essence, the strategic stakeholder management approach extends the traditional management paradigm, focused on internal participants and on suppliers and buyers as external stakeholders, to include a wide variety of other external stakeholders. This approach is especially significant when stakeholders are active and organization-stakeholder interdependence is high (as is generally the case with health care organizations). Under these circumstances, the ability to manage relationships with key stakeholders particularly affects organizational performance.

The paradigm of stakeholder management as a strategic activity is still in the formulation and theory development stage, and its application to health care organizations is growing. Nonetheless, until recently middle-range theorizing has been missing. Such theories of the middle range (Merton, 1957) permit both the researcher and the health care executive to go from the interesting but broad and abstract notion that stakeholders are important to the successful management of the health care organization to a conceptually informed and organized way to understand and systematically manage stakeholders. For example, we will specify the process of assessing stakeholders and determining the most important or key stakeholders, examine the important diagnostic dimensions that can be applied to stakeholders, and suggest the most appropriate strategies to manage different types of stakeholders. In addition, we will show how to integrate business, stakeholder management, and negotiation strategies. In other words, throughout this book we attempt to develop and extend those middle-range concepts of health care stakeholder management.

Managers in organizations might argue that the concept of stakeholders represents nothing new, since managers must deal with such individuals or groups regularly. In this book we argue that the benefit of strategic stakeholder management is its potential to organize and manage these complex relationships systematically in alignment with the strategies of the organization so that the maximum benefits and minimum damage from these relationships can be obtained. When stakeholder management is properly performed, it becomes almost invisible. The involved stakeholder is content with the relationship that exists with the organization. Contributions are maximized with minimum inducements, and the stakeholder has no reason to threaten or harm the organization.

The specific issues and topics to be addressed in this chapter include:

- The consequences of stakeholder mismanagement
- An approach to managing stakeholders *strategically*
- The increasing significance of stakeholder relationships for health care organizations
- Implications of several case studies of who (should have) mattered to organizations and why
- The stakeholder bottom line for organizations: their potential to threaten or cooperate with the organization
- The potentially threatening or cooperative exchanges inherent in organization-stakeholder relationships leading to stakeholder equilibrium or disequilibrium
- An overview of the stakeholder management process as developed in this book

Consequences of Stakeholder Mismanagement

The importance of the strategic stakeholder management approach we develop in this book can be emphasized by examining the consequences of stakeholder *mismanagement.* Stakeholder mismanagement may be viewed as (1) the absence of stakeholder management, (2) incompetence in managing the complex relationships, or (3) unethical attempts to manipulate those who have a legitimate stake in the organization's actions. Mismanagement of even one powerful stakeholder may have dire consequences for the organization. Health care executives recognize the importance that key admitting physicians have for their organizations and realize that any managerial action must be viewed in light of its effect on these key physicians. Despite this obvious fact, managers of health care organizations continually misjudge the consequences of their actions on key stakeholders. What can go wrong? We present here reported examples of stakeholder mismanagement by a large group medical practice and a hospital corporation.

Failure to recognize and manage stakeholder relationships may determine the success or failure of a health care organization, as recently experienced by Ohio's not-for-profit Cleveland Clinic when it decided to open an outpatient clinic in south Florida. The proposed clinic was to be a joint venture with the North Broward Hospital District. The clinic was to be built adjacent to Broward General Medical Center, and the center would provide surgical and other major services. However, local physicians perceived the proposed clinic as a threat and objected to it.

Cleveland Clinic was thus forced to develop plans to build its own hospital. Once again physicians and area hospital administrators objected, banded together, and lobbied to prevent a certificate of need from being issued by the state government. When the chief executive of the clinic's Florida organization, a surgeon who has performed four thousand open-heart surgeries, tried to gain hospital privileges at Broward General Medical Center, he was denied on the grounds that, among other things, he lacked enough emergency room experience. When some patients wanted to consult with the clinic, local physicians gave the patients their medical charts and told them not to come back. The bottom line was that both the area physicians and hospitals viewed the proposed clinic and hospital as threats to their patient base.

Because of political pressure the hospital district's board eventually signed a contract to permit the clinic to use Broward General. However, because of the contract, local physicians diverted patients to other hospitals, costing Broward General $3.5 million in revenues. The clinic says it may ultimately have to buy an existing hospital. Meanwhile, the vast majority of patients that come to the clinic are self-referred, prompting the clinic to add a general medical practice (Winslow, 1989).

Cleveland Clinic saw the south Florida market as way to

Figure 1. Key Stakeholders for Cleveland Clinic.

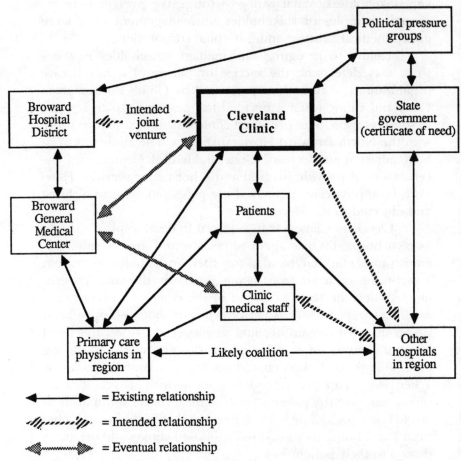

Source: information extracted from Winslow, 1989.

expand its organization. The area's population was growing and contained a large number of retirees who had the resources to pay for medical treatment. Cleveland Clinic did not foresee the potential threat that local physicians and administrators posed. The stakeholder map for Cleveland Clinic presented in Figure 1 shows how local physicians and hospital administrators were in competition for patients in the south Florida market. Proper stakeholder analysis as developed throughout this book would have shown that a coalition would be likely to develop between physicians and hospital administrators. The physicians were a powerful group of stakeholders because they were able to control the flow of patients, the most valuable resource for Cleveland Clinic or any other health care organization. The other hospitals were powerful because they could punish the hospital district by denying funded referrals to its hospital.

The Cleveland Clinic case reflects mismanagement of stakeholders by (1) failing to appreciate which other groups or organizations also have stakes in the clinic's actions and (2) having no effective strategies to manage such stakeholders' likely defensive reactions. In its proposed expansion to south Florida, the clinic should have identified the key stakeholders; assessed these stakeholders in terms of their perceptions, values, sources of power, and likely reaction to their new "competitor;" planned managerial strategies to provide inducements for these stakeholders not to oppose Cleveland Clinic's entering into this market; and been prepared to respond quickly and flexibly to unanticipated actions of the key stakeholders. Future chapters of this book will describe such management processes in detail.

Approaching Stakeholder Management Strategically

Having considered a brief example of the costly consequences of stakeholder mismanagement, what, in contrast, are some of the specific implications of the strategic stakeholder management approach that we will detail throughout this book?

Ensures Systematic Analysis of Organizational Stakeholders

- All stakeholders are identified. Identification ensures that the lack of obvious importance of particular stakeholders to the organization does not keep managers from recognizing their stakes in the organization.
- All stakeholders are assessed in terms of core values and power. Assessment is important so that stakeholder reactions can be anticipated and managed.

- Assumptions about stakeholders are surfaced. In the process, differences in assumptions by different managers are
identified, and sensitivity to issue-specific stakeholder reactions is increased. In addition, "hot buttons" that will activate stakeholders are understood.
- Only key stakeholders, not all possible stakeholders, receive
management attention. The other "marginal" stakeholders
are merely monitored. The assessment process prevents excessive use of management time and energy or other organizational resources on marginal stakeholders by focusing
management attention on crucial stakeholder relationships.
- Stakeholder groups can be segmented into more specific
subgroups. This is particularly relevant for issue-specific reactions where, for example, there are considerably different
stakes and perspectives among different segments of the
medical staff or among different third-party payers.
- All stakeholders are diagnosed in terms of potential for
threat; sources of threat are identified and monitored. The
stakeholders are also diagnosed in terms of potential for cooperation; sources of cooperation are identified and enhanced.

Enhances Organizational Strategy

- Different types of organizational strategy become better integrated. In Chapter Two, we will discuss the stakeholder
management approach as a meso level of analysis and management planning that permits the systematic linkage of three
key strategies: (1) the organization's strategy to *compete in the
marketplace;* (2) the organization's strategy to *manage its stakeholders;* and (3) the individual manager's strategy *to interact
with stakeholder representatives,* such as in negotiating a cooperative agreement or a managed care contract.
- Competitive strategy formulation is improved through anticipation of stakeholder reactions and solicitation of stakeholder input.
- Competitive strategy implementation is improved through
anticipation of stakeholder reactions and gaining of stakeholder commitment.

- Generic strategies are available to manage stakeholders so that their potential for threat is systematically reduced and their potential for cooperation is systematically enhanced.
- Generic strategies are available to better manage various interactions such as negotiations with representatives of stakeholders so that relationship outcomes are enhanced and substantive outcomes are improved.

Allows Much More Proactive Responses to Stakeholders

- The bottom line of stakeholder management is that it encourages managing relationships with stakeholders strategically and proactively, not just reacting to their demands.
- The organization systematically shares stakeholder information, perspectives, and strategies among all organizational managers who have dealings with stakeholder representatives so that they can manage on a daily basis consistent with organizational goals and strategy.

Increasing Significance of Health Care Stakeholders

In Figure 2 we present a simplified map of the stakeholders facing the typical hospital in the late 1950s. Competition then was less intense and sometimes even nonexistent, Medicare and Medicaid had not yet been passed, most hospitals were freestanding, regulation at all levels was low, health management organizations (HMOs) and preferred provider organizations (PPOs) were virtually nonexistent, physicians were the dominant stakeholders, nonprofit health institutions were self-funding, patient supportiveness was taken for granted, labor unions represented few employees, horizontal and vertical integration was rare, employers were unconcerned about employee health costs, boards were passive, philanthropy and direct private-pay patients were the norm, and third-party reimbursement was not very important. Most of the relationships between the hospital and its stakeholders were generally positive and supportive, as noted in Figure 2.

In contrast, Figure 3 illustrates how complex the typical hospital's stakeholder map has become in the early 1990s. This

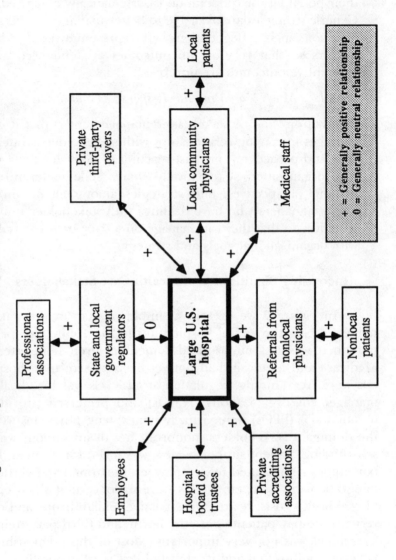

Figure 2. Simplified Stakeholder Map for Large U.S. Hospital in Late 1950s.

Figure 3. Simplified Stakeholder Map for Large U.S. Hospital in 1990s.

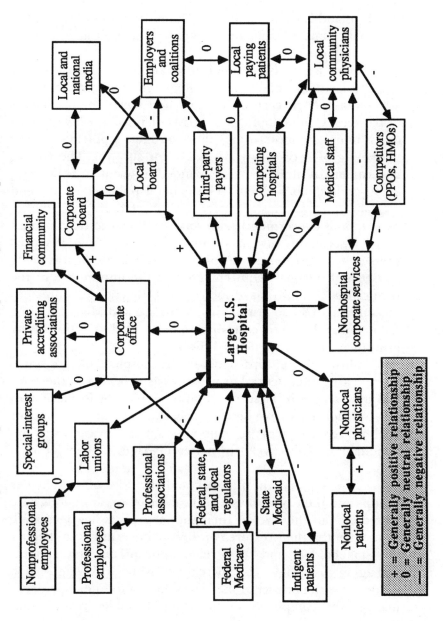

figure reflects our best estimate of hospital-stakeholder relationships and is based on our qualitative synthesis of the health
care policy and management literatures as well as interviews
with health care executives.

Many hospitals are now part of corporate chains that are
both horizontally and vertically integrated. The corporation as
a whole as well as each component unit have separate boards
of trustees. Competition on the basis of price, quality, and access is intense in most product lines. Product segmentation and
marketing of services are necessary for survival. The role of
government at all levels has expanded in terms of both regulation and reimbursement. The general public, patients, and
special-interest groups are more sophisticated and have higher
expectations concerning health services. Pressure from professional associations and labor unions is increasing. Financial
pressures are greater, since cost-based reimbursement is being
phased out. Capital requirements and the importance of the
financial community have increased. Indigent care threatens
the survival of some institutions. Medicare and Medicaid often
fail to cover the direct costs of care, but cost shifting to private
insurance has become more difficult.

Most relationships between the hospital and its stakeholders are either neutral or negative, as indicated by the zeros
and minus signs in Figure 3. A large number of formerly positive relationships have become negative. The implications for
health care executives are ominous—unless they can learn (individually or collectively) to better manage stakeholder relations.

In summary, the number and diversity of stakeholder
groups and their power vis-à-vis health care organizations have
increased, but the level of their supportiveness has decreased.
Consequently, the pressures on hospital executives to identify
key stakeholders and to develop appropriate strategies for
managing them have also increased. In the following section
we describe the impact of managers' failing to understand and
manage the complexity of hospital-stakeholder relationships
today.

Significance of Stakeholders and Their (Mis)Management: Case Studies of Who (Should Have) Mattered and Why

The management of key stakeholders in organizations goes to the heart and soul of the management function itself. It is impossible to manage strategically without actively managing key stakeholders. While health care executives intuitively realize that their real function is to identify, manage, and at least minimally satisfy their key stakeholders (Miles, 1980), this fact is usually not openly acknowledged or analyzed. The result is an emphasis on strategic management, management information systems, or marketing without any explicit consideration of *why* these activities are important in terms of gaining support or cooperation while avoiding threats from key stakeholders. This section will discuss three case studies that illustrate the importance of stakeholder managements in the overall success of health care organizations and programs. The first case concerns the federal government's unsuccessful attempt to provide mass inoculations for swine flu to the U.S. population during the 1970s. Failure to identify and manage the key stakeholders resulted in an unsuccessful program. The second case involves particularly successful attempts by Birmingham, Alabama, hospitals to deal with adverse media publicity. The third case discusses a successful attempt by an academic medical center to induce primary care physicians to refer patients to it.

Unsuccessful Stakeholder Management: Swine Flu Immunization Program. In February 1976 a few cases of swine flu, one of them fatal, appeared among army recruits in Fort Dix, New Jersey. This New Jersey case triggered a countrywide alarm, because the swine flu strain was generally thought responsible for the major lethal pandemic that swept the world in 1918–1919, killing 21.6 million people (more than 1 percent of the world population). Scientists at the National Centers for Disease Control in Atlanta recommended to the Ford administration a mass immunization program (Fottler, 1984).

On March 24, 1976, President Ford dramatically proposed a swine flu immunization program with plans to vaccinate virtually every American. The decision to vaccinate everyone in the United States was based primarily on scientific judgments that a swine flu pandemic could occur at any time. Underlying this discussion were the assumptions that (1) vaccine manufacturers could and would produce enough acceptable vaccine in a short period and (2) the public and private health care system could deliver the vaccine immediately to the entire population.

The overly optimistic nature of these assumptions became apparent once the program was implemented. The drug companies were unable to deliver the 200 million dosages by the October 29 target date. In addition, the enormous task of organizing state, local, and private facilities to deliver vaccine to 215 million Americans could not be accomplished in three months. In July drug manufacturers threatened to halt production and to withhold vaccine already produced since insurance companies were unwilling to write liability insurance covering it. Only after Congress passed legislation allowing claims to be made against the federal government was production resumed. As a result of these delays, project plans required repeated modification, and clinic locations could not be finalized. Publicity plans could not be implemented, and publicity increasingly shifted from promoting the program to responding to adverse and conflicting publicity. Volunteer participation was less than expected. Physicians were reluctant to participate because of the many uncertainties and controversies over program rationale, dosage recommendation, safety, and informed consent requirements. Many clinic sites were inaccessible. Finally, when deaths were linked to the immunization program, many states did not have facts to counter the adverse publicity.

This mismanagement of key stakeholders by the federal government shook the confidence of many Americans, including the leaders of the major corporations. These companies had originally planned to cooperate with federal officials by giving their own employees the immunizations on company premises, which would have saved much time and effort. However, as a result of delays, uncertainty concerning availability and safety of the vaccine, and lack of confidence in the program, the companies decided to curtail their plans for participation. The final death blow to the program came in early December, when more than fifty cases of a rare form of paralysis (French polio) were reported in people who had received shots. On December 16 federal officials suspended the program for what was believed to be a temporary period of time; as it turned out, the suspension was permanent.

The case illustrates a clear-cut failure in stakeholder management by the federal government in general and the Department of Health, Education, and Welfare in particular. The key stakeholders were never identified, much less actively managed. At a minimum, the key stakeholders would include the drug companies that would manufacture the vaccine, insurance companies that would insure the drug companies, employers in general who would provide facilities for employee inoculations, public health departments that would administer the local programs, local physicians who would inoculate the population, and the media that would publicize the program. If such a program is ever attempted again, federal planners should identify and collaborate with all of these key stakeholders *before* any plans are finalized. This collaboration will help to avoid implementation problems later on, *after* immunization has begun. In addition, inducements for participation by the key stakeholders need to be created *before* the program is implemented. Participation in program planning by key stakeholder representatives will help to identify such incentives or (lack thereof) while increasing future commitment to the program.

Mixed Stakeholder Management: Adverse Publicity. On October 20, 1985, a series of articles dealing with hospital-specific Medicare death rates for certain surgical procedures were published by the *Birmingham News*. Consumer groups hailed the release of the data. Basically, their position was that extremely high or low figures should cause the public and their representatives to ask questions concerning surgeon qualifications, number of cases in each category per year, unusual circumstances, death rates for non-Medicare patients, and long-term survival rates for all patients (Fottler, Slovensky, and Rogers, 1987).

Another group that particularly welcomed released of the information in Birmingham was the nineteen-million-member American Association of Retired Persons, which promotes and lobbies for the rights of senior citizens. A spokesperson of that group indicated a desire to see more complex, complete data published in the form of a handbook rather than the computer output provided to the newspaper by the U.S. Health Care Financing Administration (HCFA).

One hospital was shown to have death rates after heart surgery that were three times the Jefferson County average. The hospital responded that its own figures showed a somewhat lower death rate than the federal figures (10.06 percent rather than 11.54 percent). A spokesperson noted that their Lifesaver Helicopter Program brings in an above-average share of high-risk emergency coronary-artery bypass patients (particularly those who are older, sicker, and have more complicating conditions).

The chief of heart surgery at the hospital claimed that reporting mortality rates is dangerous because it could cause surgeons to be less likely to operate on sicker patients. He also pointed out that the hospital provides a higher than average number of reoperations (which have a higher than average mortality rate) and that all hospital death rates fluctuate widely from year to year. Medicare death rates may also be different than those for the group of patients as a whole. Consequently, mortality rate data should be standardized for case severity, data for several years should be used, and all patients should be included in the analysis.

The Alabama Hospital Association and referral hospitals in general reacted strongly and negatively, pointing out deficiencies in the HCFA data or method of analysis. However, there was not a strong response to release of the data on the part of either the general public or physicians. Most of the response occurred in the hospital community in the form of low-key discussions. None of the hospitals with lower mortality rates attempted to take advantage of the adverse publicity by attempting to lure away patients from the hospital with higher rates; they were concerned that these data could shift against them in the future.

The key stakeholders in this situation were the patients, their physicians, and the media. The media were the immediate stakeholder, while the physicians and general public were the ultimate stakeholders. Perceptions of the ultimate stakeholder were conditioned by information received through the media. In this case, the hospital took a reactive rather than proactive position. By responding to adverse publicity *after* it was released, the hospitals appeared to be in a position of trying to control the damage. Changing invalid data *before* they are publicly released is much more effective than criticizing such data *after* they are released. A proactive data management program would involve generating data from in the hospital, comparing it to local or regional averages, and generating publicity releases indicative of high-quality care. Areas of weakness could also be identified and improved.

If the hospitals had identified the general public and community physicians as major stakeholders who can be influenced by the media, management of the media would then have become a top priority because of their potential threat to major stakeholders' perceptions. The hospitals knew that the public release of death rates was coming (although they did not know when). Consequently, they could have analyzed their own data, provided explanations or justifications, and put forth the strongest case possible concerning their quality of services. These steps could (and should have) been done prior to public release of comparative mortality data by the media. While the damage to individual hospitals was not too great in this case, it very well could have been.

Successful Stakeholder Management: Physician Referrals. The University of Alabama Hospital in Birmingham is an academic medical center. As a tertiary referral institution, it is largely dependent on referrals from physicians in the south-

eastern region of the United States. The hospital's marketing
department directs a major portion of its time and resources
toward this physician population. Thus, primary care physicians in the Southeast were viewed as a major stakeholder group
who could either support the medical center through referrals
or hurt it by directing referrals elsewhere (Eudes, Divis,
Vaughan, and Fottler, 1987).

To better manage this critical stakeholder group, the
marketing department of the hospital developed a program
for referring physicians to meet the following broad objectives:
(1) build awareness of the hospital and its services, (2) establish
a channel of information and communication, and (3) pave a
route for access to the university.

The institution's program to implement these objectives
included three major services: (1) a *Directory for Referring Physicians,* (2) medical information services via telephone (MIST),
and (3) a critical care transport service. The cornerstone of this
effort was designed to build awareness of the medical center
and its services and to increase referrals. The *Directory* catalogs
the 75 departments, divisions, centers, and specialty units of
the medical center. In addition, it profiles 350 faculty members
who participate in patient care. It was sent to all Alabama physicians and all known referring physicians outside the state (in
Mississippi, Georgia, Tennessee, and north Florida). Then a
list of physicians in the twelve specialties most likely to refer to
the hospital was compiled for the same four states. These 12,000
physicians received mail announcements and reply cards so they
could request the *Directory* if desired. A print advertisement
was also published in all the southeastern states' medical journals. Physicians could receive a copy by either returning the
attached reply card or ordering it through the MIST line. Results of an audit of the program were extremely favorable. A
random sample of 600 of the 9,000 physicians who received
the *Directory* were surveyed to determine their reaction to it.
Results indicated physicians were utilizing and planning to
continue utilizing the *Directory* as a source of information and
a guide to consultations and referrals to specialists at the hospital. Physicians were also satisfied with the content and organization of the *Directory.*

Over seventy-five physicians wrote and asked for additional copies for either their home libraries or their partners, and many complimentary phone calls praising the *Directory*'s usefulness were received. An additional success measure was the number of other hospitals that have contacted the marketing department asking for assistance in developing a *Directory* for their own institutions. Even more important was the documented additional hospital revenue generated as a direct result of the *Directory:* survey reports indicated that 95 new referrals occurred in the first six months. Since the average charge per case was $7,280, the *Directory* generated an additional $691,000. The cost of the *Directory* was only $100,000, consequently the benefit:cost ratio was 7 to 1 after six months and rising. While admissions at other hospitals in the United States were declining in 1984, they were rising at the University of Alabama Hospital.

The lesson from this case study is clear. The hospital identified primary care physicians in a four-state southeastern region as a key stakeholder of the institution. This stakeholder was inherently neither supportive nor threatening, but it could be either. It could be supportive if it could be induced to increase referrals to the hospitals. Alternatively, it could be hostile if it lacked information about the hospital, received little or no communication, or perceived low quality of service to referred patients. In that case, referrals from existing referring physicians might decline and other primary case physicians might never refer patients. The survival of the hospital might be in jeopardy. Active assessment and management of key stakeholders is required for hospital survival. Failure to involve even one key stakeholder such as primary care physicians could make the difference between success and failure in an increasingly competitive environment.

Managing Organization-Stakeholder Relationships

In the next sections we will examine the nature of the "exchanges" inherent in organization-stakeholder relationships. In particular, we will be concerned with the implications of these exchanges for the stakeholder's impact on the organizations. The key dimensions of that impact are the extent to which a given stakeholder does (or could) *threaten* the organization and the extent to which that stakeholder does (or could) *cooperate* with the organization.

Exchanging Organizational Inducements for Stakeholder Contributions. A key concern of those who have studied organizational power issues has been the willingness of potential organizational participants to join and to remain in the organization (for example, Barnard, 1938; March and Simon, 1958; Mintzberg, 1983). In general, participants must be convinced through appropriate *inducements* to make their *contributions* to the organization rather than to some *alternative* organization. *Inducements* are resources (tangible and intangible) possessed by the organization that are desired or needed by the participants. Although inducements are typically thought of as economic (wages, benefits), they can also be noneconomic (status, power). *Contributions* are resources possessed by the participant that are desired or needed by the organization. Contributions are typically thought of as items such as labor, technical skills, or managerial expertise but could also include items such as legitimization or capital investment.

It should be noted that the values and perceptions of the internal and external stakeholders as well as the organization itself heavily influence the definitions of contributions and inducements. In addition, there are typically internal conflicts in the organization about appropriate inducements to stakeholders. There are also conflicts in stakeholder groups and organizations concerning appropriate contributions to organizations. In both cases, there is likely to be considerable disagreement over the appropriate "exchange rate" even if the types of inducements or contributions are agreed on.

The power of participants is a reflection of the organization's need for their contributions and the availability of suitable alternatives to the organization. The power of the organization is a function of the potential or actual participants' need for the inducements and the availability of suitable alternatives to the participants. Simon (1957) and his colleagues (Simon, Smithberg, and Thompson, 1950) have called this approach *organizational equilibrium* theory. An organization is "solvent" or will be able to continue to exist only so long as the participants' contributions and inducements are in equilibrium.

For example, in health care this equilibrium has been disturbed over the past few years as the nursing shortage has grown. Hospitals need to offer increased inducements relative to competition to recruit and retain sufficient nurses to staff their units. There are now more ambulatory care competitors seeking nurses together with declining nursing school enrollments and a stagnant overall suppʹy of nurses. This means nurses today (1990) have more attention if they are dissatisfied with the inducements:contributions ratio of their current employer. Hospitals have responded to this situation by increasing their inducements (economic and noneconomic) while modifying the nurse's job to make it more attractive.

This organizational equilibrium approach focuses primarily on individuals *in* the organization and their contributions to the organization. Here we are proposing extending that power analysis to the macro level and looking externally and at the interface in a way comparable to the internal analysis. This might be called a *stakeholder equilibrium* approach. Contributions of stakeholders might include political support, favorable publicity or word-of-mouth support, referrals, donations, capital investments, various business or other services, and reimbursement for services provided by the organization.

In dealing with stakeholders, health care executives are in effect providing more or less inducements of various kinds to obtain necessary contributions (cooperation) from the stakeholders. In turn, stakeholders are applying more or less pressure to obtain valued inducements from the organization for their contributions. To continue to exist (or be solvent), the contributions by stakeholders and the inducements by the organization must be in equilibrium. At a minimum, the inducements must not exceed the contributions *over the long term*. The potentially cooperative exchange relationship—or stakeholder

Figure 4. Stakeholder Equilibrium Between Organization
and Stakeholder.

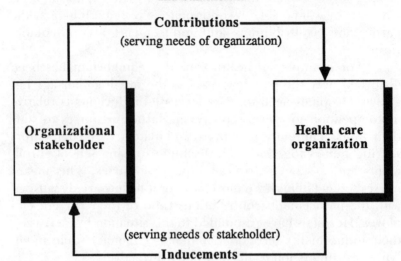

equilibrium—between the organization and its stakeholder is
shown in Figure 4.

*Defending Against Stakeholder "Discontributions" Through
Organizational Inducements and "Disinducements."* In the original inducements-contributions approach, an individual could
choose to participate and make his or her contributions. The
individual could also choose to not participate or to withdraw
his or her contributions by leaving the organization. Thus, the
only way the individual could harm or otherwise threaten the
organization was through withdrawal of contributions or ter-
mination of the relationship.

However, when one considers organization-stakeholder
relationships (other than those with internal participants), several differences emerge:

- By their very nature, stakeholders have a stake in the organization that probably will not disappear. Therefore, they
  cannot or will not simply go away. *The organization has relationships with them whether or not its managers want to.*
- Stakeholders do not always have contributions to make to

organizations, even if they want to. For example, special-interest groups may want inducements such as changes in policies or more open access to care from the organization but may not have contributions—just demands—to make. Indigent patients may not have any contributions desired by a hospital due to their inability to pay; however, the hospital could provide indigent patients with inducements they want (for example, free care). Thus, there is no real or potential exchange. As an extreme example, animal rights groups that break into research laboratories at medical centers have a stake in the organization's policy governing animal use in research but no contribution to make toward meeting the medical center's goals.

- Competitors also have a clear stake in what the organization does but are not likely to make any contributions. In fact, they are likely to take actions that can harm or undermine the organization. Many regulatory bodies make demands for inducements (often expensive actions taken to comply with regulations) but offer no real contributions.

As a result of these differences, we have extended the inducements-contributions notions to include their opposites: discontributions and disinducements. *Discontributions* are actions that explicitly threaten or actually harm the organization or are in some other way dysfunctional to the organization. In some cases, they could represent a constant threat to organizational viability by negatively affecting the organization's market share. Alternatively, they may cause ongoing public-relations problems through pressures of various kinds. In any case, stakeholder actions of this type are likely to be very nonsupportive of the organization.

Disinducements are defensive strategic actions, such as comparable moves, legal injunctions, or increasing security, that prevent or offset stakeholder discontributions. Of course, it is also possible to reduce discontributions using inducements, such as changes in policies desired by the stakeholder. The potentially threatening exchange relationship between the organization and its stakeholder is shown in Figure 5. Whether the health

Figure 5. Potentially Threatening Exchange Relationship Between Organization and Stakeholder.

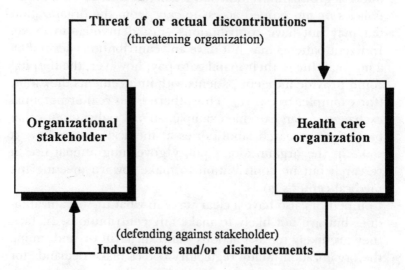

care organization should use inducements or disinducements depends on the organization's assessment of the costs and relative effectiveness of each.

For example, a county hospital in the South recently had to decide how to handle indigent patients who complained about newly initiated procedures to determine the patients' eligibility for Medicare, Medicaid, and other insurance programs *prior* to the provision of services in the hospital's outpatient clinic. Obviously, these indigent patients had no contribution to make to the hospital. However, they could and did threaten the hospital by complaining to the news media and the county commission. The adverse publicity and pressure from those county commissioners representing the minority community left the hospital chief executive officer (CEO) with two alternatives. He could either provide the inducements desired by the indigent patients (that is, return to the old system in which insurance coverage was ascertained *after* service was provided) or pursue a disinducement defensive strategy. The latter alternative was chosen by the CEO as he went before the county commission and granted interviews with the media in which he argued that the county commission should only be *setting policy* and should not be telling management how to run the hospital on a *day-to-day basis*. The new policy is still in effect, and the CEO has been feuding over this issue with one county commissioner and with other minority community representatives for some time.

Health care researchers have experienced a unique relationship with stakeholder groups making discontributions to their organizations. Animal rights groups have been attacking research facilities through both legal and terrorist-type actions. These groups, determined to protect animals used for research, have broken into research labs, stolen animals, and vandalized facilities. They have also filed complaints against the research labs with the National Institutes of Health, which fund such research (Barlow, 1989). The directors of these research labs can respond with contributions. Such a plan might involve making donations to these animal rights groups along with allowing an animal rights group member to have a position on the board, thus coopting the group. However, it is more likely that research labs will respond with disinducements such as defense of their practices to the National Institutes of Health, publicity about the value of their research, and increased security in their research labs.

However, not all disinducements are effective, and some are clearly unethical. Although we will save a detailed discussion and case presentation of the National Healthcare scandal until the final chapter, in that widely known case (see, for example, Beam, 1987; Lutz, 1989) stakeholders and other investors who had a legitimate stake in the organization were not provided with valid financial information. In terms of our approach, the company provided disinducements (misinformation) to investors, and the investors, in turn, responded by initiating discontributions (a class-action lawsuit). In addition, however, there were other stakeholder victims who were also mismanaged. The health care executives in the individual hospitals were pressured to alter their financial results. Many quit or lost their jobs as a result of the ensuing company shakeout. Patients found their access to health services reduced as facilities everyone had previously believed to be financially viable were shut down.

The bottom line in this case was a violation of the bond

of trust that must exist between a health care organization and its key stakeholders. These stakeholders need to have confidence in the information provided by the organization. Otherwise, the inducements:contributions ratio is upset. Contributions needed by the organization will not be forthcoming. Such a situation can threaten the viability of the organization, as it did in the case of National Healthcare.

Stakeholder power will be discussed at length in Chapters Three and Four. Here it is important only to recognize that power, to a great extent, is a reflection of the dependence of the health care organization on the stakeholder. The dependence of the organization is, in turn, a function of the need the organization has for the stakeholder's contributions and the availability and cost (in terms of inducements) of suitable alternatives to the health care organization. For example, the power of the physicians on a hospital medical staff (a key stakeholder for most health care organizations) is a function of the hospital's dependence on the physicians for crucial contributions in terms of inputs (for example, patients), the conversion process (for example, use of hospital beds), and output (for example, hospital services provided).

Likewise, the organization's power is a reflection of the dependence of the stakeholder on the organization. The dependence of the stakeholder is itself a function of the need of the stakeholder for the inducements the organization has to offer as well as the availability and costs (in terms of contributions) of suitable alternatives. For example, the power of a hospital vis-à-vis the physicians on its medical staff is a function of the physicians' dependence on the hospital for crucial inducements in terms of inputs to their practices (for example, patients provided by a hospital-run physician referral service or staff association with a prestigious hospital), the conversion process (for example, hospital facilities made available to the physician), and output (for example, treatment of the physicians' patients).

"Stakeholder Bottom Line" for Organization: Potential to Threaten or Cooperate

In Chapter Three, we will address in detail two key dimensions of organization-stakeholder relationships that provide simplifying diagnostic perspectives on the multitude of stakeholders facing executives: their *potential to threaten* the organization and their *potential to cooperate* with it. Here we will briefly introduce these two dimensions since they are essential to our basic approach.

Potential for Threat in Organization-Stakeholder Relationship. Hostility in terms of applying extensive pressure appears as a key variable in several formulations of organization-environment-strategy relationships (Khandwalla, 1973; Miller and Friesen, 1978). Physicians, for example, are sometimes explicitly identified as a group that does or could apply extensive pressure impacting on effective strategic management by hospitals (Sheldon and Windham, 1984). Looking at the current or anticipated threat inherent in the relationship with a particular stakeholder or group of stakeholders is similar to developing a worst-case scenario and protects managers from unpleasant surprises.

The level of threat in the relationship is a function of not only the stakeholder's overall power but also the particular stakeholder's relevance for any particular issue or decision confronting the organization's managers. Thus, threatening relationships reflect one of two kinds of situations: attempts to make significant discontributions to the organizations such as discussed above and demands for special organizational inducements desired by the stakeholder, presumably in exchange for the stakeholder's contributions. This situation is threatening when there are stakeholder threats to provide the same contributions to an *alternative* organization instead (or in addition).

This situation is different from the normal exchange relationship focusing on potential for cooperation since it also introduces a clear potential to threaten the organization by denying it needed resources and providing them to another such as a competitor. Health care organizations' relationships with physicians are often of this second kind and contain a potential for threat in an otherwise cooperation relationship.

In the Cleveland Clinic example, the power of local physicians to channel patients away from hospitals involved with the clinic was not perceived as a threat. However, the clinic was not able to give the hospitals adequate contributions to offset the threat to the hospitals presented by local physicians who had the power take away contributions (send patients elsewhere).

We are arguing that the organization's managers need to systematically anticipate and evaluate the actual or potential threats in its relationships with stakeholders and, in some cases, evaluate threats that face their supportive stakeholder. These threats may be focused on obtaining from the organization inducements that may or may not be provided. These desired inducements may induce financial resources, participation in decision making, and enactment of particular organizational policies. Alternatively, they may focus on undermining the fundamental viability of the organization.

Potential for Cooperation in Organization-Stakeholder Relationship. Because managers often emphasize the types and magnitude of pressures (or even threats of extreme discontributions) that stakeholders put on the organization, the second dimension of cooperation level in the organization's relationship with its stakeholders is easily ignored. We feel that this dimension should be equally emphasized as managers attempt stakeholder diagnosis as it more clearly directs attention to potential stakeholder management strategies that go beyond the merely defensive or offensive in confronting stakeholder pressures. Diagnosing this dimension suggests the potential for using more cooperative strategies. These strategies focus on cooperation in stakeholder relationships in terms of the actual or potential contributions valued and needed by the organization.

For example, two competitors facing a common threat of dis-contributions from a given stakeholder, such as a third com-petitor who has purchased a helicopter to aid in rural market penetration, may well be potential allies in counteracting such a move by sharing the cost of a joint venture helicopter of their own.

Another example of competitors joining together against a common threat is occurring as hospitals merge to reduce the bargaining power of PPOs. PPOs have been able to demand price concessions from hospitals in markets where several hos-pitals compete for market share. With unprofitable hospitals falling by the wayside, the remaining hospitals can merge. The PPO is left with one dominant organization with which to ne-gotiate and is in a very weak position since it cannot threaten to send its members elsewhere. However, stakeholder manage-ment does not end for hospital administrators planning to im-plement this strategy. The Antitrust Division of the Justice De-partment is becoming increasingly active in investigating such mergers. As of June 1989, the Justice Department had taken two rural hospital merger cases to court and won one of them (Zwanziger, 1989). Health care executives need to anticipate the likely reaction of regulators—who represent the "public's" stake—to prospective mergers.

One may look at the cooperation or cooperative poten-tial of a relationship in a fashion parallel to that for looking at actual or potential threat. However, in this case one looks at a best-case scenario and in so doing may discover new possibili-ties otherwise ignored because of fundamental assumptions and perspectives.

The current support or cooperative potential to be found in the organization's relationships with a stakeholder is to a great extent a function of the level of contributions the stake-holder can make to the hospital and the stakeholder's rele-vance for any particular issue or decision facing the hospital. The more resources the stakeholder controls and could (or does) provide to the organization, the higher the level of potential (or actual) cooperation. Next, we investigate how a manager can maximize cooperation and reduce threat through his or her daily stakeholder interactions consistently with overall competitive strategy.

Strategic Stakeholder Management Process: Overview

In this book we focus on further developing systematic and strategic stakeholder management approaches. In Figure 6, we display stakeholder management in this broader perspective by attempting to portray the complexity of managing stakeholders strategically. The implications for contributions and discontributions resulting from well or poorly managed exchange relationships are also displayed. This book elaborates the pieces of the stakeholder management puzzle depicted in Figure 6.

We discuss such activities as stakeholder assessment as only one part of the overall stakeholder management process in Chapter Three. In turn, stakeholder management cannot be effective without integrating it into still broader strategic management. As discussed briefly in the next section of this chapter and in detail in Chapter Four, executives need to diagnose key organizational stakeholders in terms of their potential to threaten or cooperate with the organization. These key diagnostic dimensions are shown in Figure 6.

In Chapter Four we also discuss the formulation of stakeholder management strategies based on stakeholder assessment and diagnosis and look at which managers are responsible for implementing strategies for which stakeholders. Chapter Five looks at an important managerial issue in all strategy implementation—negotiating with stakeholder representatives. We further address specific issues and techniques in strategy implementation in Chapter Six. Chapters Seven and Eight focus on the details involved in the strategic management of specific key stakeholders.

The current degrees of threat and cooperation result in the contributions and discontributions from key stakeholders and provide the context for the strategic stakeholder management process shown in Figure 6. How well stakeholders are managed during the stakeholder management process will af-

Figure 6. Strategic Stakeholder Management Process.

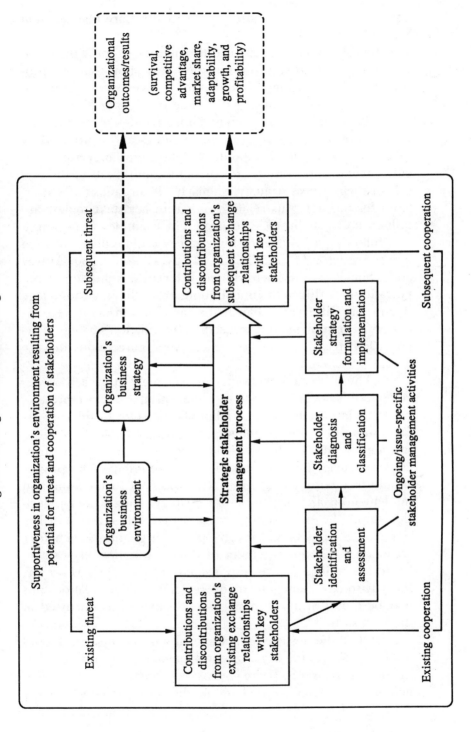

fect the subsequent potential to threaten or support the organization. The feedback loops in the figure show that this process should be constantly updated in the dynamic world facing health care organizations, as discussed in Chapter Nine.

Stakeholder management both provides input into the health care organization's business strategy and is affected by that strategy. Some stakeholder relationships may represent either major opportunities for or significant threats to the success of the business strategy. Similarly, the organization's strategies for managing its relationships with key stakeholders are influenced by its business strategy. For example, an organization following a cost leadership strategy is quite different than one pursuing a differentiation strategy. (Porter, 1980; Autrey and Thomas, 1986). Each will see different stakeholders as important, want different contributions from them, and manage them quite differently than if the same organization were attempting to implement a focused differentiation strategy (Porter, 1985) based on buyers' and payers' perceptions of care quality.

The strategic stakeholder management approach we develop in this book, informed by the illustrative data we present, has some important managerial implications for health care organizations and their managers. Clearly, all health care organizations should explicitly assess, diagnose, and develop strategies to manage their key stakeholder relationships. This process should be integrated fully into the process of formulating and implementing the organization's strategy. Each strategic decision should be examined in terms of the likely reaction of key stakeholders and should involve plans for gaining stakeholder acceptance. The management of the organization's key stakeholders is ultimately the responsibility of the CEO. However, the day-to-day management of key stakeholder relationships may be found in many management activities, as discussed in the next section.

Of all the possible organizational stakeholders, which ones will be *relevant* to the organization's managers depends on what the particular *issue* is. If the issue is cost containment, the stakeholders who are concerned will be different than on the issue of access to health care. On the issue of quality of care, the relevance for a particular stakeholder may again be different. The analysis of the nature of the relationships will probably be different on those three issues as well. We will look at issue-specific stakeholder management in detail in Chapters Four and Seven.

Stakeholder management is both an *ongoing* and an *issue-specific* activity for health care managers. This is reflected in Figure 6. One cannot assume that a stakeholder who is supportive on one issue will be supportive on every issue, or that one who is nonsupportive on one issue will be that on another. Both opportunity and danger await health care organizations encountering a wide range of stakeholder relationships that are generally characterized by what might be called *dynamic ambiguity*—that is, organizations facing a large number of stakeholders with a high potential for cooperation *but also* high potential for threat.

The success of managing key stakeholders should be evaluated continuously, and adjustments in organizational structure or personnel made when appropriate. Managers should recognize that who matters, why they matter, and how they can be managed vary, for example, in different types of hospitals as well as in different nonhospital health care organizations. Equally important, these factors also depend on the specific issue being addressed.

The next chapter presents some key conceptual issues of particular interest to the more research-oriented reader but also relevant to the practitioner trying to put all the pieces together on any given day. The practitioner can be further guided by the resources at the ends of Chapter Three through Five. These resources provide some systematic tools that can be used to implement the stakeholder management approach we present throughout this book.

Our goal in conducting the stakeholder-management-in-action study described in the next chapter and in developing and presenting this strategic stakeholder management approach is to help managers avoid stakeholder mismanagement pitfalls by:

- Developing a competitive (corporate, business, or functional) strategy after assessing the organization's mission, opportunities, and threats in the external environment; internal strengths and weaknesses; and stakeholder relations
- Identifying and assessing the power of key stakeholders necessary to implement the competitive strategy
- Identifying stakeholders who could potentially use organizational resources with little or no potential to make contributions to the organization
- Maintaining positive relationships with supportive stakeholders
- Identifying and soliciting appropriate contributions that each key stakeholder needs to provide in order for the organization to successfully implement the competitive strategy
- Identifying and providing the inducements needed to elicit the necessary contributions from key stakeholders
- Defending against threatening stakeholders or changing the relationship so that the stakeholder becomes less threatening
- Managing key stakeholders who could be either threatening or supportive so that the threat is minimized and the contributions are maximized
- Monitoring stakeholders who appear to have potentially little power so that any changes in their potential will be observed
- Defining explicit strategies that can be communicated throughout the organization so that stakeholder management becomes a familiar tool

The *strategic* stakeholder management process that we describe represents a new and potentially more powerful approach to the management of health care organizations than what has existed up to this point. In particular, it is more consistent with what "good managers" actually do on a day-to-day basis through intuition and trial and error. Our approach systematizes these intuitive insights by providing both a conceptual framework and details on how to actually do it.

❈❈❈❈❈❈❈❈❈❈❈❈❈❈❈❈❈❈❈❈❈❈❈

CHAPTER 2

Understanding
The Foundations of
Strategic Stakeholder Management

As indicated in Chapter One, health care as well as other organizations have faced increasingly turbulent environments and have attempted to become increasingly *strategic* in their management (Johnson and Johnson, 1986; Smith and Reid, 1986; Coddington and Moore, 1987; Shortell, Morrison, and Friedman, 1990). However, there is often little clear connection between what health care managers do in their day-to-day activities—in the actual practice of management—and the abstract organizational strategies that have been formulated to permit the health care organization to accomplish its mission and goals in today's and tomorrow's environment.

Specifically, managers may find it difficult to meaningfully integrate the overall organizational issues with the activities generated by their in boxes, meetings, and telephone calls. Overall environmental and organizational conditions seem far removed from daily interaction situations. In addition, overall organizational strategies to achieve competitive advantage hardly appear relevant to the strategy used in interacting with others in the memos, meetings, and the phone calls resulting from the press of events from early morning until the end of the workday or even much later. Finally, the results experienced by managers from interaction with others may have little apparent direct impact on how well the organization does (as opposed to how well managers are evaluated by the organization). For example, does a "successful" phone call have any real impact on return on investment? The feedback from a negotiation episode may be quite immediate, while the results from organizational strategy are often not evident—even over an extended period—and are certainly not clear in the short run.

One symptom of the fundamental, turbulent, and in some cases revolutionary change that has occurred is the fact that health care executives must daily respond to an increasing number of active and powerful stakeholders. Much of the manager's time is spent negotiating, meeting, or otherwise interacting, in person or in writing, with representatives of such stakeholders. As a result, stakeholders now exert influence on issues ranging from governance to financial reimbursement to patient services. As the realities of health care management change, different perspectives for developing alternative models and approaches to management are also needed.

This gap in management practice is also reflected in the management theory designed to inform management practice. Management research has long been divided between the study of organizations in relationship to their environment (*macro research*) and the study of individuals and groups in the organizations (*micro research*). This separation of levels has divided organizational behaviorists and theorists. This distinction carries over into the strategic management field.

Bourgeois (1980) defines two types of strategy. The first strategy refers to decisions about which type of product or markets with which to be involved. This is usually called *corporate strategy* (Wheelen and Hunger, 1989). The second type of strategy is concerned with how to compete in a given market or product once the first decision has been made. This is known as *competitive strategy* at the strategic business unit level (Wheelen and Hunger, 1989). As mentioned in Chapter One, we will use *competitive strategy* throughout this book to refer to both kinds of macro strategy.

Thus, *strategy at the macro level,* is concerned with the type of business in which to be as well as the scope and competitive advantage of the strategy content. *Strategy at the micro level* is concerned with approaching behavioral processes with clear strategies in mind (such as negotiating strategically). These micro-level strategies (and their effective implementation) may well, in turn, impact the effective implementation of corporate or competitive strategy (at the macro level). For example, an executive may formulate an overall strategy to negotiate a particular contract with a key supplier of products or services. This strategy may be designed to achieve certain goals during the course of negotiations. If the executive succeeds in negotiating according to that strategy, that is, successfully implements that micro-level strategy, that micro-level behavior may have considerable impact on the successful implementation of a macro-level strategy that requires the organization to "differentiate" its services (Porter, 1980; Autrey and Thomas, 1986; Whitehead and others, 1989). If that supplier's cooperation in providing scarce products or services is essential to making that competitive strategy work, micro-level negotiation strategy leading to a mutually acceptable contract is clearly linked to successful implementation of the macro-level competitive strategy of differentiation.

Strategic management theory has not effectively linked strategic functioning at the macro level to behavioral processes at the micro level. In this chapter, we argue that to clearly understand (1) the relationships between abstract strategy and daily management practice and (2) the formulation and implementation of strategy, it is necessary to introduce another set of concepts that integrate these two levels of reality. We contend that the missing conceptual link that permits the systematic linking of macro and micro levels of reality—and analysis—is found at the *meso,* or middle, level of analysis between the well-known macro and micro levels (Hage, 1980). In this chapter, we argue that that meso-level theory can be found in the form of the stakeholder management approach.

This approach has increasingly shown its value in understanding and managing health care organizations (Keele, Buckner, and Bushnell, 1987; Blair and Whitehead, 1988; Blair, Savage, and Whitehead, 1989; Fottler and others, 1989; Blair, Slaton, and Savage, 1990). We believe that it is now time to systematically link these concepts to both macro-level strategic management and micro-level behavioral focuses of past research and practice. We then present an argument for using a stakeholder management approach to facilitate both strategic management theory as well as strategic management performance in organizations.

We provide an integrative approach to health care strategic management, ranging from strategy to process and combining micro and macro perspectives. The result is a conceptually based framework for linking *day-to-day health care management practice* to *abstract competitive strategic orientations* (for example, being a "prospecter" rather than a "defender") (Shortell, Morrison, and Friedman, 1990) or *abstract competitive strategies* (for example, being a "focused differentiater," not the "low-cost producer") (Porter, 1980, 1985). This linkage is possible by focusing on the importance of organization-stakeholder relations, strategic management of stakeholders, and stakeholder interactions. The issues to be addressed in our integrated strategic approach include

- Identifying concepts from the stakeholder management literature that can be used to develop this linkage
- Using the stakeholder approach to integrate strategy at macro and micro levels
- Identifying the problems in integrating planned strategy with day-to-day managerial practice by delineating the problematical linkage of strategic issues across different levels of analysis
- Integrating top-down (deliberate/planned) and bottom-up (emergent) approaches to multilevel strategy using stakeholder management as the linchpin
- Developing the concept of stakeholder interaction episodes as a way to focus on only *strategically relevant* management behavior
- Illustrating how competitive stakeholder management and negotiation strategies can be integrated for a hospital
- Delineating the impact of stakeholders on competitive business strategy formulation and implementation in the managed care industry

- Discussing stakeholder management as the integrating focus for multiple management activities
- Discussing the implications of this approach for research and practice

Managing Organizations Strategically

In the following section of this chapter, we will look at strategy at three different levels of analysis. Two of these are better understood than the third. Macro-level strategy is the best and serves as a model to discuss the other two. Micro-level analysis of behavioral processes such as negotiation and conflict management and prescriptions for practitioners who need to negotiate or resolve conflicts are increasingly becoming strategic in tone. In a parallel fashion to these two levels of strategy, we will elaborate the underlying concepts and implications of a third: stakeholder management strategy. We will argue throughout this chapter that stakeholder strategy permits the systematical linkage, both conceptually and practically, of macro and micro strategies. This linkage is provided through the development of the strategic stakeholder management approach at the meso or middle level of analysis. We will discuss the meso level at length later in this chapter. Abstract as this may seem, it will become clearer as we examine the pieces of this intellectual problem, which has significant day-to-day managerial implications.

Macro-Level Strategy. Our model of strategy at the macro level as well as the other two basic models representing the stakeholder and micro levels of analysis used in this chapter are all based on the same research paradigm. This model is an extension of the model presented by Fahey and Christensen (1986). This paradigm consists of three basic elements: *conditions, strategy content,* and *results.* To this basic model, we have added *assessment of the conditions* and *realized strategy.* These five elements are connected in the following manner: Some assessment is made of the existing conditions, planned strategy is formulated based on this assessment, the actual or "realized" strategy (which may or may not differ from the planned strategy) is put into place and leads to results, and finally these results feed back into the conditions that start the cycle over again. In the next sections we will look at strategy from traditional macro and micro perspectives. We will also address the role of the stakeholder approach in integrating these perspectives.

Macro-level planned strategy formulation is represented in our model (shown in Figure 7) by *competitive strategies*. This basic paradigm indicates that strategy is developed after the *environmental conditions* have been *assessed*. At this level, managers responsible for strategic planning in the organization attempt to create overall *corporate and competitive strategies* that will most closely align the organization with the environment. The tighter the fit between the organization and the environment, the more successful the organization will be in achieving the desired results. This paradigm of *planned strategies* is based on the economist's view of rational decision making (Murray, 1978). Such a view assumes that decision makers possess comprehensive knowledge of the environment and are acting to attain some agreed-on goal such as profit maximization.

Figure 7. Managing Strategically at Macro Level of Analysis.

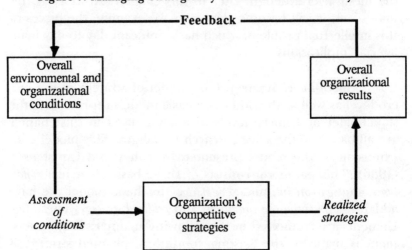

At the macro level, many environmental and organizational conditions affect the formulation of specific competitive strategies. These conditions also have considerable impact on the results of these planned strategies—given their appropriateness in terms of the organization's strengths and weaknesses and the threats and opportunities in the environment. A pure type model of planned strategic management would indicate that strategy is developed at the apex of the organizational hierarchy. Members of the organization would have knowledge of this strategy, and the strategy would drive their actions. In addition, the *planned strategy* would also be the actual or *realized strategy* that would impact on (if not completely determine) *overall organizational results.*

However, people involved in strategy formulation and implementation activities do not operate in a vacuum, nor are all planned strategies ever realized. Managers do not directly deal with dimensions of the environment such as complexity, munificence, or even a category such as suppliers. What they deal with every day is other people. These people represent different parts of the organizational environment. *Thus, macro environmental reality actually appears to the manager doing his or her daily tasks as people who represent themselves or other individuals, groups, and organizations that hold a stake in the decisions and actions of the manager's organization.*

Middle-Level Strategy: Approaching Stakeholder Management Strategically. Because of their mission, health care organizations are at the center of the social, economic and ethical crosscurrents surrounding health care delivery (Johnson and Johnson, 1986; Smith and Reid, 1986; Coddington and Moore, 1987). As such, they have a large number of divergent and frequently conflicting stakeholders. These stakeholders have become increasingly activist during the last decade in their effort to influence the way health care organizations operate. One daily implication of this increasingly dynamic health care environment is that managers must respond to—and attempt to manage—this ever-increasing number of active and powerful stakeholders (Fottler and others, 1989).

Thus, in addition to the potential for the strategic management function to be coopted through unintended micro-level decisions, actions, and interactions, the realized competitive strategy is susceptible to being influenced or coopted by activist stakeholders. For example, consider how the following factors have intensified the complexity of health care organization-stakeholder relationships:

- Increased forms and numbers of joint ventures
- Increased multiinstitutional forms of health care organizations
- Complicated networking relationships with suppliers and other organizations
- Growth of employees as owners of organizations
- Growth of special-interest groups
- Increased government (national and international) regulation
- Increased employee and patient expectations

As indicated in Chapter One, the stakeholder management literature has become increasingly more strategic in its approach (Freeman, 1984; Fottler, 1987; Blair and Whitehead, 1988; Blair, Savage, and Whitehead, 1989; Carroll, 1989; Whitehead and others, 1989; Blair, Slaton, and Savage, 1990). That is, there has been more and more interest in attempting to develop strategies to manage stakeholders, not just identify which ones are important. Underpinning this emerging stakeholder management paradigm, shown in Figure 8, is the fundamental approach to strategic management research reflected in the macro strategy paradigm discussed above.

There are many barriers to successful and full implementation of planned stakeholder management strategy. Further, there is a high likelihood that the strategy may have to be adapted based on information that emerges during attempts to make the strategy work or be adapted through political maneuvers of internal stakeholders, and what strategy the organization realizes actually ends up following may be quite inconsistent with the planned strategy. In any case, it is the

**Figure 8. Managing Stakeholders Strategically at Middle Level
of Analysis.**

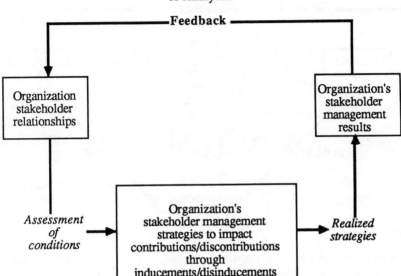

realized stakeholder management strategy—for good or ill—
that has successful or less successful results in managing stakeholder environments.

Micro-Level Strategy. Strategic approaches to interaction
appear increasingly throughout the micro-level management
literature. This level of management research is concerned with
individuals interacting with other individuals. At the micro level
of analysis, *interaction situations* (conditions) such as negotiation
and crisis management can be approached strategically. Strategic formulation on how to most effectively interact leads to
the *interaction strategies.* Such strategies are very different in focus but not in logic from the macro-level strategy discussed
above. These strategies are used to deal with manager-other
interactions. They are not necessarily related to the macro
strategies, although we will argue that when dealing with representatives of important stakeholders they *should* be related.
These strategies on negotiating, for example, include collaboration, subordination, and competition (Savage, Blair, and

Figure 9. Managing Strategically at Micro Level of Analysis.

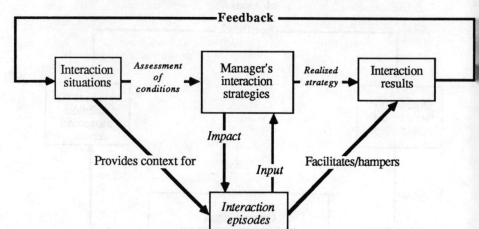

Sorenson, 1989). As Figure 9 shows, when these interaction strategies are *realized,* they are expected to produce *interaction results.* Although the macro-level strategy may be more commonly thought of as strategy in the management literature, the practitioner is much more likely to be using micro-level interaction strategies in day-to-day activities.

At the micro level, the same basic research paradigm applies, as shown in Figure 9. Behavioral researchers in areas such as negotiation have taken explicitly strategic approaches to this micro-level phenomenon (for example, Lax and Sebenius, 1986). At this level, the paradigm implies that interaction situations serve as the conditions that affect the strategies (such as collaboration, subordination, and competition) to be used by executives to negotiate, manage conflict, or otherwise interact with others in or outside the organization. Such interaction strategies obviously involve management attempts to balance stakeholder inducements and contributions. The realized strategies lead to the results of the interactions. Results of specific negotiation, for example, depend on both the appropriateness of the strategy in terms of both the executive's and the other party's desired outcomes (Savage and Blair, 1989).

Interaction Episode. Micro-level interaction is inherently episodic. In a parallel fashion to the earlier concept of role-taking episodes of Katz and Kahn (1966), we look at actual interaction between managers and others in episodic terms as developed by Savage, Blair, and Sorenson (1989) and Savage and Blair (1989). The interaction episode is represented at the bottom of Figure 9. The *interaction episode* is where the actual communication takes place between the manager and other people. The manager in this episode may be the CEO of the company or a lower-level manager. This micro level of strategy is *not* meant to represent the lower levels of management but rather strategic interactions between people, that is, interpersonal behaviors that are influenced by strategy-based choices on the part of one or more participants. The interaction episode will be developed further in this chapter as we focus on interactions with key organizational stakeholders and their representatives.

Integrating Multiple Types of Strategies: Practical and Conceptual Challenges

Micro- versus *macro*-level distinctions represent conceptually clear—but artificial—designations in management, and they have proven useful for theorists because they are conducive to parsimonious study and organization of the research literature. However, this dichotomous classification may not be helpful to the practitioner facing highly complex management situations. Managers and other members of the top executive team, as we will illustrate shortly, may find that macro and micro theories of strategy fail to address certain key aspects of everyday management situations. Indeed, the management literature has indicated that the strategy process cannot simply be described with either macro or micro theory but may be better characterized by terms such as *muddling through* (Lindblom, 1959).

It is important that macro and micro *levels of analysis* should not be confused with strategic (higher-level managers) and operational (lower-level managers) *hierarchical levels* in the organization. Both macro and micro strategies can be formulated and implemented by the same persons, such as an organization's chief executive officer. In fact, implicit or explicit micro strategies are *formulated* by all managers who interact with significant parties affected by the organization's macro strategy, although most may only be asked or directed to help *implement* that macro strategy.

The tension between macro and micro levels of strategy is captured in the continuum anchored on one side by planned strategy and on the other side by emergent strategy. On one hand, the planned strategy approach ignores the reality of pressures from internal and external sources that managers face as a macro strategy is realized. On the other hand, if managers ignore macro-level strategy and concentrate only on micro-level strategy, then the organization may suffer from a lack of clear direction. Managers concentrating only on strategy that emerges from what is actually happening in the organization (on "where the action is" rather than on planning staffs or the board room) allow negotiations or other interaction episodes to drive the direction of the organization. Viewed in its ideal form, this latter approach leads to an emergent formulation and realization of a macro strategy. Such macro strategy is not planned but emerges as a pattern from the micro-level interactions of managers with strategically significant others. Emergent strategy may eventually be formally articulated in documents, but this represents, in many ways, a *post hoc* rationalization of an often chaotic process.

As a result, the management literature suffers from a lack of integration of the micro and macro approaches. In essence, a link is needed between the macro level of analysis provided by organizational and strategic management theory and the micro level of analysis provided by theories of organizational behavior. The problematical nature of that linkage is indicated in Figure 10. The top part of this figure reflects the organization's (macro) competitive strategy. The bottom part of the model reflects a corresponding strategic perspective

Figure 10. Problems Linking Macro Competitive and Micro Interaction Strategies.

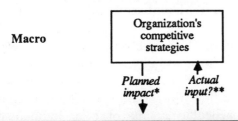

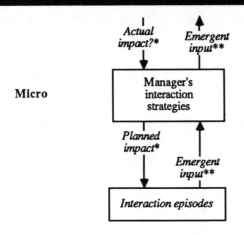

*   = Deliberate/planned impact on strategy implementation

**   = Emergent patterns as input to strategy formulation/reformulation

toward (micro) organizational behavior, including the concept of interaction episodes.

Figure 10 also illustrates several types of barriers to effectively linking these two levels of strategy. Some barriers may be *political* and reflect power games or other influence processes that distort or present such a linkage. Other barriers may be primarily *conceptual* and reflect an inability of executives to actually tie together what happened at the strategic management retreat they attended last week and what they have to do today. Still other barriers may be found to result from poor *communication* downward (in the organization) of overall competitive strategy and what that should mean for operational units.

Hence, for all of these reasons, the *actual impact* of planned macro competitive strategy on the day-to-day behavior of managers and other organizational participants is unclear. Communication flow upward (in the organization) is also problematical. In particular, results of what happens when managers actually have to deal with people who are *themselves* (or who represent others who are) important to the success of the competitive strategy are very likely not effectively communicated upward. As a result, the implications of these interactions for assessing the appropriateness of overall competitive strategy may not be known by higher-level managers. Thus, the actual input for strategy formulation and reformulation from micro, day-to-day activities is unclear.

More specifically, there are several distinct but related areas in which problems may arise in the linkage between macro and micro levels of strategy analysis:

- Problems may arise for an organization if environmental and organizational conditions are not considered prior to encounters with boundary-spanning members in the manager's own organization as well as interactions with members from other organizations. To varying degrees, executives can choose both to create opportunities for interactions and to avoid or inhibit interactions with significant others. When these micro-level choices are not rationally linked to macro-level conditions, interaction opportunities that could further the organization's goals may be lost or obstructed. Moreover, other interaction situations, if not proactively inhibited, may actually threaten the organization, negate the organization's strategy, or divert the organization from accomplishing its goals.
- Problems also arise when the assessment of conditions at the macro level of analysis are decoupled from assessment at the micro level. The assessing of an interaction situation,

divorced from consideration of the overall conditions, may lead a manager to optimize gains in that interaction that may be suboptimal for the organization. Given the top management team's diverse and numerous encounters with others, it is likely that macro-level conditions may not be at the forefront when they assess the opportunities and threats of each interaction.

- Interaction strategies not linked to organizational strategies may possibly negate, delay, or radically change the intended macro strategy. This problem, of course, builds on the prior two problematical linkages. Moreover, its impact depends on the interaction episode where the partial implementation of an organizational strategy actually occurs. Additionally, the interaction episode can provide input for modifying interaction strategies based on the information obtained from and the decisions made with significant others.

- Without a clear linkage to the macro level, vital information from micro-level interactions may not be used to modify the organization's strategy. Conversely, such information may be overinfluential if the prior linkage of macro- to micro-level strategy is very weak. In the first case, the organization reduces its ability to change a strategy midstream to accomplish its objectives; in the second case, the organization overcorrects its strategy to such a degree that it again may lose sight of its original objectives.

- Finally, the lack of linkages between the realized strategy and results at the micro level and at the macro level can exaggerate the incongruities noted previously. The worst case entails feeding back a realized strategy and organizational results totally decoupled from the realized strategy and interaction results of the top management team. Problems at these points would certainly lead to dysfunctional and pathological organizational strategizing.

It is very appealing for managers as well as scholars to look at models of strategy formulation and implementation that show planned strategy becoming realized strategy and having the intended results. This ideal model is also the basic theoret-

ical underpinning of the strategy paradigm we have been using. On one hand, this simplistic approach ignores the reality
of pressures faced by managers from influences in and outside
the organization as they attempt to implement the strategy so
that it is realized. On the other hand, if managers ignore the
macro-level strategy and concentrate only on micro-level strategy, then the organization may suffer from lack of direction.
A manager concentrating only on strategy at the micro level
may allow negotiations or other interaction episodes with other
parties to drive the overall direction of the organization. The
approach might be viewed as having no particular or at best a
purely emergent formulation and realization of macro strategy. This latter form of macro strategy was not planned but
emerged as the result of patterns in micro-level behaviors of
managers with strategically significant others.

Stakeholder Management as a *Meso*-Level Phenomenon

Although the management literature is rich with theory,
it can be difficult to implement. Therefore, we propose an integration of theory that bridges the gap left by previous management theorists. We argue that a strategy paradigm similar
to the macro and micro applies at the meso level (Hage, 1980).
Researchers examining the relationships of health care or other
organizations with their key stakeholders have taken explicitly
strategic approaches to this phenomenon (Freeman, 1984; Keele,
Buckner, and Bushnell, 1987; Blair and Whitehead, 1988; Blair,
Savage, and Whitehead, 1989; Fottler and others, 1989; Blair,
Slaton, and Savage, 1990).

As illustrated earlier in Figure 9, we believe that neither
the practitioner nor the researcher has had systematic theory
or practical guidance to tie everyday working activities to macro-level strategic management. To fill that gap, we propose
the stakeholder management approach. We argue that stakeholder analysis represents the *meso* (middle) level of analysis
argued for by Hage (1980). We believe these concepts can bridge
the current separation of micro-level behavioral phenomena

from macro-level organization and environment strategic phenomena.

This *middle level of analysis* should not be confused with *middle-range theory* (as opposed to grand theory) described and advocated by Merton (1957). Middle-range theory's primary contribution is that it is formulated at a level of abstraction close enough to empirical reality that the theory's concepts remain highly relevant for understanding and guiding individual managerial behavior (such as negotiating effectively) or broader organizational processes (such as formulating competitive strategy). Nevertheless, middle-range theory does systematically move beyond the merely descriptive to an explicitly analytical level and develops concepts that organize and help us understand many seemingly disparate phenomena.

Middle-range theory can be and has been developed for any level of analysis—from macro to micro. Examples of middle-range theory development on stakeholder phenomena can be found in both the generic management literature (Mason and Mitroff, 1981; Freeman, 1984; Carroll, 1989) and in the specific health care management literature (Blair and Whitehead, 1988; Blair, Savage, and Whitehead, 1989; Fottler, Phillips, Blair and Duran, forthcoming; Blair, Slaton, and Savage, 1990). This entire book represents, in many ways, a deliberate attempt at developing integrated middle-range theory dealing with significant behavior in and between organizations and their participants.

At the meso level of analysis, some sort of relationship (condition) exists between the organization and the stakeholder. This organization-stakeholder relationship impacts on stakeholder management strategies such as proposed by Blair and Whitehead (1988) and discussed at length in Chapter Four. To manage key stakeholders, managers must first seek those stakeholders who are likely to influence the organization's decision. Then executives must make the two critical assessments about these stakeholders introduced in Chapter One: (1) *their potential to threaten the organization* and (2) *their potential to cooperate with it.* When determining this stakeholder bottom line, managers should account for such factors as its relative power, the specific context and history of the organization's relations with it, and those other key stakeholders influencing the organization (Blair and Whitehead, 1988). These activities are key elements in the process of assessing the stakeholder elements in the organization's environment (conditions) prior to the formulation of stakeholder management strategy.

At this level, existing relationships between organizations and their key stakeholders (Fottler and others, 1989) are the conditions that affect the content of strategies, such as *collaboration, involvement, defense* and *monitoring,* used by executives to manage those stakeholders. The results of the attempt to manage stakeholders strategically are based on (1) the appropriateness of those strategies in terms of the stakeholders' overall potentials for threat and cooperation and (2) the extent to which the planned strategy is realized or, alternatively, (3) the emergence of an unplanned, nondeliberate, but appropriate strategy that is then realized (Blair and Whitehead, 1988).

The development and use of middle-range theory, focusing on stakeholders at the meso level as phenomena between overall organizational/environmental conditions and micro interaction situations, permit researchers and the health care executives to go from the interesting but abstract notion that stakeholders are important to the organization to a conceptually informed and organized way to understand and manage key stakeholders. Even more important, meso-level stakeholder management provides a model that allows analysis of the impacts of micro and macro levels on each other through examination of meso-level phenomena as they impact the content and process of strategy.

Using the Stakeholder Approach to Integrate Strategy at Macro and Micro Levels

Figure 11 illustrates how we believe the meso level of analysis fits between the macro and micro levels. The bosses in the middle of each level represent that level's strategy. Although not shown in our model, remember that each level has

Figure 11. Integrating Macro and Micro Management Strategies with Stakeholder Concepts and Strategies.

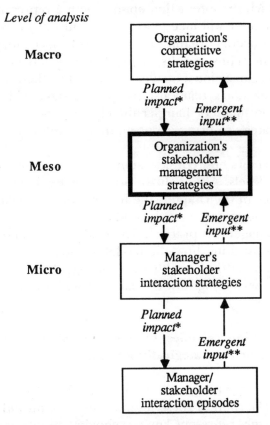

*   = Deliberate/planned impact on strategy implementation

** = Emergent patterns as input to strategy formulation/reformulation

the assessment of conditions between conditions and strategy and has realized strategy between strategy and results. However, the levels do not exist independently from each other. The vertical arrows in the model represent impacts and inputs that connect the levels.

The conditions of the lower levels take place in the context of the upper levels. Thus, whatever conditions exist between an organization and its stakeholder are affected by the overall environmental conditions. In fact, *environmental reality,* we argue, *is manifested concretely as organizational stakeholders.* In turn, organization-stakeholder relations provide the context for the situation in which the interaction episode with a representative of the stakeholder will take place. The results of micro-level strategy affect overall organizational results by facilitating or hampering them. Thus, results of individual negotiations will affect overall organizational results—mediated by their impact on the organization's relationships with its stakeholder, which will in turn facilitate or hamper the effectiveness of the realized macro strategy to bring about desired overall organizational results.

This model shows how consideration of stakeholders affects the different levels. Although we briefly discuss interaction episodes earlier in the chapter, the introduction of stakeholders into the integrated model produces the means to reconceptualize management practice. The rest of this chapter is devoted to demonstrating how the model ties together and to providing examples from health care management situations. We begin by examining how crucial stakeholder interaction episodes can be.

Stakeholder Interaction Episodes: Only Certain Managerial Behavior Is Strategically Relevant

Although executives interact with many people throughout the day, only a portion of these interactions are with individuals who effectively represent key stakeholder groups and organizations. From the stakeholder management perspective, this distinction between interactions with key stakeholders and interactions with others is crucial because it allows managers to focus their strategic efforts. However, executives should be wary of thinking that key stakeholders are only those who have displayed an *active* interest in and an ability to influence the organization's decisions. Key stakeholders may be *inactive,* or their interest may be *latent* because a significant issue has not yet been raised by the organization. Such interests may, however, become salient during an interaction episode involving such issues.

As a result, it is not uncommon for managers to interact with a large and diverse group of stakeholders who are frequently confrontational, high in threat, and low in cooperation. Without a guiding managerial framework that links ongoing pressures to interact with broader strategic issues, undesirable, conflicting, or compromising outcomes are likely. These undesirable results occur because of *ad hoc* responses during particular stakeholder interaction episodes.

A stakeholder interaction episode may range from a scheduled one-on-one encounter to a large, formal press conference to an informal telephone conversation. Furthermore, such episodes may be as complex as negotiating the staffing of an outpatient surgical center or as simple as informing medical equipment suppliers of new bidding requirements for items previously under special contract. Each episode, no matter the length of its duration, influences future interaction episodes by changing the relative threat of and degree of cooperation between the health care organization and the stakeholder.

The micro level of analysis illustrated in Figure 11 demonstrates those aspects of the situation and the stakeholder interaction episode that shape both strategies and results. The reader should note that Figure 11 depicts the interaction episode somewhat differently than does Figure 9. In Figure 10, we focus on only *interaction episodes with representatives of key stakeholders*—not all possible interaction episodes—as the ones crucial for linking macro and micro strategies.

Existing levels of threat and cooperation influence the interaction strategies chosen by the health care manager and the target stakeholder (as well as other possible stakeholders involved in a particular issue). Both the organization's and the stakeholder's strategies may also be influenced by possible coalitions between the target stakeholder and other stakeholders that may or may not be acceptable to the organization's managers (Blair, Savage, and Whitehead, 1989).

The stakeholder interaction episode depicted at the bottom of Figure 11 influences the stakeholder interaction strategy. This immediate "reality test" either reinforces the current stakeholder interaction strategy or provides reason for changing it. This influence continues upward to affect the stake-holder management strategy well as the overall organizational strategy. These influences occur over a time period that may range from very short to relatively long.

Strategic management has long recognized that results should be evaluated. Most models of management processes include a feedback loop indicating this evaluation. Although not pictured directly, recognition of the importance of this type of feedback is intended to be implicit in our simplified model. The influence of the stakeholder interaction episode does not necessarily occur just through the feedback loops at each level—micro, meso, and macro. Our model implies that health care managers can, and in fact often do, alter overall organizational strategy based on the immediate feedback they receive from stakeholder interaction episodes, which provide a needed check on how realistic and "implementable" strategy is. This feed-back affects stakeholder interaction strategies and stakeholder management strategies, thereby indirectly affecting overall or-ganizational strategies.

On the practice side, we advocate, therefore, that after each episode and prior to the next episode the health care manager reassess the stakeholder interaction strategy, the stakeholder management strategy, and the organization's com-petitive strategy. To determine if a stakeholder-sensitive strat-egy at any level of analysis should be changed, managers must monitor the actions and responses of the stakeholder. These stakeholder reactions will help the executive determine whether strategically relevant elements are undergoing unanticipated changes.

How the stakeholder acts and responds will signal not only the stakeholder's perceptions of the interaction, but also the stakeholder's strategy. An unanticipated stakeholder strat-egy may indicate that the manager inaccurately assessed the levels of threat or cooperation or failed to anticipate other pos-sible interaction alternatives.

As mentioned earlier, the organization's stakeholder management strategies are driven by the organization's overall competitive and interaction strategies. However, changing stakeholder management strategies also affect the content of the overall competitive strategies. Stakeholder strategies can be seen as a mediating linkage between the organization's corporate or competitive strategy on the macro level and the interaction strategy on the micro level. These changing overall competitive strategies result from the emergent processes and patterns driven most fundamentally by interactions with stakeholder representatives.

Integrating Multiple Types of Strategies: Example

Managers have many daily interactions with stakeholders or their representatives. These incidents have a very personal quality. However, interacting with stakeholders should not be an interpersonal act isolated from other managerial issues and strategies. A common type of interaction involves negotiating to accomplish organizational goals. Given that the stakeholder as the other party to the negotiation has a stake in the organization's decisions and actions, strategies for negotiating during interaction with a stakeholder need to be connected to two other types of organizational strategies: the organization's overall competitive strategy and its strategy for managing each stakeholder. This interactive process of linking three levels of organizational strategy is depicted in Figure 12.

These strategic linkages move away from the exclusively micro level of analysis and interpersonal focus of most negotiation research, grounding the negotiation process in broader organizational processes. An in-depth theoretical perspective on these multiple analysis levels is provided in the next section. Here our concern is with illustrating the day-to-day managerial implications of such linkages.

For example, the senior management team of a large urban hospital might face many empty beds, perhaps because of the prospective payment system's pressure for shorter lengths of stay. Whatever the cause, they might decide that this can be remedied primarily through capturing a larger share of the tertiary care referral market. Their thinking reflects the generic business strategy of *market penetration*. That is, they plan

Figure 12. Linking Three Levels of Hospital Strategy.

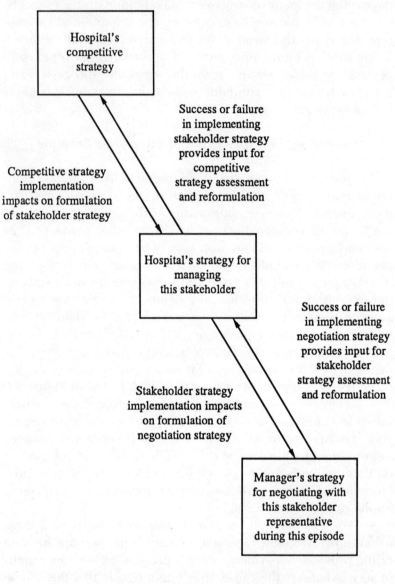

Strategy formulation and implementation   ————————▶

◀———————— Feedback for strategy assessment and reformulation

to grow through expanding the hospital's share of an existing market (tertiary care referrals) using the same products (beds and services to provide tertiary care). Further, they have identified the key stakeholders impacted by that strategy—and essential to its success—to include the rural hospitals and rural primary care physicians in the hospital's secondary market area. Both of these stakeholders are, as we will call them in Chapter Four, mixed-blessing stakeholders because they are high on both the potential for threat and the potential for cooperation. We will suggest that the most appropriate management strategy for this type of stakeholder is *collaboration*.

To collaborate effectively, the hospital might set up a department of regional services. The vice-president for regional services would negotiate collaborative ventures with rural hospitals and members of their medical staffs. Such ventures would be sought to reduce the stakeholders' actual threat and to increase their cooperation. A combination of high threat and high cooperation represents a moderately favorable negotiating situation (discussed at length in Chapter Five). During the negotiations with these stakeholders, the strategies used by the vice-president for regional services must further the urban hospital's goals for effective stakeholder management and overall business strategy.

As the arrows in Figure 12 indicate, implementing the overall business strategy affects the hospital's stakeholder management strategy; carrying out the stakeholder management strategy influences the hospital's negotiation strategy. In turn, the success of a negotiation strategy helps reformulate the strategy for managing a stakeholder. Similarly, the success of the stakeholder management strategy provides valuable input for evaluating the original business strategy.

To continue our example, the vice-president would negotiate with the rural hospitals through their representatives, such as administrators, and the physicians' representatives, such as the chiefs of the medical staffs. Should the chosen negotiation strategy fail, it may call into question both the business and stakeholder management strategies. For instance, the basic collaborative stakeholder management strategy might not be effective because the hospitals' and medical staffs' levels of actual threat or unwillingness to cooperate were underestimated. Further, it may indicate that a simple market penetration business strategy is not adequate. Alternatively, successful negotiation resulting in improved relationships and increased tertiary care referrals may suggest that both the stakeholder management strategy and the business strategy were well formulated.

Another example of these linkages would be a manager in another urban hospital with a strategy to penetrate the rural referral market following a competitive strategy of differentiation based on its unique tertiary care capabilities and management expertise needed by the rural hospital. That manager may have anticipated that a rural hospital stakeholder would be willing to negotiate collaboratively about the purchase of management services from the urban hospital. However, the rural hospital threatens to seek management services from a competitor and demands a lower price.

At this point, the urban executive must assess how this demand for lower costs will affect not only the *stakeholder interactions strategy of collaborative negotiation* but also the *stakeholder management strategy of involving a (presumably) supportive stakeholder* and the *competitive strategy of market penetration through differentiation*. As with the previous example, the reciprocal vertical arrows in the center of Figure 12, which link all three levels of strategy, point to the interaction of these three strategic levels.

Stakeholder Impacts on Macro Competitive Forces and Strategy: The Managed Care Industry

Throughout this book, we look at ways of systematically identifying, diagnosing, and formulating overall strategies to manage stakeholders and even at developing specific strategies to interact effectively with them. In this section, we extend Porter's (1980, 1985) well-known macro model for competitive analysis by incorporating stakeholder concepts. Porter's focus was not on the individual, group, or even individual organization. He was concerned with whether the industry (or specific segment of a broader industry) was strategically "attractive." If managers were to determine that an industry is attractive to move into or to stay in (a *corporate strategy* decision), then Porter (1985) suggested one of four "generic strategies": cost leadership, differentiation, cost focus, and differentiation focus as a *competitive strategy* for a particular organization or a particular strategic business unit focused on that industry or industry segment.

Our purpose here is not to repeat his analysis or the many adaptations of his work (for example, Autrey and Thomas, 1986; Whitehead and others, 1989) but to illustrate for a particular industry the multiple levels of strategy we have been addressing in this chapter. In addition, we further develop stakeholder analysis by examining different types of stakeholder impacts on competitive strategy and articulating the implications of managing stakeholders strategically. In this section we examine competitive strategy concepts in the context of a particular element or segment of the overall health care industry—managed care. As Whitehead and others (1989) have done, we will refer to and analyze managed care as an *industry*, because of its clear difference from other industry segments in health care such as the "hospital industry." Here, we specifically focus on HMOs in the managed care industry.

Stakeholders and the Strategic Attractiveness of the HMO Industry

Macro Perspective. Several structural elements in the environment affect the level of competition in an industry (Porter, 1980; Autrey and Thomas, 1986). Porter directed analytical attention to five potentially threatening "competitive forces." More specifically, the *strategic attractiveness* of any industry and the intensity of competition to be found there are affected by

- Competitive rivalry among existing firms
- Risk of entry by potential competitors
- Bargaining power of suppliers

- Bargaining power of buyers
- Threat of substitute products

It has been argued by Whitehead and others (1989) that, for the most part, HMOs have pursued a cost leadership competitive strategy—particularly vis-à-vis fee-for-service (FFS) delivery systems. The major question for HMOs is whether they have a viable strategy and a sustainable competitive advantage. The competitive situation is changing. Traditional health care systems have responded to the cost leadership strategy because of pressure not only from HMOs but also from Medicare's prospective payment system and from indemnity insurance companies. HMOs face rivalry from each other, from new HMO entrants (particularly the more easily formed and capitalized independent practice associations [IPAs]), and from preferred provider arrangements (PPAs) and other cost-effective FFS substitutes. In addition, HMOs are confronting the growing power of buyers-payers and suppliers as more alternatives are available to them. Many employers are cutting the number of HMO plans offered to their employees while turning to alternative networks of doctors and clinics, often organized by insurers (Shellenbarger, 1990). We will not address strategic issues for HMOs in detail here, since our purpose is primarily to illustrate strategy linkages. Readers interested in recent analyses using Porter's perspective should consult Whitehead and others (1989) or Topping and Fottler (forthcoming).

These structural elements in the environment affecting the strategic attractiveness in an industry represent a macro perspective on HMOs as organizations competing in a specific industry. Next, we examine how this perspective is enhanced by the addition of the meso or stakeholder level of analysis.

Meso Perspective: HMOs and Their Stakeholder Bottom Line. Various studies of the hospital industry using Porter's competitive analysis have been conducted recently (Sheldon and Windham, 1984; Baliga and Johnson, 1986; Autrey and Thomas, 1986). Whitehead and others (1989) have modified and applied these general notions to the managed care industry. Here, we extend their competitive analysis (which used stakeholder concepts) to illustrate the broader issues on which this chapter is focusing. Although competitive analysis looks at the power potential of key stakeholders, how that power might be used is not well developed in this approach. We argue that the levels of support provided by key stakeholders is just as important as if not more important than the levels of bargaining or other power available to those stakeholders. Power and support are relevant to our analysis since they are components on the stakeholder bottom line—*the potential to threaten the organization or to cooperate with it.* Stakeholder supportiveness affects how and whether power is used by stakeholders, thus ultimately determining the strategic vulnerability of HMOs.

In our analysis, we have followed the distinction between health care buyers and payers made by Baliga and Johnson (1986) in their application of competitive analysis to the hospital industry. Thus, we examine key buyer stakeholders such as current HMO enrollees as well as potential enrollees who receive their health care in FFS settings. Employers are key third-party payer stakeholders, including both those who have made HMOs/IPAs available to their employees and those who have not. Other potential key payer stakeholders would include the federal government (Medicare HMOs), state governments (Medicaid HMOs), and insurance companies (with or without their own HMOs). Supplier stakeholders include physicians who are currently practicing full or part time in group or staff model HMOs or the newer IPA model. Also included are physicians who are currently engaged only in FFS practice but who represent potential HMO/IPA practitioners, that is, potential suppliers of professional labor to HMOs or to HMO substitutes such as PPAs.

The effects of competitive forces and stakeholder supportiveness on HMOs in the managed care industry are depicted in Figure 13. In this figure we have modified and extended the competitive analysis framework by incorporating stakeholder concepts and applying the amplified strategic framework to HMOs. We have also translated the impact of Porter's threatening competitive forces into the specific types

Figure 13. Stakeholders and Their Potentially Threatening Actions as Competitive Forces Impacting Organizations in the Managed Care Industry.

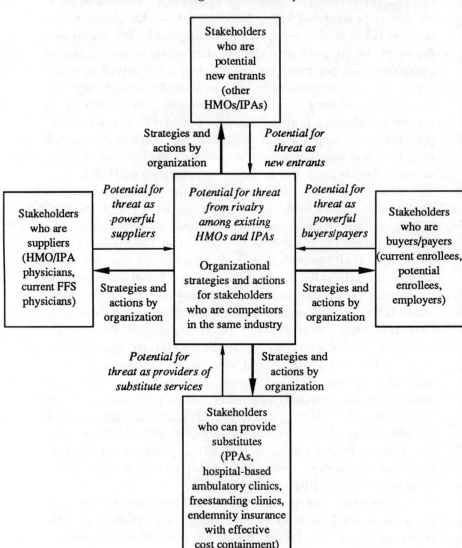

Source: Adapted from Porter (1980, p. 4) for the HMO industry and extended from Whitehead and others (1989, p. 67) to include stakeholder concepts and organizational actions.

of potential threats from stakeholder groups and organizations that provide the day-to-day managerial reality to abstractions like competitive forces. We have also indicated that organizations in the industry might well take potential stakeholder management actions to attempt to control these competitive forces. By managing the key stakeholders whose demands and potential actions create the "force," these actions by organizations—individually or collectively—would, thereby, make the industry more attractive.

Porter's analytical framework focuses on the attractiveness of an industry as a whole, not a specific organization. Here we are able to translate these industrywide competitive forces into the actual stakeholders with which a particular organization in that industry must deal. More specifically, our modified concept of the factors affecting the *strategic attractiveness* of the managed care industry and the intensity of competition includes:

- Potential for threat from *competitive rivalry* among existing HMOs with a stake in each other
- Potential for threat from *stakeholders that are potentially new entrants* into the managed care industry (such as hospitals or insurance companies) or into the organization's specific markets (such as existing staff, group, or network model HMOs or the newer organizational form of IPAs) with market presence elsewhere
- Potential for threat from *powerful supplier stakeholders* such as physicians who practice in HMOs or FFS physicians who serve as potential suppliers of professional labor to HMOs or their substitutes
- Potential for threat from *powerful buyer stakeholders* such as enrollees or potential enrollees, or *powerful payers* such as employers
- Potential for threat from *stakeholders that can provide substitute products or services* such as PPAs, hospital-based ambulatory care clinics, freestanding ambulatory clinics, indemnity insurance with cost containment through second opinions, precertification procedures, and the like

Although HMOs have received substantial attention in the literature, until recently there have been few strategic analyses of these managed care systems. Now we are beginning to see articles warning that the HMO industry as a whole is strategically vulnerable because of a lower-than-desirable level of support from key stakeholders. These issues have been addressed in depth by Whitehead and others (1989) and Topping and Fottler (forthcoming) in their respective analyses of key HMO stakeholders, including the implications for strategic vulnerability and competitive strategy.

Here, our purpose is to present an overview of the relevance of key stakeholders and the stakeholder management approach to a more inclusive analysis by expanding traditional concepts of competitive strategy. We further suggest in Figure 13 that organizations (individually or collectively as an industry) can and do develop strategies and take actions to attempt to manage these key stakeholders. Some of these strategic stakeholder management actions by HMOs will be illustrated when we discuss generic stakeholder strategies in Chapter Four.

Micro Perspective. Although we will not elaborate on the macro strategic issues confronting HMOs, it is clear that the kinds of negotiation or other interaction challenges facing other health care organizations face HMOs as well. In fact, they often *are themselves* key stakeholders for other health care organizations such as hospitals, group medical practices, and reference laboratories. In addition, they may be interacting with many other key stakeholders, for example, insurance companies, employers, and government health programs, shared with other organizations such as hospitals. To deliver care contracted for, they must actually interact on an ongoing basis with stakeholders from patients and their families to the physicians and other health care personnel. Interaction, in these cases, may focus primarily on carefully monitoring, reviewing, and attempting to control utilization of health care services. The linkages between the three levels of HMO strategy parallel those we have just seen in the discussion of the urban hospital and its negotiation with key stakeholders to implement a competitive strategy.

Impact of Managing Stakeholders Strategically

Shown in Figure 14 are the *analytical* and *action* components of stakeholder management and their impact on exchange relationships, resulting in stakeholder equilibrium or disequilibrium. Management of the organization's stakeholders is accomplished by *assessment and diagnosis* as well as *formulation and implementation of a stakeholder management strategy.* Organizations can *systemically analyze* and *strategically manage* the equilibriums of contributions/discontributions and inducements/disinducements that exist between the organization and its stakeholders.

The section to the right in Figure 14 indicates that the exchange relationships that exist between the organization and its stakeholder *should* reflect the results of a variety of actions that are components of the strategic stakeholder and management process. Stakeholder management actions also have an impact on overall organizational results and outcomes through their effect on stakeholder equilibrium or disequilibrium in contributions and inducements. Note that key stakeholder satisfaction (See Figure 14 under "Organizational outcomes/results.") is an overarching organizational outcome resulting, to a great extent but not exclusively, from strategic stakeholder management actions. The corresponding impact of the appropriateness of competitive strategy is also noted in Figure 14—including its effect on stakeholder satisfaction.

Strategic stakeholder management can be thought of as

- A necessary ingredient that needs to be considered and integrated into the organization's formulation and implementation of its business strategy
- The strategic application of inducements to obtain valued stakeholder contributions or support that facilitates attainment of strategic objectives

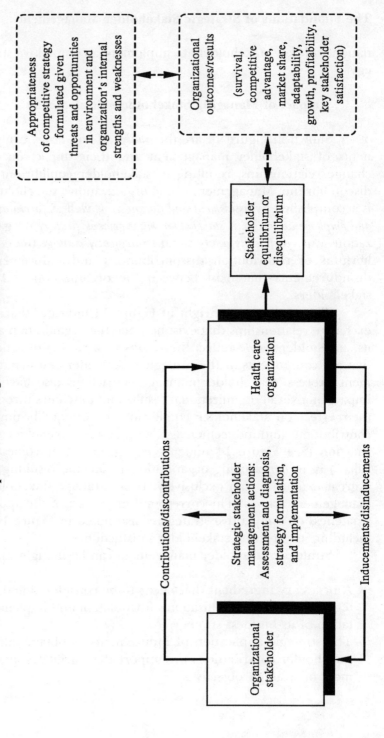

Figure 14. Impact of Strategic Stakeholder Management Actions on Stakeholder Equilibrium or Disequilibrium and Implications for Organizational Outcomes/Results.

- The strategic application of disinducements to protect the organization from stakeholder discontributions that threaten attainment of strategic objectives
- A search for more attractive alternative sources of needed contributions or support through the assessment and diagnosis of stakeholders
- An attempt to reduce the expenditure of inducements to stakeholders while maintaining the same level of contributions
- An attempt to reduce the expenditure of disinducements to stakeholders without increasing the level of discontributions
- An attempt to increase the total acquisition of stakeholder contributions or support without increasing the level of discontributions

Of course, the nature of the inducement and contribution exchange will not always be equitable—or at least not be equitable as viewed by either the organization or the stakeholder or both (Blau, 1964). In addition, the exchange partners' perceptions of "better" alternatives is crucial (Thibault and Kelley, 1959).

From Abstract to Concrete:
Stakeholder Approach Focuses and Integrates Multiple
Management Activities Relevant for Competitive Strategy

As illustrated in Figure 11, we believe that today's manager has had little theory to tie everyday working activities to the macro level of strategic management. We proposed in Figures 12 through 14 that stakeholder management can be used at a meso level of analysis to integrate—both analytically and practically—micro-level management content and process activities with their counterparts at the macro level. This integration occurs when executives approach managing key organizational stakeholders strategically by effectively assessing, diagnosing, and formulating and implementing strategies that impact stakeholders contributions or discontributions through *strategically* exchanging inducements and disinducements for them.

Success in steering through a dynamic and conflictual environment might be as much a consequence of its stakeholder interaction strategies—and the facility of its managers in interacting with stakeholders—as of any other factor. In short, during this decade of frequent strategic realignment in the health care industry, stakeholder interaction consistent with overall strategic goals has become a key skill for the manager. Every manager interacts with others to resolve conflicts, implement projects, or create opportunity. Whether dealing with representatives of key stakeholder groups such as the president of the medical or professional staff, department managers, or suppliers, managers should consider carefully how to handle these interactions. Such diverse stakeholders require a manager capable of successfully interacting with individuals, groups, other organizations, and various stakeholder coalitions.

Stakeholders vary in their significance for, and potential impact on, the strategic management process. For each strategic decision situation, organizations typically face a diverse set of stakeholders with varied, frequently conflicting, interests and goals. Although a set of key stakeholders will typically affect a particular strategic decision, their ability and desire to influence specific strategies vary greatly. However, any strategy depends on creating a support base among stakeholders.

Hence, strategy formulation and implementation are, to a great extent, the results of either explicit or implicit interaction with various internal, interface, and external stakeholders. Since the costs associated with, and ultimate success of, a competitive strategy partly depend on the response of key stakeholders, we advocate that executives approach interaction with them as a conscious decision process and explicitly link their actions to overarching business strategies. The relationships between the organization and its key stakeholders are important not only in formulating meso-level stakeholder management strategies but also in formulating and implementing strategy at both the macro and micro levels.

Successful stakeholder interaction goes beyond basic interpersonal skills. Health care managers should be sensitive to potential and existing coalitions of internal stakeholders, as well as potential and existing coalitions among external stakeholders, whenever they interact with a particular stakeholder. Additionally, managers should recognize that the results of their interaction with stakeholders depend on the political astuteness and authority of the representatives with whom they actually meet or talk. These concerns are compounded by the fact that stakeholder interactions should be explicitly integrated with the organization's overall competitive strategies and its stakeholder management strategies.

The notion of strategic stakeholder management and its connection to both macro and micro organizational processes promises to extend both strategic management and behavioral theory. Researchers should focus on the connections between the macro and micro levels. Use of stakeholder management strategies by practitioners should be examined to determine if they improve the performance of organizations by allowing the organization to alter macro-level competitive strategy when stakeholders prove to be at odds with the original strategy and develop stakeholder strategies that prove effective over time.

As indicated earlier in this chapter, we see stakeholder management as an integrative approach that links a wide range of management activities usually addressed separately. The common linkage of these management tasks is that all are involved in managing relationships with key stakeholders.

Table 1 displays the key stakeholder relationships focused on by multiple management activities. The stakeholder management approach concentrates on *strategically managing* relationships with all key organizational stakeholders.

Thus, stakeholder management is, in part, strategic management, marketing, public relations, human resource management, and many other executive activities. Some of this is intuitive for experienced and successful managers. Much of this intuition is based on experiencing the consequences of well—or poorly—managed stakeholder relationships and learning what inducements elicit contributions and what discontributions require what kind of disinducements. Managing stakeholders

Table 1. Stakeholder Management: Integrating Existing Management
Activities.

Management Activity	Key Stakeholder Relations Focused On
1. Strategic management	Competitors, suppliers, buyers/payers, corporate office
2. Marketing	Potential patients representing different market segments, physicians and other referral sources
3. Guest relations	Employees, patients and their families, physicians
4. Board relations	Board of trustees, stakeholders represented by board
5. Physician relations	Medical staff, community physicians
6. Public relations	Community, media, special-interest groups
7. Government relations/public issues management	Local, state, and federal government agencies; local, state, and federal elected officials; special-interest groups
8. Financial management	Third-party payers, financial institutions, corporate office
9. Organizational politics and design	Organizational managers, other employees, corporate office
10. Quality assurance/utilization review	Accrediting/licensing agencies, third-party payers, physicians
11. Operations management	Employees, suppliers
12. Information management	Organizational managers, other employees, third-party payers, accrediting/licensing agencies, corporate office
13. Risk management	Insurance companies, courts/trial lawyers, regulatory agencies
14. Human resource management	Employees, labor unions

strategically, however, requires that all key relationships be examined systematically and diagnostically and that explicit strategies be formulated and implemented to maximize stakeholder cooperation and minimize threat. This book provides a systematic and strategic way to make day-to-day managerial activities consistent with the organization's overall competitive strategy through focusing on managing its key stakeholders.

We encourage executives to integrate their interaction, stakeholder, and business/corporate strategies. We believe that the strategic stakeholder management approach provides sound advice for practitioners who must manage their way through interacting with their many stakeholders.

Stakeholder-Management-in-Action Study

Our empirical research approach for this book, the stakeholder-management-in-action study, incorporates qualitative and quantitative data gathered in a systematic but exploratory fashion. These complementary approaches facilitated our developing and extending the understanding of the stakeholder management approach for health care organizations in general and for hospitals in particular. Although our data collection was not limited to hospitals, they represent the most complex organizations from a management perspective, generally have the greatest number and variety of stakeholders, and have the most complete, systematic, and strategic approach to stakeholder management. Hence, we have focused in great part on different types of hospitals or hospital corporations but have also included examples from our research with other types of health care organizations such as group practices, HMOs, ambulatory surgery and imaging settings, nursing homes, and academic medical centers.

Our data collection was designed to enhance the development of strategic stakeholder management concepts and was not intended to be a complete description and analysis of all health care stakeholders and how they are dealt with by every type of organization. Thus, stakeholder management theory and practice are informed by these data rather than systematically tested by them. In other words, this book presents both a conceptual *and* a limited empirical exploration of health care organization-stakeholder relationships, including the assessment and strategic management of key stakeholders and their stakes in these organizations.

As part of our research to systematically determine key health care stakeholders and how they should be managed, a survey instrument was administered to sixteen hospital administrators at a symposium in Sandestin, Florida, sponsored by the Department of Health Services Administration at the University of Alabama, Birmingham, in August 1987. Table 2 indicates the respondent characteristics from this exploratory study and the nature of the hospitals they represent. Most respondents are CEOs or assistant administrators, and the hospitals they represent are quite diverse in terms of control, type of hospital, bed size, system affiliation, and resource availability. As compared to hospitals in the southeastern United States, they are generally representative with a slight overrepresentation of public hospitals and underrepresentation of religious hospitals.

In addition to this pilot survey, we enhanced and supplemented the theory-building aspects of our research with an initial look at the complexity of empirical reality—not easily captured in pencil-and-paper survey instruments—through qualitative interviews. These interviews were designed to further our understanding of how particular management actions and practices in specific organizations related to both their chosen business strategies and their conceptions of those with a stake in their organizations and how these stakeholders should and could be managed, that is, what implicit or explicit strategies were being used.

We conducted in-depth, semistructured qualitative interviews with thirty senior executives, primarily in health care organizations in the Southwest and the southeastern United States. Executives included CEOs, chief operating officers, chief financial officers, associate administrators, assistant administrators, vice-presidents of marketing, vice-presidents of corporate services (services involving for-profit ventures and hospital-

Table 2. Pilot Survey Respondent Characteristics.

Respondent Characteristic	Number	Percent
Position		
CEO	10	61
Assistant administrator	5	33
Department head	1	6
Hospital control		
Investor owned	5	31
Not for profit	5	31
Public	6	38
Type of hospital		
University medical center	3	19
Specialty hospital	1	6
General hospital	12	75
Number of beds		
1–99	3	19
100–199	3	19
200–299	4	25
300+	6	37
System affiliation		
Freestanding	8	50
System members	8	50
Resource availability		
Stable or increasing	10	63
Decreasing	6	37

physician outpatient joint ventures), vice-presidents for human resources, and directors of public relations and regional services. In addition, we interviewed representatives of health care venders and insurance companies. These interviews represented two academic medical centers, two children's hospitals, two religious hospitals, two investor-owned hospitals, two nonprofit community hospitals, one nursing home, one HMO, several ambulatory settings, and one insurance company. All of these institutions had diversified to some degree, and six of the hospitals were part of a multiinstitutional system. An average of two interviews with different executives per institution were conducted. In addition, several executives were interviewed several times to extend our depth of understanding of what they do, why, and with what consequences. This limited qualitative study was intended to give us insights into the range of actual organizational practices and strategic linkages, not to provide precise estimates of behavioral parameters.

These interviews helped us to determine

- What generic and specific competitive strategies the organization was pursuing and why
- What generic stakeholder management strategies they were implicitly or explicitly following and why
- The degree to which stakeholder management practices were integrated with competitive strategy
- The specific practices implemented to reinforce both competitive and stakeholder strategies
- The interaction strategies followed to manage those practices

The examples used throughout this book are based on real situations and reflect actual stakeholder issues and managerial behavior. To protect the confidentiality of our respondents in the qualitative interviews, details in the examples have often been disguised and are not identified by organizational name. For the same reason, we only rarely use direct quotations, even though the interviews were taped and transcribed with the respondents' consent. Nevertheless, the situations we discuss reflect the everyday reality facing health care managers. In those cases where public information was available through the *Wall Street Journal, Modern Healthcare, Hospitals,* or other media sources, we have specified which organization we are using to illustrate the stakeholder management issue addressed.

We encourage other researchers to test and to extend the strategic approach presented in this book through both empirical and conceptual research. We also suggest that theoretical extensions of this approach address the implications for understanding emergent strategy (Mintzberg, 1988a, 1988b) and the broader organizational strategy enactment (Weick, 1979).

Stakeholder management represents a new way of thinking for many health care executives. Given the importance of the key stakeholders for overall business strategy, successful implementation of the stakeholder management concept should provide a competitive advantage. Our research indicates a definite need for a *systematic and strategic* emphasis on stakeholder management by health care executives.

While most organizations in our study claimed to have an explicit stakeholder management strategy, the examples provided by the respondents indicated that most were ignoring the majority of their stakeholders and focusing on only one of three whom they deemed of critical importance. The most common stakeholders mentioned in terms of explicit management strategies included the corporate office, medical staff, and board of trustees.

Few organizations have fully developed an integrated, articulated strategic approach for managing their key stakeholders. For most organizations, at best, executives' stakeholder management perspectives are incomplete, and their approaches to stakeholder assessment and management are underdeveloped and haphazard; at worst, they display a total lack of explicit awareness of and involvement in a systematic and effective management approach. Throughout this book, we articulate and detail the overall approach and specific tools and techniques that facilitate managing stakeholders strategically.

❊❊❊❊❊❊❊❊❊❊❊❊❊❊❊❊❊❊❊❊❊❊❊❊❊❊❊❊❊❊❊

CHAPTER 3

Identifying and Assessing
Key Health Care Stakeholders

In Chapters One and Two we focused on stakeholder management as an integrative management approach necessary for dealing with conflicting demands from the increased number of stakeholders to which health care executives must respond. We argue here that an increasing proportion of health care stakeholders have neutral or negative relationships with health care organizations. In addition, the power of such stakeholders vis-à-vis the health care organization is increasing. In this chapter, we identify and assess the power and values of key stakeholders of today's health care organizations.

The steps in our approach to stakeholder assessment include identifying organizational stakeholders, determining key organizational stakeholders, examining the balance of power, assessing stakeholder sources of power and key values, and examining issue-specific stakeholder concerns. Since relevant stakeholders vary for different types of organizations, we examine alternative stakeholder assessment by determining who matters in different types of hospitals and nonhospital health care settings.

These steps will be covered in this chapter, which includes several case studies of who mattered and presents the first of three resources in this book. This resource, the "Stakeholder Identification and Assessment Toolkit," can be used by any manager in any kind of organization to apply the approach we develop in this chapter.

Who Matters? Identifying Organizational Stakeholders

The purpose of identifying stakeholders is to determine the relative influence that they may or should have on managerial decisions. Stakeholders' influence can constrain management and limit strategic choices. Knowing the players is an important first step in determining how health care managers should behave if their organizations are to realize their competitive strategies.

Three approaches may be useful in identifying stakeholders if one conducts empirical research on an organization. First, the organization's publications may be examined to determine which stakeholders are recognized as important and have an impact on decisions. Second, one might examine what is written in public sources about an organization and its relationship with stakeholders. Third, one might ascertain the organization's perspective on stakeholders through interviews and survey questionnaires. In fact, these methods would also serve as sources of information for a detailed staff study to be presented at an annual strategic management retreat.

However, the practitioner who is thrust into a situation or role must be able to conduct a quick assessment of stakeholders. Such a practitioner can quickly use the relatively simple and straightforward but analytically powerful approaches we present here. If the assessment techniques and tools are understood and become an integral part of the way managers think, they will be able to view the world around themselves— in and outside their organizations—with new clarity.

The following list shows the typical stakeholders in a large U.S. hospital. These stakeholders are categorized into three groups: internal, interface, and external.

Internal Stakeholders

Management
    Top managers
    Physician managers/medical director
    Nonclinical managers (marketing, financial)

Clinical functional managers
Clinical unit managers
Nonmanagement employees
Professional
Paraprofessional
Support personnel

Interface Stakeholders

Nonmanagement medical staff
On staff only at this hospital
Also on staff at other hospitals
Partners in joint venture with hospital
Hospital board
Trustees with policy authority
Advisory only
Parent companies/organizations/religious orders
Stockholders/taxpayers/contributors

External Stakeholders

Hospital suppliers
Competitors
Other hospitals
Physicians (for outpatient services)
Alternative delivery systems (HMOs, PPOs)
Other alternatives (freestanding outpatient surgery, diag-
nostic or instant care centers)
Related health care organizations
Clinics
Nursing homes
Pharmacies
Smaller hospitals
Government regulatory/licensing agencies
Federal
State
Local
Private accreditation associations
(for example, Joint Commission on Accreditation of Health
Care Organizations)

Professional associations
  (for example, for certification of hospital professionals)
  National
  State
  Local
Unions
  National/international
  Local
Patients
  Private pay patients
  Insured patients
    Pay through prospective payment
    Pay through retrospective payment
    Pay at full rate
    Pay at discounted rate
  Indigent patients
    Residents
    Nonresidents
  Patient families
Third-party payers
  Governments
    Federal
    State
    Local
  Insurance companies
  Employers
  Business coalitions
  HMOs (as purchasers of hospital services)
Media
  Local
  National
Financial community
  Including joint venture investment partners
Special-interest groups
  (for example, American Association of Retired Persons, vet-
    erans' organizations for VA hospitals, or Alcoholics
    Anonymous for psychiatric/substance-abuse programs)
Religious organizations

Denominational organization (synods, dioceses)
Local churches/pastors
Local community

Internal stakeholders are those that operate almost entirely in the generally accepted bounds of the organization and typically include management, professional, and nonprofessional staff. Management attempts to manage these internal stakeholders by providing sufficient inducements to gain continual contributions from these stakeholders. The stakeholders determine whether the inducement is sufficient for the contribution they are required to make. This is partly determined by the alternative inducement—contribution offers received from competitive organizations.

Unless both the organization and the stakeholder believe such an agreement will be mutually beneficial and of fair value (relative to alternatives), agreement will not be reached or sustained. Under conditions of scarce resources, the exchange partners can be expected to attempt to obtain as high an inducement as possible while giving as low a contribution as possible. Restructuring the situation (for example, providing a better compensation and benefit package) is the way the organization may induce or persuade employees to make the needed contribution. Alternatively, individuals in the organization also engage in manipulation, bargaining, and coalition activity to protect both their own interests and those of the coalition (also including external coalitions such as unions or professional associations) to which they belong.

Interface stakeholders are those which function both internal and external to the organization, that is, those who are on the interface between the organization and its environment. The major categories of interface stakeholders include the medical staff, the hospital board of trustees, the corporate office of the parent company, and stockholders, taxpayers, or other contributors. These tend to be among the most powerful stakeholders in health care organizations but are easily misunderstood because they are thought of as "us" or "them" when they are both—and neither.

As in the case of internal stakeholders, the organization must offer each interface stakeholder sufficient inducements to continue to make appropriate contributions. However, the inducements can be more complex than in the case of internal stakeholders because of the lack of a structured human resource systems and management authority. Examples include such inducements as professional autonomy (medical staff), institutional prestige or political contacts (hospital board), good financial returns (corporate office), access (taxpayers), and special services or benefits (contributors).

Finally, the hospital must respond to a large number and wide variety of *external stakeholders* including suppliers, competitors, related health organizations, government agencies, private accrediting associations, professional associations, labor unions, patients, third-party payers, the media, the financial community, special-interest groups, and the local community. Whereas the internal and interface stakeholders are at least supportive of the hospital, many of the external stakeholders are seen as neutral, nonsupportive, or even openly hostile by the health care executives we interviewed.

External stakeholders fall into three categories in their relationship to the health care organization. Some *provide inputs* to the organization, some *compete* with it, and some have some *special interest* in how it functions. The first category includes suppliers, patients, third-party payers, and the financial community. The relationship between the organization and these external stakeholders is a symbiotic one since the organization depends on these stakeholders for its very survival. These stakeholders, in turn, depend on the organization to take their outputs. Without the organization or others like it, the stakeholders providing inputs could not survive. The degree of dependence of the organization on these stakeholders (and vice versa) depends on the number and relative attractiveness of alternative providers of similar goods and services.

Consequently, the relationship between the organization and its stakeholders providing necessary inputs is one of mutual dependence. As such, the two parties cannot or do not want to do without one another. However, they may experience conflict as to how to cooperate. For example, a hospital and its patients may conflict over the price charged for certain services, but neither wishes to sever all relationship with the other.

The second category of external stakeholders (competitors) seek to attract the focal organization's dependents. These competitors may be direct competitors for patients (for example, other hospitals) or they may be competing for skilled personnel (for example, related health organizations). Competitors do not necessarily need one another to survive. While cooperation between hospitals and their competitors has increased in recent years, so too has competition. Competitiveness, rather than cooperation, best defines the nature of the relationship, at least most of the time.

The third category of external stakeholders (special-interest groups) includes any organization concerned with those aspects of the organization's operations that affect the stakeholders' interests. The major special-interest groups impacting hospitals are government regulatory agencies, private accrediting associations, professional associations, labor unions, the media, the local community, and various political-action groups such as the American Association of Retired Persons (AARP). Due to the nature of the special interest, conflict most often defines the nature of this relationship. The conflict is most often solved by compromise and, in some cases, overt collaboration.

Why Do They Matter? Determining Key Organizational Stakeholders and Balance of Power

While the previous section indicates the wide range of possible stakeholders for hospitals, it would be impossible and unnecessary to consider all of them. Some stakeholders are generally influential and powerful, others are only influential and powerful regarding certain issues, and still others lack influence and power. Executives do not have time to consider all possible stakeholders, so it is important for them to focus on the most important ones.

Why are some stakeholders more important than others? In this book we argue that there are several basic reasons for stakeholders to matter to the organization:

- Their contributions are essential to implementing the organization's competitive strategy.
- Their demands for inducements place severe strain on the organization.
- Their attempts to confront the organization with significant disinducement threaten its viability.
- Their contributions can be easily switched to another organization.

All of these factors affect stakeholders' potentials for threat and cooperation and, therefore, their overall supportiveness. In the sections to follow, we look at both the extent of stakeholder power and where it comes from as well as the values that impact on how that power will likely be used.

Balance of Power

Table 3 indicates that our pilot survey respondents felt that the balance of power is shifting toward the stakeholders and away from the hospital. Moreover, managers perceive there

Table 3. Balance of Power, Degree of Consensus, and Use of Explicit Stockholder Management Strategies.

Category	Number	Percent
Balance of power		
Increasing power for stakeholders	10	63
No change	1	6
Increasing power for hospital	5	31
Degree of consensus among stakeholders		
Very little	4	25
Some	10	63
Very much	2	12
Explicit stakeholder management		
No	4	25
Yes	12	75

to be very little or only some consensus among stakeholders concerning the mission, goals, and priorities of the hospital. While most hospitals claimed to have an explicit stakeholder management strategy, the examples provided indicated most were ignoring most of their stakeholders and focusing on one of three whom they deemed of critical importance. The most common stakeholders mentioned in terms of explicit management strategies included the corporate office, medical staff, and board of trustees.

Table 4 shows the key stakeholders identified by respondents in response to an open-ended question. In addition to listing all stakeholders listed by the respondents, the first col-

Table 4. Key Hospital Stakeholders Identified by Hospital Administrators.

Key Stakeholders Identified (I, IF, E)*	Percent of Respondents Identifying Stakeholder (n = 16)	Total Score	Percent Indicating Stakeholder Increasing Power
1. Medical staff (IF)	94	124	40
2. Patients (E)	81	83	77
3. Hospital management (I)	50	65	62
4. Nonphysician professional staff (I)	56	58	67
5. Board of trustees (IF)	44	56	43
6. Federal government (E)	37	55	67
7. Corporate office (IF)	44	48	50
8. Nonprofessional staff (I)	44	38	27
9. Third-party payers (E)	31	33	100
10. Elected public officials (E)	25	26	50
11. Political pressure groups (E)	19	15	—
12. Local business/industry (E)	19	14	—
13. Accreditation (licensing agencies) (E)	12	13	—
14. Medical school officials (IF)	12	12	—
15. Other hospitals (E)	12	10	—
16. State government (E)	6	9	—
17. Health maintenance organizations (E)	19	6	—
18. Media (E)	6	5	—
19. Labor unions (E)	6	2	—

    * E = External stakeholder
      IF = Interface stakeholder
       I = Internal stakeholder

umn lists the percentage of respondents listing each particular stakeholder. The second column indicates the total score for each stakeholder defined as the number of mentions times the perceived degree of power. For example, if a particular stakeholder was mentioned four times and the degree of power was eight (on a ten-point scale) in two cases and six in two others, the total score is 28 $(2 \times 8) + (2 \times 6)$. The third column indicates the percentage of respondents (if mentioned by at least 25 percent of respondents) who indicated a particular stakeholder was increasing power (vis-à-vis their hospital).

While these results from a limited sample of hospital administrators should not be viewed as definitive in any sense, they are probably *suggestive* of the identity of most of the key stakeholders and their relative power and resultant importance to the organization. In addition, the findings are consistent with the in-depth qualitative interviews we conducted with senior health care executives.

One stakeholder not listed here is church organizations (for example, synods or dioceses) or religious orders, which obviously have a great deal of influence in religious hospitals. This omission is due to the lack of religious hospital respondents in our sample.

The ordering of the various stakeholders in terms of their degree of influence will obviously vary depending on the nature of the hospital. For example, the corporate office is only of moderate importance for the sample as a whole; however, only 50 percent of the sample hospitals were part of a corporate chain. For those hospitals, it was one of the two or three most important stakeholders. For the others, it was of no importance whatsoever.

Table 4 indicates that the *medical staff* is the most important stakeholder for our respondents. It was listed by 94 percent and had the highest total score. However, only 40 percent indicated that the medical staff was increasing its power, with the rest indicating no change or a decline. Note, however, that both the evaluation of the importance of each stakeholder and the trend in stakeholder power are based on the subjective judgments of the administrator respondents. *Patients* were the second most influential stakeholder and were increasing in influence. This reflects the increasing competition for funded patients among hospitals and the recent emphasis on hospital marketing.

The next three key stakeholders were *hospital management,* the *nonphysician professional staff,* and the *board of trustees.* However, none of these achieved the degree of consensus as did the medical staff and patients. They were listed by only 44 to 56 percent of the respondents. Most of those respondents thought both management and the professional staff were increasing their power (perhaps somewhat at the expense of the medical staff). However, they also thought the board was losing power (perhaps due to the failure of some boards to keep up with recent changes in the industry).

The *federal government* was the next key stakeholder identified by our respondents based on the government's role in funding and regulating Medicare, Medicaid, and the state health-planning efforts. The Medicare prospective payment system, in particular, has been influential in modifying hospital management practices (see, for example, Smith and Fottler, 1985). While the federal government is listed by only a minority of our respondents, those who did list it considered it very powerful; hence, the relatively high score (55) indicates an important stakeholder.

The *corporate office* is of critical importance to those hospitals that have a corporate office but of no importance to freestanding institutions, which constitute half our sample. There is no trend for it to become either more or less important over time. The reason for the rather high ranking of the corporate office is obvious; the corporate office hires the hospital's CEO (with concurrence of the local board) and evaluates her or his performance. Moreover, the institution has to operate within the constraints (budgets, policies, and so on) imposed by the corporate office.

The next key stakeholder identified by our respondents was the *nonprofessional staff.* However, most felt these stakeholders were declining in influence as a result of their plentiful supply and the fact that they are easily replaced.

Third-party payers, like Blue Cross–Blue Shield and other

insurance companies, were next in terms of their importance. All respondents indicated third-party payers were increasing in power and influence. The implication is that this stakeholder will be of even greater importance in the future. The significance of this stakeholder is obvious. The third-party payer negotiates contracts with employers and enforces these contracts regarding insured individuals who use hospital services. Denial of claims may be costly for the hospital.

Elected public officials are another key stakeholder identified by a minority of our respondents. Obviously, these individuals play some role for all hospitals but are particularly important for hospitals that receive significant public funding. Examples would be public hospitals run by state and local governments and Veterans Administration hospitals.

None of the other stakeholders listed were identified by 20 percent or more of the respondents. These other stakeholders included political pressure groups, local business and industry, accrediting/licensing agencies, medical school officials, other hospitals, state government, health maintenance organizations, the media, and labor unions.

It should be remembered that this listing provides averages for all hospitals represented by our respondents and therefore does not represent any one particular hospital. Consequently, any one of the stakeholders identified by less than 20 percent of the respondents could be a key stakeholder for a given hospital at a specific time. For example, the *media* could become a significant stakeholder if a particular hospital experienced very high death rates in particular diagnosis-related group (DRG) categories if such data were reported to the media by the U.S. Health Care Financing Administration (Fottler, Slovensky, and Rogers, 1987). The resulting negative publicity could adversely affect the hospital's image and its ability to market services in the local community.

Assessing Stakeholders' Sources of Power and Key Values

Table 5 indicates the sources of power and values of the top ten key stakeholders identified in Table 4. This information represents our synthesis of managerial perceptions and is derived from both the questionnaires and the in-depth personal interviews. As already noted in Table 3, the values of key stakeholders are at least partly incompatible.

The *medical staff* obviously admits patients, controls the patient care process (including the use of resources), and provides the major services of the institution. The high degree of dependence of the hospital on these physician inputs makes the medical staff the single most important hospital stakeholder. However, the physician surplus, which is predicted to increase over the next decade, has reduced the absolute power of physicians since more physicians are competing for a smaller number of medical staff openings.

In addition, physicians are in a position of mutual dependence since they need to admit their patients and practice their craft in a hospital. However, in most larger communities, they are affiliated with several hospitals and may shift patients from one to another if their needs are not being met.

Table 5. Sources of Power and Values of Key Hospital Stakeholders.

Key Stakeholder	Sources of Power	Key Values
1. *Medical staff*	1. Admits patients 2. Controls patient care process 3. Controls use of resources 4. Provides key services	1. Clinical quality 2. Patient access 3. Medical training 4. Support services 5. Physician autonomy
2. *Patients*	1. Choose provider 2. Influence public perceptions	1. Clinical quality 2. Service quality 3. Access 4. Low cost to patient
3. *Hospital management*	1. Controls operations 2. Influences or controls budgets	1. Institutional leadership 2. Cost containment 3. Profitability
4. *Nonphysician professional staff*	1. Possesses critical skills 2. Controls support services	1. Clinical quality 2. Personal independence and influence 3. Professional ethics

Key Stakeholder	Sources of Power	Key Values
5. Board of trustees	1. Possesses formal authority and control 2. May veto decisions 3. May discharge CEO	1. Community needs 2. Institutional pride/image 3. Profitability 4. Overall effectiveness
6. Federal government	1. Regulates 2. Controls reimbursement	1. Consistency with regulations 2. Cost containment 3. Patient access
7. Corporate office	1. Controls resources 2. May veto decisions	1. Cost containment 2. Profitability 3. Market share
8. Nonprofessional staff	1. Provides necessary services 2. Impacts patient perceptions	1. Adequate salaries 2. Job security 3. Job satisfaction
9. Third-party payers	1. Negotiate rules regarding reimbursement for insured patients 2. Enforce rules regarding reimbursement	1. Reimbursement based on provision of insured service 2. Market expansion
10. Elected public officials	1. Exert political influence/pressure 2. Control funding	1. Service to constituents 2. Cost containment 3. Positive image

The key values of the medical staff regarding the hospital include high clinical quality (sometimes identified as the latest in high technology), convenient access for patients, medical training programs, adequate support services, and physician autonomy. The medical staff is not generally concerned with the requirements of external regulators or supportive of internal administrative mechanisms to contain costs or enhance profitability.

The sources of power for *patients* include their ability to choose providers (physicians, hospitals, and ambulatory facilities) and the ability to influence other potential patients regarding these choices. Like physicians, they are concerned with clinical quality and patient access. Unlike physicians, they are also concerned with service quality (for example, amenities) and a low cost to the patient. They are concerned with containing those costs that directly impact on them but less concerned about costs absorbed by others (third-party payers, managed care programs).

Hospital management controls operations and influences or controls budgets. Their values include cost containment, profitability, and institutional leadership. The latter can cover a wide range of activities that may be compatible or incompatible with the values of other key stakeholders. Management's emphasis on cost containment and profitability often creates an uneasy truce between it, the medical staff, and the professional staff.

The *nonphysician professional staff* possesses critical skills necessary to health service delivery. Obviously, different professional occupations are more or less critical in a given institution. Moreover, supply and demand in the labor market can also influence how much power a given professional group exerts in a hospital. For example, in the late 1980s the shortage of nurses enhanced the power of the nursing staff to obtain concessions from hospitals. Professional staff members are concerned with clinical quality, personal independence and influence, and an environment which is consistent with their professional ethics. They want to be treated as professionals.

The *board of trustees* is a key stakeholder due to its formal authority. The board alone possesses formal authority and control, may veto administrative proposals or decisions, and may discharge the CEO. The board usually represents a broad spectrum of influential citizens in the community and therefore is concerned with community needs identified by these board members. The board is also interested in increasing or maintaining the hospital's image and pride, profitability, and overall effectiveness (as judged by other influential individuals and groups).

The *federal government* is powerful because it regulates and controls reimbursement under the Medicare program and influences reimbursement under the Medicaid program. Its main concerns are the hospital's consistency with federal regulations, cost containment, and patient access (particularly for uninsured, indigent patients).

The *corporate office* controls resources and may disapprove of individual hospital decisions not compatible with corporate goals or strategies. It is concerned with cost containment, profitability, and market share in the profitable markets. A high market share in an unprofitable market such as indigent care would not be viewed favorably.

The *nonprofessional staff* provides necessary services and impacts patient perceptions of the hospital on the basis of how well such services are delivered. Concerns of the nonprofessional staff include adequate salaries, job security, and job satisfaction. The nonprofessional staff is less powerful than the professional staff as a result of not possessing unique skills that are difficult to recruit and replace. However, they could become more powerful if they are unionized or engage in strikes and slowdowns to force the administration to consider their demands.

Third-party payers negotiate the rules regarding reimbursement for their insured patients and then enforce these rules. The ability to deny payment and to reduce the income of hospitals is the source of power. Third-party payers are concerned that reimbursement be based on an insured service that has actually been delivered. They are also concerned with expanding their own market. The latter is usually done by meeting the needs of employers and employees for health insurance packages that cover desired services with a competitive premium.

Finally, *elected public officials* exert pressure or influence in areas that affect them or their constituents. Since all hospitals receive some public funding, the threat to cut the budget of programs that provide such funding is a concern for hospitals. The funding threat is obviously greater in the case of public hospitals. Elected public officials are concerned with hospital service to their constituents, cost containment, and a positive community image.

Examining Issue-Specific Stakeholder Concerns

Table 6 provides a *stakeholder issue matrix* for a hypothetical health care organization such as those developed by Freeman (1984) for other industries. In this hypothetical matrix, we have listed the ten key stakeholders discussed above along with local business and industry, the media, and competitors. We see the hypothetical issues presented as typical for many organizations. The degree of concern with various issues from offering a new service to the amount of financial return the organization receives would vary widely among the thirteen stakeholders. It is, therefore, very important for health care executives to identify the key stakeholders who would be most concerned *with each particular issue,* anticipate their concerns and likely reaction, take steps to alleviate these concerns, and manage the entire process of implementing change with the stakeholders in mind. For any specific organization some of these issues will be particularly critical for realizing corporate or competitive strategy; some will be less so. None of the key stakeholders would be equally concerned with all issues, and management needs to keep this in mind when formulating and implementing strategies. The use of such a stakeholder issues matrix will permit health care executives to be more proactive in anticipating and dealing with likely stakeholder reactions— especially to issues essential for overall effective competitive strategy formulation or implementation.

Health care managers need to be concerned with identifying and managing *all* of their key stakeholders who might have an interest in any particular issue faced by the institution, especially if the issue is central to overall competitive success. These key stakeholders vary by type of hospital and between hospitals and other health service organizations. In the following sections, we will provide some illustrations of key stakeholders in specific types of health care organizations.

Table 6. Stakeholder Issues Matrix for Hypothetical Health Care Organization.

Stakeholder	New Services	Truth in Advertising	Patient Death Rates	Price Policy	Clinical Quality	Service Quality	Financial Return
1. Medical staff	2	4	2	4	1	3	5
2. Patients	2	1	1	3	1	1	5
3. Hospital management	1	4	2	2	3	2	1
4. Nonphysician professional staff	2	2	2	4	2	3	4
5. Board of trustees	2	3	2	3	2	3	2
6. Federal government	5	2	1	1	2	4	4
7. Corporate office	2	4	3	3	3	4	1
8. Nonprofessional staff	4	5	4	5	3	3	4
9. Third-party payers	4	4	3	1	2	3	2
10. Elected public officials	2	2	2	2	3	2	3
11. Local business/industry	2	1	2	1	2	3	2
12. Media	4	2	1	3	3	3	3
13. Competitors	1	1	3	2	3	2	5

1 = Critically important to stakeholder
3 = Somewhat important to stakeholder
5 = Of no concern to stakeholder

Who Matters in Different Types of Hospitals?

The discussion in the previous section indicates the key stakeholders identified by administrators in a wide variety of hospitals. However, it does not describe stakeholders in any one type of hospital. Nor does it necessarily describe key stakeholders in other types of health care organizations.

This section will describe the key stakeholders in a wide variety of hospitals (although, of course, not all kinds): (1) academic medical center, (2) small rural hospital, (3) multiunit religious hospital system, (4) local government hospital, and (5) Veterans Administration (VA) hospital. For reasons of brevity, other types of hospitals such as the specialty psychiatric facility or the investor-owned multiinstitutional system have not been included. Our purpose here is show the range and variability of hospital stakeholders as identified by our questionnaire, our interviews, and literature concerning these different types of hospitals.

Academic Medical Center. Figure 15 illustrates some of the key stakeholders in an academic medical center supported partly by state funding. Key competitive strategies often involve differentiation based on quality of care, physician bonding, and development of centers of excellence (Coddington and Moore, 1987). The state legislature provides some funding and approves appointments to the university board of trustees. The medical center hospital is under the medical school administration, and the medical staff includes many medical school faculty members. In addition to state funding, the medical center receives funding from medical research funding agencies and patients who are referred by hospitals and primary care physicians in the region. The two-way arrows indicate that the stakeholder both influences and is influenced by the hospital.

On a particular issue, such as the amount of uncompensated indigent care facing medical center managers, coalitions among stakeholders may form because of their similar values or interests. In Figure 15 we show such a coalition between the

Figure 15. Key Stakeholders in Academic Medical Center.

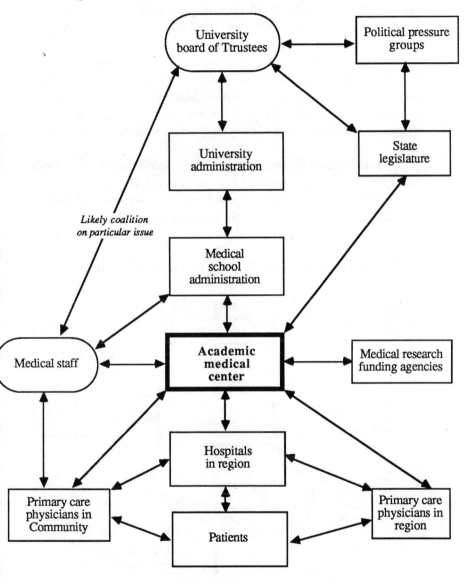

medical staff and the board of trustees. A coalition among these key stakeholders is likely to be powerful and to impact overall competitive strategy. The communication between these two stakeholder groups effectively bypasses the bureaucratic chain of command by backchanneling issue-relevant information and thus activating this latent coalition. To display this likely coalition, we have modified the map by placing the stakeholders in rounded boxes and linking them with a wider arrow to show stronger ties than those connecting other stakeholders.

Small Rural Hospital. A key stakeholder map for a small rural hospital is illustrated in Figure 16. Key strategies for survival will include aggressive marketing of services, physician bonding, and networking with a major medical center (Cod-

Figure 16. Key Stakeholders in Small, Freestanding Rural Hospital.

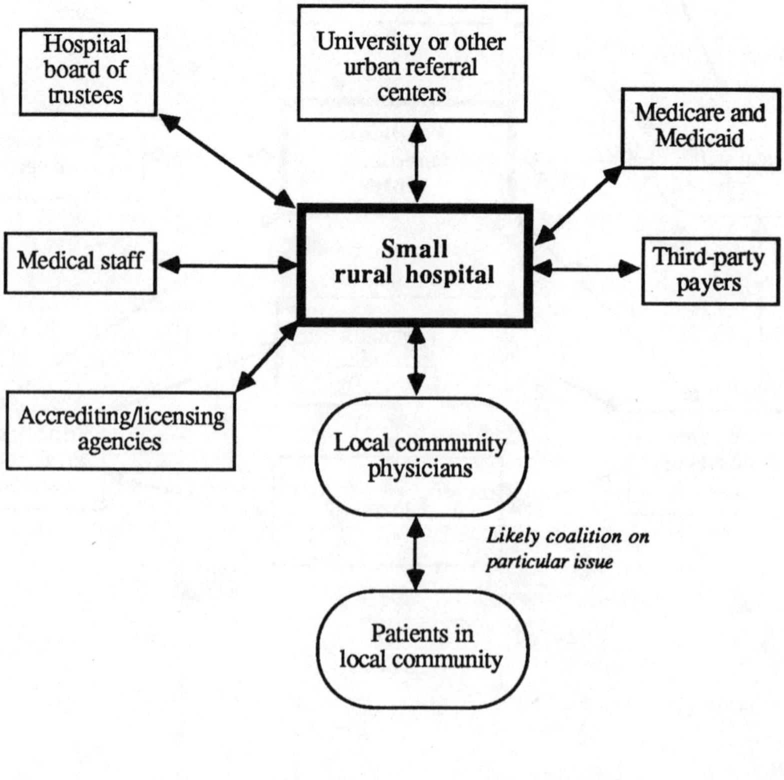

dington and Moore, 1987). Linkages are established with the university medical center to provide necessary tertiary medical care. Helicopters are often used to facilitate transfers of emergency patients from rural hospitals. Physician bonding is done with both its own medical staff and other local physicians in the community. Patients will be drawn from the immediate area. Medicare and Medicaid patients are important because there is usually a shortage of insured or self-pay patients in rural areas. The accreditation/licensing agencies are more critical here than in most other hospitals because small hospitals have a more difficult time meeting the minimum standards.

In Figure 16, local community physicians and patients are shown as likely to form a coalition on a particular issue. One example might be an attempt to induce the hospital to provide a particular service or to provide already available services on a different schedule.

Multiunit Religious Hospital System. Figure 17 provides a key stakeholder map for a multiunit religious hospital system. Key business strategies for this type of institution often include diversification, aggressive marketing, downsizing some units, and developing centers of excellence (Coddington and Moore, 1987). The church or religious order affects the hospital through its ability to approve trustees to the system board. In some cases, the church also provides some funding and becomes more directly involved in policy decisions. Since it is a multiunit system, the corporate office is a major stakeholder for each individual hospital. The corporate office approves budgets, strategic plans, and key executive appointments. It holds individual hospitals accountable for achieving particular corporate goals and objectives. Of course, the hospital also receives certain system services and functional directives, such as personnel policies and procedures.

Patients are referred to the individual hospital through both community physicians and HMOs or PPOs. The individual hospital cooperates with other system hospitals through mechanisms such as joint purchasing agreements. They also interact with competitive nonsystem hospitals both by compet-

Figure 17. Key Stakeholders in Multiunit Religious Hospital System.

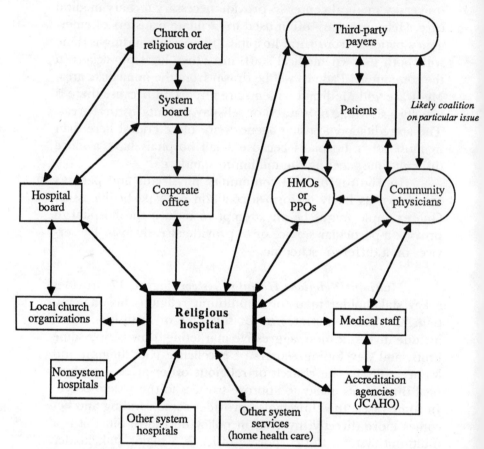

ing for the same markets and by sometimes forming joint ventures. Joint ventures with members of the medical staff are also becoming more common (Blair, Slaton, and Savage, 1990; Shortell, Wickizer, and Wheeler, 1984; Snook and Kaye, 1987).

Additionally, we have identified another likely issue-specific coalition using the same mapping technique previously described. Figure 17 shows that third-party payers such as employers may seek to manage their health benefits costs by collaborating with local or national HMOs or by cooperating with insurance companies offering PPO arrangements. These managed care organizations may have or be seeking contracts with community physicians who are key stakeholders for the hospital. However, the types of physicians included in HMOs and PPOs can affect hospital admissions either positively or negatively. As Greer (1984, 1986) has pointed out, physicians who are "community specialists" are much more likely to admit patients to one preferred hospital than are "community generalists" or "referral specialists." Thus, on an issue such as whether to contract with a given HMO or PPO, the hospital needs to examine both the membership or the potential stakeholder coalition as well as its power.

Local Government Hospital. The stakeholder map for a local government hospital, shown in Figure 18, indicates the major role of political stakeholders. In the typical situation, the local community, political pressure groups, indigent patients, and the hospital board pressure the local government unit (county commission or city council) to provide certain services to certain populations. Since the proportion of insured patients is low, the Medicare and Medicaid programs are important stakeholders. In many situations, the local government contracts with a management service corporation to manage the facility. This company, in turn, both becomes a stakeholder and also manages other stakeholders. There is also a tendency for indigent patients (and their representatives) to form a coalition with certain members of the county commission or city council to pressure the hospital for various concessions.

Note the role of the county judge in determining whether county funds will be used to pay the local government hospital for services provided to indigent patients residing in another (usually rural) county. If the hospital seeks approval of the county judge *prior* to receipt of services, the expenditures will usually be authorized. However, if the hospital attempts to collect money from the county *after* the services are delivered, approval is problematical in many cases.

Figure 18. Key Stakeholders in Local Government Hospital.

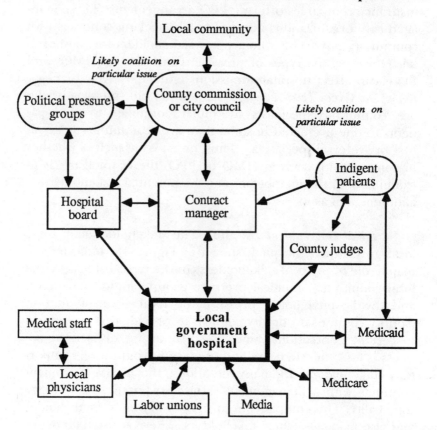

Veterans Administration Hospital. A VA hospital also exists in the public sector and is subject to political pressures from Congress, veterans' organizations, and the VA hospital system itself, as illustrated in Figure 19. The typical VA hospital is also affiliated with a medical school, which provides it with residents for the various clinical areas. Coalitions are often formed between veterans' political pressure groups, congressional committees, and the Veterans Administration. The focus on such coalitions is often to increase appropriations, modify eligibility for services, or add additional services.

Figure 19. Key Stakeholders in Veterans Administration Hospital.

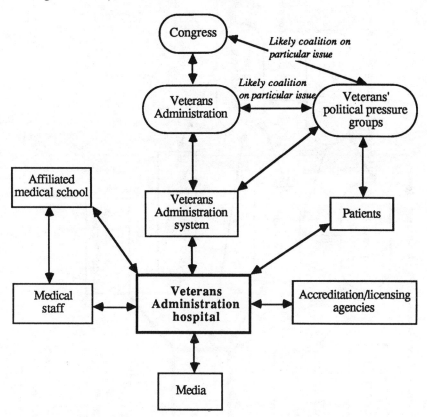

Who Matters in Nonhospital Health Care Settings?

There are many kinds of health care settings besides the hospital. This section describes the key stakeholders in several (but not all) types of nonhospital health care organizations: (1) nursing home, (2) health maintenance organization, (3) free-standing ambulatory clinic, and (4) ambulatory clinic that is part of a joint venture.

Nursing Home. Figure 20 illustrates a key stakeholder map for a nursing home affiliated with a corporate chain. The corporate board influences the corporate office, which in turn de-

Figure 20. Key Stakeholders in Nursing Home.

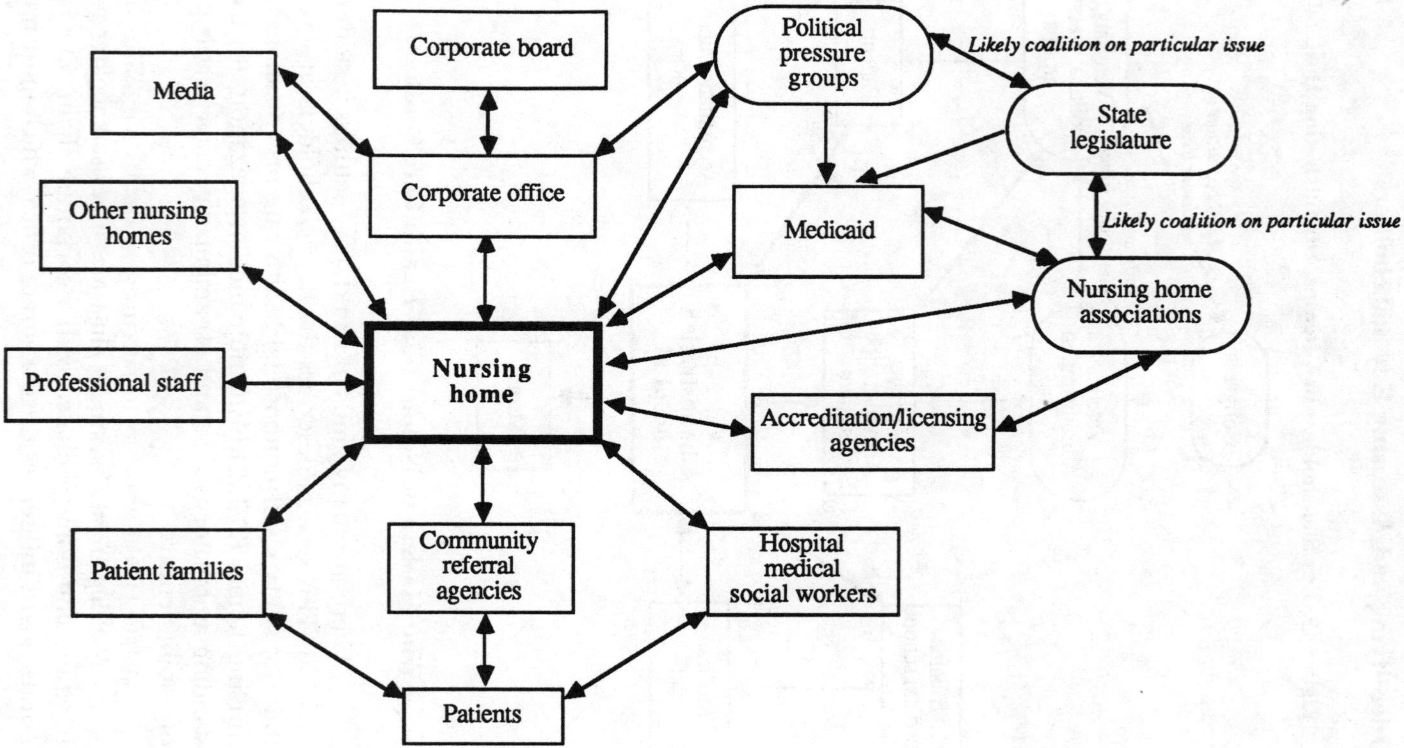

termines budgets and sets goals for the individual nursing home. However, the unique aspect of this stakeholder map is that this is the only health organization where physicians are not a key stakeholder. Instead, patients are directed to the nursing home by community referral agencies, medical social workers, and their own families.

The Medicaid agency at the state level is a major stakeholder since a significant proportion of most nursing home patients are on Medicaid. The daily rates allowed under that program have a significant impact on survival of the home. Consequently, the nursing home associations and other political pressure groups often form a coalition to lobby their state legislators to increase funding and liberalize provisions of the Medicaid program. Professional staff are another major stakeholder (particularly registered nurses). Their significance is due to the difficulties nursing homes experience in recruiting and retaining them as a result of relatively low wages and fringe benefits as well as poor or stressful working conditions.

Health Maintenance Organization. The key stakeholder map for an HMO is shown in Figure 21. Some type of corporate sponsor (hospital, insurance company, third-party payee, corporation, or medical foundation) usually sponsors the HMO by providing the initial investment. This sponsor is seeking a target rate of return on its investment. The HMO also needs to negotiate a contract with one or more local hospitals to provide hospital care to enrollees. Recruiting and retaining patient enrollees is a significant challenge that requires working with physicians and the corporate community as well as dealing directly with the local community. The more critical business strategy task for a new HMO is to secure agreements with local employers to offer the HMO as an option to their employees. The presence of an employer coalition can greatly influence negotiations with employers in the corporate community.

The HMO also has to recruit and retain a medical staff to provide services. Obviously, the recruitment of physicians is easier in an IPA model, since physicians maintain their individual offices and merely treat enrollees for the prenegotiated fee.

Figure 21. Key Stakeholders in Health Maintenance Organization.

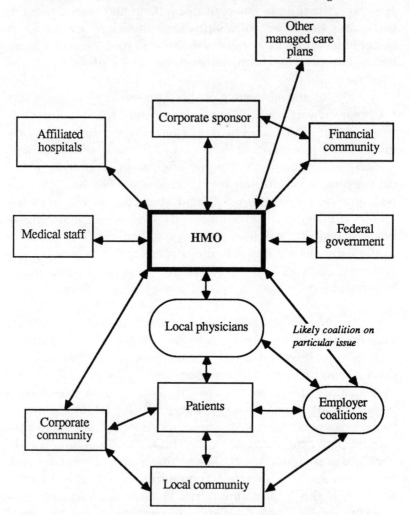

The federal government is another key stakeholder since it defines which HMOs are eligible for federal funding. The corporate community and employer coalitions may form a coalition to pressure the HMO to contain costs, provide data, or develop new service packages.

Ambulatory Clinic (Freestanding and Joint Venture). The key stakeholder map for a freestanding ambulatory clinic is shown in Figure 22. The corporate sponsor is the corporation or partnership that provided the initial investment to start the clinic. The clinic draws its patients from the local community

Figure 22. Key Stakeholders in Freestanding Ambulatory Clinic
(Possible Joint Venture Also Shown).

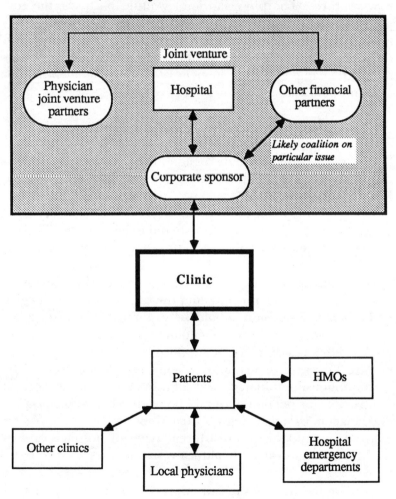

and competes with HMOs, other clinics, local physician office practices, and hospital emergency departments.

In Figure 22 we have added a shaded box at the top. This box indicates additional stakeholders who would impact on the freestanding clinic if it were a joint venture. As we will see in Chapter Six, joint ventures are increasingly important as a way for hospitals to attempt to manage their physician stakeholders as well as a mechanism to obtain needed capital for new ventures. The physician joint venture partners, the corporate sponsor, and other financial partners may form a coalition if the clinic's performance, rate of return on investment, or patient volume is inadequate. Such a coalition might attempt to change top management or top management strategies and policies.

Summary and Managerial Implications

On the basis of the discussion in this chapter, the following managerial guidelines for health care organizations are formulated:

- All health care organizations should explicitly identify their major stakeholders and each stakeholder's major issue or concern.
- This process should be fully integrated in the process of formulating and implementing the organization's strategy.
- Each major decision should be examined in terms of the likely reaction of key stakeholders and plans for gaining stakeholder acceptance or support.
- The success in managing each key stakeholder should be continuously evaluated, and adjustments in organizational structure or personnel should be made when appropriate.
- Managers should recognize that who matters is not always the same and varies in different types of hospitals and in different nonhospital health care settings.

The specific steps in our approach to stakeholder assessment include (1) identifying organizational stakeholders, (2) determining key organizational stakeholders and the balance of power, (3) assessing stakeholder sources of power and key values, and (4) examining issue-specific stakeholder concerns.

In this chapter, we look at how health care executives can diagnose the different key stakeholders and formulate management strategies for dealing with them more specifically. Concluding this chapter is a resource, the "Stakeholder Identification and Assessment Toolkit." This is the first of our toolkits designed to facilitate executives' systematic analysis of *who matters* to their organization and why.

Resource: Stakeholder Identification and Assessment Toolkit

Exhibit 1: Identifying Those Individuals, Groups, or Organizations with a Stake in the Organization. Exhibit 1 provides a form to assist managers in identifying stakeholders and then determining whether they are "key" (significant in helping the organization attain its strategic objectives). In addition, the evaluator will determine whether each particular stakeholder is internal, interface, or external to the organization.

Exhibit 2: Stakeholder Map Form. Exhibit 2 provides a form for the manager to develop his or her own stakeholder map similar to those shown throughout this chapter. External stakeholders may be placed at the top of the map with interface stakeholders in the middle and internal stakeholders at the bottom.

Exhibit 3: Key Stakeholders and Their Power. To assess the power of the key stakeholders identified in Exhibit 1, Exhibits 3 and 4 are provided. Exhibit 3 provides a form for the manager to indicate each key stakeholder's overall power level as well as stakeholder power trends (whether it is increasing or decreasing).

Exhibit 4: Sources of Key Organizational Stakeholders' Power. Exhibit 4 can be used to identify the stakeholders' source of power. Typically, the sources of power include control of financial resources, patients, needed skills, and political support, although their relative importance will vary from stakeholder to stakeholder.

Exhibit 5: Core Values of Key Stakeholders. Exhibit 5 provides a form to identify the core values of each key stakeholder. It is important to know these core values to determine which issues are likely to be important to each key stakeholder as well as how each is likely to respond to particular stakeholder management strategies, to be discussed in the next chapter.

Exhibit 6: Organization Stakeholder Issue Matrix. Exhibit 6 provides an organization stakeholder issue matrix that allows the manager to identify and list various issues facing the organization. Each key stakeholder is then assessed in terms of how important each issue is to them.

Exhibit 1. Identifying Those Individuals, Groups, or Organizations with a Stake in the Organization.

Instructions: Using the examples given in this chapter, identify all stakeholders who are relevant to your organization. Then circle whether each stakeholder is internal, external, or interface and whether each is key or not.

Organization Name _____

Organizational Stakeholder	Stakeholder Is			Is Stakeholder Key?	
1. _____	Internal	External	Interface	Yes	No
2. _____	Internal	External	Interface	Yes	No
3. _____	Internal	External	Interface	Yes	No
4. _____	Internal	External	Interface	Yes	No
5. _____	Internal	External	Interface	Yes	No
6. _____	Internal	External	Interface	Yes	No
7. _____	Internal	External	Interface	Yes	No
8. _____	Internal	External	Interface	Yes	No
9. _____	Internal	External	Interface	Yes	No
10. _____	Internal	External	Interface	Yes	No
11. _____	Internal	External	Interface	Yes	No
12. _____	Internal	External	Interface	Yes	No
13. _____	Internal	External	Interface	Yes	No
14. _____	Internal	External	Interface	Yes	No
15. _____	Internal	External	Interface	Yes	No
16. _____	Internal	External	Interface	Yes	No
17. _____	Internal	External	Interface	Yes	No
18. _____	Internal	External	Interface	Yes	No
19. _____	Internal	External	Interface	Yes	No
20. _____	Internal	External	Interface	Yes	No

Exhibit 2. Stakeholder Map Form.

Stakeholder map for: _____

Instructions: Using the examples of stakeholder maps in this chapter, construct a key stakeholder map for your own organization. Place external stakeholders at the top of the exhibit, interface stakeholders in the middle, and internal stakeholders at the bottom. Indicate any likely coalitions among these stakeholders with a heavy line.

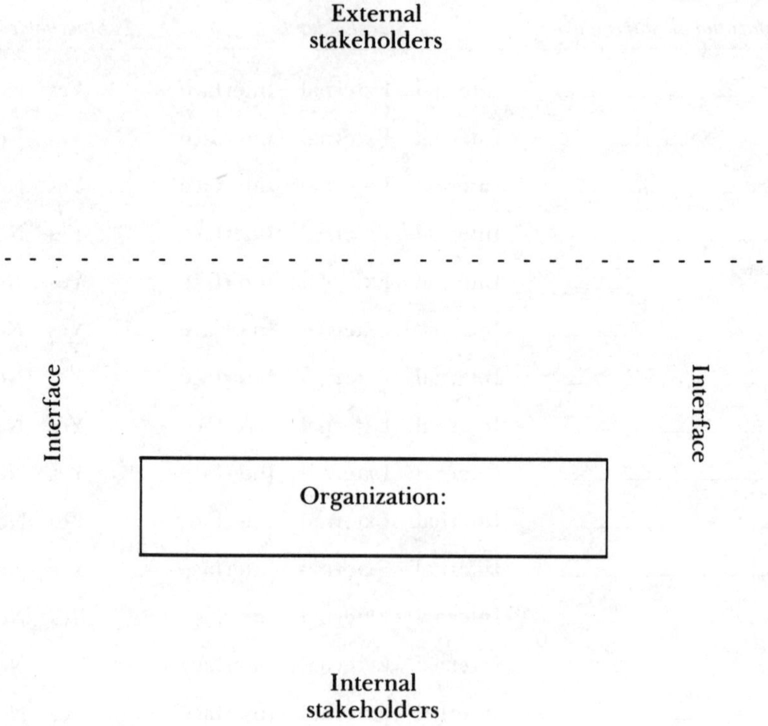

External
stakeholders

- -

Interface   Interface

```
┌─────────────────────────────────────────┐
│            Organization:                  │
│                                           │
└─────────────────────────────────────────┘
```

Internal
stakeholders

Exhibit 3. Key Stakeholders and Their Power.

Instructions: Using the examples given in this chapter, identify all stakeholders who are relevant to your organization. Then circle whether each stakeholder is internal, external, or interface and whether each is key or not.

Key Stakeholder	Overall Power Level	Stakeholder's Power
1. _____	VG G M L VL	INC SAME DEC
2. _____	VG G M L VL	INC SAME DEC
3. _____	VG G M L VL	INC SAME DEC
4. _____	VG G M L VL	INC SAME DEC
5. _____	VG G M L VL	INC SAME DEC
6. _____	VG G M L VL	INC SAME DEC
7. _____	VG G M L VL	INC SAME DEC
8. _____	VG G M L VL	INC SAME DEC
9. _____	VG G M L VL	INC SAME DEC
10. _____	VG G M L VL	INC SAME DEC

VG = Very great   VL   = Very little
G   = Great   INC   = Increasing
M   = Moderate   SAME = No change
L   = Little   DEC   = Decreasing

Exhibit 4. Sources of Key Organizational Stakeholders' Power.

Instructions: Using Table 5 as a guide, list your key stakeholders and their sources of power.

Key Stakeholder	*Stakeholder's Sources of Power*
1. _____	1. _____
	2. _____
	3. _____
	4. _____
2. _____	1. _____
	2. _____
	3. _____
	4. _____
3. _____	1. _____
	2. _____
	3. _____
	4. _____
4. _____	1. _____
	2. _____
	3. _____
	4. _____
5. _____	1. _____
	2. _____
	3. _____
	4. _____

6. _____   1. _____
                                     2. _____
                                     3. _____
                                     4. _____

7. _____   1. _____
                                     2. _____
                                     3. _____
                                     4. _____

8. _____   1. _____
                                     2. _____
                                     3. _____
                                     4. _____

9. _____   1. _____
                                     2. _____
                                     3. _____
                                     4. _____

10. _____   1. _____
                                     2. _____
                                     3. _____
                                     4. _____

Exhibit 5. Core Values of Key Stakeholders.

Instructions: Using Table 5 as a guide, list your key stakeholders and their core values.

Key Stakeholder	Core Values
1. _____	1. _____
	2. _____
	3. _____
	4. _____
2. _____	1. _____
	2. _____
	3. _____
	4. _____
3. _____	1. _____
	2. _____
	3. _____
	4. _____
4. _____	1. _____
	2. _____
	3. _____
	4. _____
5. _____	1. _____
	2. _____
	3. _____
	4. _____

6. _____ 1. _____
2. _____
3. _____
4. _____

7. _____ 1. _____
2. _____
3. _____
4. _____

8. _____ 1. _____
2. _____
3. _____
4. _____

9. _____ 1. _____
2. _____
3. _____
4. _____

10. _____ 1. _____
2. _____
3. _____
4. _____

Exhibit 6. Organization Stakeholder Issue Matrix.

Instructions: Using Table 6 as a guide, list your key stakeholders and the major issues facing your organization. Then indicate for each issue whether each particular stakeholder views the issue as "critically important," "somewhat important," or "not at all important."

	Issues				
Stakeholder	*1*	*2*	*3*	*4*	*5*
1. _____	___*	___	___	___	___
2. _____	___	___	___	___	___
3. _____	___	___	___	___	___
4. _____	___	___	___	___	___
5. _____	___	___	___	___	___
6. _____	___	___	___	___	___
7. _____	___	___	___	___	___
8. _____	___	___	___	___	___
9. _____	___	___	___	___	___
10. _____	___	___	___	___	___

*Indicate on line:
1 = *Critically important to stakeholder*
3 = *Somewhat important to stakeholder*
5 = *Not at all important to stakeholder*

xxx

Strategies for Managing Key Stakeholders

In Chapters One through Three, we looked at stakeholders as those individuals, groups, and organizations with an interest in the actions of an organization. We examined their power and their ability to influence the health care organization and the achievement of its corporate and competitive strategic objectives. Because health care organizations affect stakeholders through the policies and actions they pursue, they must become better able to manage their relationships with relevant stakeholders to successfully implement their corporate/competitive strategies. Each of these stakeholders has expectations for the organization and its managers and can oppose or support its actions (Blair and Whitehead, 1988).

The analogy of the health care seesaw with too many on it seems particularly appropriate for health care executives who daily attempt to balance conflicting stakeholder demands and pressures. This balancing problem is increasing because the number of stakeholders and their influence on health care managers are also increasing, as we have seen in Chapters One and Three.

Organizations in the health care industry have to rethink their strategies and operations as they face increasing, and potentially conflicting, demands for effectiveness and efficiency from internal, external, and interface stakeholders. Although much of the health care management literature focuses on how to enhance efficiency and effectiveness, on a daily basis effective managers do *not* try to either minimize costs or maximize quality. Nor do they try to meet the demands of *all* stakeholders. Rather, they *minimally* satisfy the needs of *marginal* stakeholders while they *maximally* satisfy the needs of *key* stakeholders (Fottler, 1987). Achieving given levels of efficiency and effectiveness is only a *means* to achieve what administrators really desire: *satisfaction of key stakeholders.*

In Chapter One, we focused on stakeholder management as an integrative management approach necessary for dealing with conflicting demands of the type indicated above. In this chapter we develop a diagnostic framework designed to identify and analyze four types of relevant stakeholders for today's health care organization, and we present and discuss five strategies to manage key stakeholders.

The steps in our strategic approach to stakeholder management include

- integrating business and stakeholder management strategies
- diagnosing key stakeholders in terms of potential for threat and for cooperation
- mapping the different types of stakeholders
- formulating generic strategies for stakeholder management
- formulating, adapting, and reformulating specific stakeholder management strategies in response to specific issues facing the organization
- identifying managerial responsibilities for different stakeholders
- monitoring stakeholder behavior and changing stakeholder diagnoses and strategies as needed

We will first describe these generic processes. Then we will provide specific implementation guidelines for these processes.

Integrating Business and Stakeholder Management
Strategies

As we have argued, trying to manage stakeholders should not be an isolated act. Given that the stakeholder has a stake in the health care organization's decisions and actions, strategies for managing a stakeholder need to be connected to its overall business strategy. Stakeholder management integrates in a systematic way what managers often deal with separately: strategic management, marketing, human resource management, public relations, organizational politics, and social responsibility. This integrative perspective assumes that an organization requires some degree of consensus among key stakeholders about what it should be doing and how it should be done.

Here we provide more detail concerning the connection between business strategy and stakeholder management strategy discussed in Chapter Two. In Chapter Five, we will also include negotiation strategy as a guide to managing a specific type of interaction with stakeholder representatives. Implementing the overall business strategy affects the organization's stakeholder management strategy. In turn, the success of the stakeholder management strategy provides valuable input for evaluating the original business strategy.

For example, because of market share pressures in its traditional markets, assume that the senior executives and board of a large urban hospital decide that the hospital should diversify to exploit new business opportunities (see Coddington and Moore, 1987, for a discussion of diversification as one of ten market-driven strategies). To do so, they further decide to open a freestanding ambulatory surgicenter. They realize that there may be conflict between some of the services that surgery center would offer and the office-based ambulatory surgery done by some of their most prominent admitting surgeons.

Since these physicians represent key hospital stakeholders, business strategy is not fully independent of stakeholder management. The executives in this hospital further decide that they should explore joint venture possibilities with these physicians. This represents a reasonable stakeholder management strategy, as we will see below. Thus, implementing their business strategy impacts on the formulation of stakeholder strategy.

In turn, the success or failure of the joint venture with these physicians (as a stakeholder management strategy) will provide important input into assessing the effectiveness of the hospital's diversification strategy and into reformulating overall business strategy if necessary. Remember, the hospital probably could have diversified through setting up the ambulatory center by itself without joint venturing with physicians. In fact, joint ventures of this kind may well cause considerable problems for the hospital in managing this set of surgeons (as hospital stakeholders) if the joint venture (where they are also stakeholders) is not successful financially. Joint ventures—as a specific type of collaborative stakeholder management strategy—will be discussed at length in Chapter Seven.

Diagnosing Key Stakeholders in Terms of Potential for Threat and for Cooperation

To manage stakeholders, health care managers must be involved in a continuous process of internal and external scanning when making strategic decisions. They must go beyond the traditional issues in strategic management such as the likely actions of competitors or the attractiveness of different markets. They must also look for those external, internal, and interface stakeholders who are likely to influence the organization's decisions. As introduced in Chapter One, managers must make two critical assessments about these stakeholders: their potential to threaten the organization and their potential to cooperate with it (Freeman, 1984; Blair and Whitehead, 1988).

Diagnosing Stakeholder's Potential for Threat. Hostility or threat appears as a key variable in several formulations of organization-environment-strategy relationships (Miller and Friesen, 1978). Physicians, for example, are sometimes explicitly identified as potential threats to effective strategic management by hospitals (Sheldon and Windham, 1984). Looking at the potential threat of stakeholders is similar to developing a worst-case scenario and protects managers from unpleasant surprises.

The stakeholder's relative power was discussed at length in Chapter Three. Stakeholder power and its relevance for any particular issue confronting the organization's managers determine the stakeholder's potential for threat. Power is primarily a function of the dependence of the organization on the stakeholder (Pfeffer and Salancik, 1978). Generally, the more dependent the organization, the more powerful the stakeholder (Korukonda and Blair, 1986). For example, the power of staff physicians is a function of the hospital's dependence on those physicians for patients, alternative sources of patients, the use of hospital beds, and the provision of hospital services.

Diagnosing Stakeholder's Potential for Cooperation. Because stakeholder analyses emphasize the types and magnitude of threats that stakeholders pose for the organization, the second dimension of potential for cooperation is often ignored. We suggest it should be equally emphasized since it allows stakeholder management strategies to go beyond the merely defensive or offensive. Health care organizations should find cooperative potential particularly relevant because it may allow them to join forces with other stakeholders and better manage their respective environments.

Assessing the potential for cooperation is also similar to scenario development, here a best-case one. The stakeholder's dependence on the organization and its relevance for any particular issue facing the organization determine the stakeholder's cooperative potential. Generally, the more dependent the stakeholder on the organization, the higher the potential for cooperation. Often, however, the organization and the stakeholder may be very interdependent. For example, in a small town with a limited number of physicians and one hospital, the hospital and the physicians usually have high levels of mutual dependence. Although the hospital may encounter potential threats from some physicians who send patients to another hospital in a larger city, it may also have cooperation from most other physicians who want to keep the patients in the community.

Factors Affecting Potentials for Threat and Cooperation. Besides power, other factors also affect the level of a stakeholder's potential for threat or cooperation. In Table 7, we provide a list of stakeholder characteristics health care executives should examine when diagnosing the potential for threat or cooperation. These factors were developed from our interviews with health care executives described in Chapter Two.

Table 7 focuses on four major factors: control of re-

Table 7. Factors Affecting Stakeholder's Potentials for Threat and Cooperation.

Factor	Increases or Decreases Stakeholder's Potential for Threat?	Increases or Decreases Stakeholder's Potential for Cooperation?
Stakeholder controls key resources (needed by organization)	Increases	Increases
Stakeholder does not control key resources	Decreases	Either
Stakeholder more powerful than organization	Increases	Either
Stakeholder as powerful as organization	Either	Either
Stakeholder less powerful than organization	Decreases	Increases
Stakeholder likely to take action (supportive of the organization)	Decreases	Increases
Stakeholder likely to take nonsupportive action	Increases	Decreases
Stakeholder unlikely to take any action	Decreases	Decreases
Stakeholder likely to form coalition with other stakeholders	Increases	Either
Stakeholder likely to form coalition with organization	Decreases	Increases
Stakeholder unlikely to form any coalition	Decreases	Decreases

sources, relative power, likelihood and supportiveness of potential stakeholder action, and coalition formation. For each factor, there are two or three different basic situations possible. Lines in Table 7 separate the specific situations according to each major factor. Generally, only one situation from each of the four factors will apply to a given organization's relationship with a particular stakeholder. The exceptions would be if the stakeholder is likely to take *both* supportive and nonsupportive actions or likely to form a coalition with *both* the organization and other stakeholders, potentially nonsupportive to the organization. We also indicate whether the presence of a specific situation in each factor will probably *increase, decrease,* or *either* increase or decrease each type of potential. After one has looked at the probable impact of the relevant situation on overall cooperative or threatening potential, then it is a qualitative judgment on the part of a manager to weight the relative importance of the four factors in making a final stakeholder diagnosis most appropriate for that organization at that time.

Some of the factors in the table follow up our detailed discussion in Chapter Two. They are concerned with the relative power of the stakeholder vis-à-vis the hospital in general or with specific power resulting from control over key resources (Mintzberg, 1983). Others concentrate on the kind of action the stakeholder might take. Is that action likely to be supportive or counteractive? Is the stakeholder likely to form a coalition with other stakeholders or, instead, with the manager's own organization?

Exactly how a factor will affect the potential for threat or cooperation depends on the specific context and history of the organization's relations with that stakeholder and those with other key stakeholders influencing the organization. For example, a manager may be able to assess the cooperative or threat potential of the medical staff only in the context of how competing institutions are managing their medical staff *and* in the context of how the organization has treated its medical staff in the past. By carefully considering the factors in Table 7, executives can fine-tune their analyses and management of stakeholders.

An example of a stakeholder unlikely to take any action regarding nursing home patients is physicians. Physicians do not play a major role in either admitting or treating nursing home patients. Consequently, they have both a low potential for threat *and* a low potential for cooperation.

Alternatively, an example of a stakeholder controlling key resources needed by a nursing home is the state Medicaid agency. Since most patients in nursing homes do not have the resources necessary to pay their own nursing home expenses, most depend on Medicaid. This means the individual home (and the nursing home association) views the Medicaid agency as posing *both* a significant threat *and* a high potential for cooperation (if they can work together to increase state funding for the program).

Classifying Different Types of Stakeholders

The two dimensions—potential for threat and potential for cooperation—map stakeholders into a diagnostic framework. As discussed in the previous section, these two dimensions of classification serve as summary measures of stakeholder supportiveness or lack thereof and incorporate information from multiple factors. Using these two dimensions, we can characterize four types of health care stakeholders as shown in Figure 23. It should be noted that there is a dynamic process occurring at all times so that stakeholders initially categorized in one cell might be moved to another cell as a result of

- What the organization does or fails to do
- What the stakeholder does or fails to do
- What new information the organization has that would change the classification
- What the issue facing the organization and its stakeholders is (as discussed below, in detail)

Type 1: Mixed-Blessing Stakeholder. We see the mixed-blessing stakeholder as playing a particularly key role. Here,

Figure 23. Diagnostic Typology of Organizational Stakeholders.

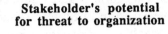

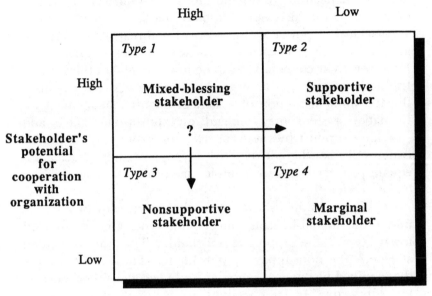

the health care executive is facing a situation where the stakeholder is high on both types of potential: threat and cooperation. For example, in a well-managed hospital, stakeholders of the mixed-blessing type would generally include not only the medical staff but also other physicians not on the staff, insurance companies, insured patients, and hospitals with complementary but not competing services. Physicians are probably the clearest example of this type of stakeholder. Although they can do much for a hospital, they can also threaten it because of their general control over admissions, the utilization and provision of different services, and the quality of care.

Some special-interest groups are also a mixed blessing. For substance-abuse programs, groups such as Alcoholics Anonymous (AA) or Narcotics Anonymous (NA) have a significant stake in the program and its therapeutic approach. Such groups can enhance referrals to the program, or they can undermine the same program in the recovering community and greatly impact its clinical and financial viability.

City services and utilities are often mixed-blessing stakeholders for health care organizations. They provide very necessary services to increasingly technical facilities, affording them a great deal of power and potential for threat if they are unable or unwilling to provide the level of service necessary. However, their cooperation can be instrumental in the successful implementation of an organization's strategy. For example, the full implementation of a state-of-the-art management information system may depend on appropriate cable and switching support by the local telephone company. A similar issue would be whether the power company could provide adequate power circuits for complex medical technology such as linear accelerators.

Figure 23 also shows a question mark with two arrows under the mixed-blessing stakeholder type. One is directed toward type 2, the supportive stakeholder. The other is pointed at type 3, the nonsupportive stakeholder. These arrows imply that a mixed-blessing stakeholder could become either more or less supportive. In later sections, we will look at appropriate stakeholder management strategies for each type of stakeholder. In so doing, we will emphasize how to manage this mixed-blessing stakeholder most effectively.

Type 2: Supportive Stakeholder. The ideal stakeholder is one who supports the organization's goals and actions. Managers wish all their stakeholders were of this type. Such a stakeholder is low on potential threat but high on potential cooperation. Usually, for a well-managed hospital, its board of trustees, its managers, its staff employees, its parent company, the local community, and nursing homes will be of this type. In many large medical centers with multiple health care facilities, a common support facility such as a power plant, laundry, or parking consortium typifies the concept of the supportive stakeholder.

Type 3: Nonsupportive Stakeholder. Stakeholders of this type are the most distressing for an organization and its managers. They are high on potential for threat but low on potential for cooperation. Typical nonsupportive stakeholders for hospitals include competing hospitals, freestanding alternatives such as urgi- or surgicenters, employee unions, the federal government, other governmental regulatory agencies, indigent patients, the news media, and employer coalitions. Special-interest groups may often prove a nonsupportive stakeholder, as in the case of prolife demonstrations that have slowed or halted normal business, particularly for ambulatory women's centers.

Type 4: Marginal Stakeholder. Marginal stakeholders are high on neither threat nor cooperative potential. Although they potentially have a stake in the organization and its decisions, they are generally not relevant for most issues. For a well-run hospital, typical stakeholders of this kind may include volunteer groups in the community, stockholders or taxpayers, and professional employee associations. However, certain issues such as cost containment or access to care could activate one or more of these stakeholders, causing their potential for either threat or cooperation to increase.

Issue-Specific Stakeholder Diagnosis. Not everyone will agree with the set of stakeholders we have used as examples for each type. There is a very good reason to be uncomfortable with such global classifications of particular stakeholders. The most important issues facing organizations and their managers—at a given time—change constantly. Of all the possible stakeholders for a given health care organization, the ones who will be *relevant* to its managers depend on the corporate/competitive strategies being persuaded as well as the particular *issue*, as noted in Chapter Three. If the issue is *cost containment,* the stakeholders who are concerned will be different than if the issue is *access to health care.* The *diagnosis* of the relevant stakeholders in terms of the four stakeholder types will probably be different on these two issues as well. Later in this chapter we present a detailed example of a large hospital in Houston and how it responded to a specific complex issue involving multiple stakeholders.

This issue specificity suggests that stakeholder diagnosis

is an ongoing activity for health care managers. Managers cannot assume that a stakeholder who is supportive on one issue will be that on every issue, or that a stakeholder who is nonsupportive on one issue will be so on another. Both opportunity and danger await the organization from its stakeholders, especially from those of the mixed-blessing type.

Moreover, whatever the classification of a particular stakeholder on a specific issue, managers should *explicitly* classify stakeholders to surface inadvertent managerial biases. For example, if a manager identifies all stakeholders for any particular issue as nonsupportive, then the manager should critically examine her or his assessment of the relationship between the organization and its stakeholders. Also, if a particular stakeholder is always thought of as the same in terms of threat and cooperation, it suggests that the manager may both be missing opportunities for capitalizing on *potential* for cooperation and also be running the risk of being blindsided by underestimating the *potential* for threat on a specific issue.

Formulating Generic Strategies for Stakeholder Management

Stakeholder diagnosis of the type attempted in Figure 23 suggests some generic strategies for managing stakeholders with different levels of potential for threat and cooperation. In Figure 24, we present a fourfold typology of such strategies. Since executives continually manage a wide variety of stakeholders (in terms of their potential for cooperation and threat), all executives need to use a *combination* of strategies at any one time. Chapters Six through Nine closely examine these generic strategies in terms of specific strategies and tactics that managers can implement to manage particular stakeholders. The presentation in this section provides an overview of these strategies and some of their applications.

Strategy 1: Collaborate with Mixed-Blessing Stakeholder. The mixed-blessing stakeholder, high on the dimensions of potential threat and potential cooperation, may best be managed through collaboration. If executives seek to maximize their

Figure 24. Generic Stakeholder Management Strategies.

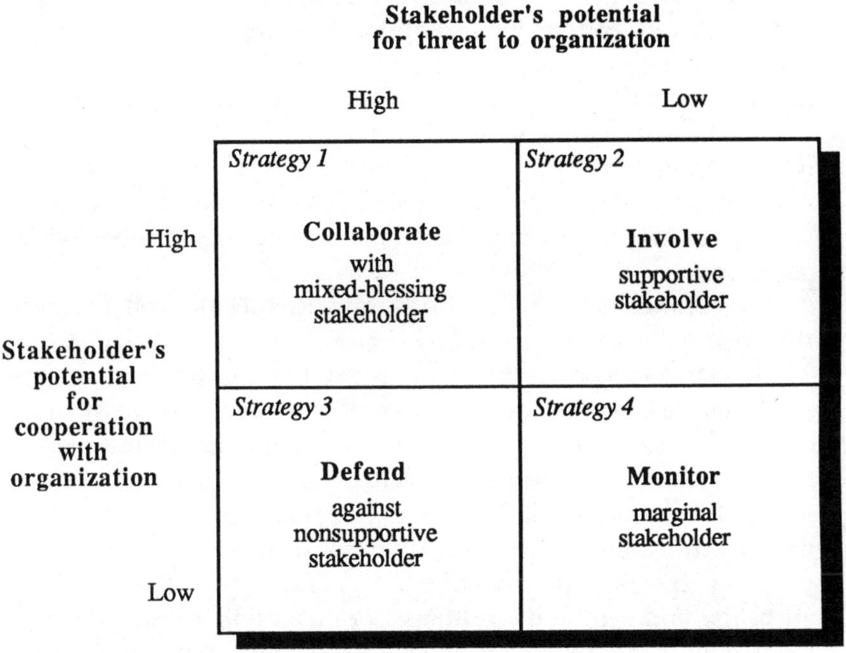

**Stakeholder's potential
for threat to organization**

	High	Low
High	*Strategy 1* **Collaborate** with mixed-blessing stakeholder	*Strategy 2* **Involve** supportive stakeholder
Stakeholder's potential for cooperation with organization	*Strategy 3* **Defend** against nonsupportive stakeholder	*Strategy 4* **Monitor** marginal stakeholder
Low		

potential for cooperation, these potentially threatening stake-holders will find their supportive endeavors make it more dif-ficult for them to oppose the organization. A variety of joint ventures or other collaborative efforts up to and including mergers are possible (see, for example, Mancino, 1984; Snook and Kaye, 1987; Coddington and Moore, 1987; Coile, 1990).

For example, a hospital might form a joint venture with a group of its medical staff to build a freestanding surgicenter or imaging center. Such collaboration stops the physicians from building a center themselves and thus from competing with hospital-based surgery or diagnostic procedures. The hospital can contribute its name and capital resources, while the physi-cians presumably will send their patients to the hospital when inpatient services are needed. Both the hospital and the phy-sicians will benefit. Chapters Six and Seven are devoted to looking at the implementation of collaborative strategies with this key stakeholder group.

Insurance companies represent another mixed-blessing stakeholder. Here the value of a collaborative strategy seems to be well recognized. For example, Partners, the recent joint venture between Aetna Insurance and the Voluntary Hospitals of America, involves the insurance company, the hospital, and the medical staff in a nationally marketed, collaborative PPO (Coddington and Moore, 1987). Such a PPO may even help a participating hospital to manage a nonsupportive stakeholder such as an employer or, particularly, an employer-business coalition.

Substance-abuse programs often explicitly collaborate therapeutically and practically with groups such as AA and NA. They may incorporate AA's twelve-step program into their treatment approach and encourage the groups to meet at the organization's facility—even groups that do not include patients in the organization's program.

Collaboration with the local transit authority in the planning of transportation routes, times, and the need for handicapped accessible equipment helps to increase ridership for the authority and can be instrumental in increasing access to a facility. This access may be primarily for patients, but it also may impact employees and students in the case of a large teaching or research facility.

For the mixed-blessing stakeholder, effective collaboration may well determine the long-term stakeholder-organization relationship. In other words, if this type of stakeholder is not properly managed through a collaborative strategy, it could become a nonsupportive stakeholder.

Strategy 2: Involve Supportive Stakeholder. By involving supportive stakeholders in relevant issues, health care executives can maximally capitalize on these stakeholders' cooperative potential. Because these stakeholders pose a low threat potential, they are likely to be ignored as stakeholders to be managed, and their cooperative potential may therefore be ignored as well.

Involvement differs from *collaboration* in that *involvement* further activates or enhances the supportive capability of an already supportive stakeholder. The emphasis here is not on reducing threat, since its potential is low. Instead, this strategy attempts to capitalize on the already existing potential for co-operation by converting even more of the *potential* into *actuality*. *Collaboration,* in contrast, involves much more give-and-take on the parts of the organization and the stakeholder. Collaboration may require the organization to give up or expend certain key resources or change important policies to gain stakeholder support by either lowering threat or increasing cooperation.

Managers can operationalize the involvement strategy by using participative management techniques, decentralizing authority to clinical managers, or engaging in other tactics to increase the decision-making participation of these stakeholders. For example, hospital executives might invite clinical managers to participate in the analysis and planning for eliminating redundant programs. The clinical managers will more likely become committed to achieving such an organizational objective than if they had not been involved in establishing it. A key requirement for the success of this type of strategy is the ability of the managers to enlarge their vision of ways to further involve supportive stakeholders in higher levels of cooperation.

Nonmanagerial professional and support employees represent another class of stakeholders who belong in this category and for whom an involving strategy might be effective (see, for example, Counte, Barhyte, and Christman, 1987). Employees do not pose a great deal of direct threat to the organization, although union activism, the perception of poor third-shift conditions, and human resource shortages can make their continued service problematical under certain circumstances. Yet their cooperative potential may not have been fully tapped.

Many group practices and hospitals are explicitly involving their supportive employee and in-house volunteer stakeholders in training them to manage mixed-blessing stakeholders such as funded patients, patients' families, and physicians. They are doing this through guest- or customer-relations programs designed to enhance the management of one or more potentially threatening stakeholders by increasing the cooperative potential of a key internal stakeholder.

Two other recent managerial approaches reflect the involvement strategy we recommend. The first is an adaptation of some aspects of Japanese management and American participative and operations management called quality (control) circles. Quality circles represent a straightforward example of the involvement strategy, presenting a means of managing employee relations and improving productivity while more closely linking the employee to the organization and its objectives (Blair and Whitehead, 1984; Cornell, 1984; McKinney, 1984; Phillips and others, 1990).

The second managerial approach is explicitly strategic and focuses on systematically linking human resource management systems and practices to overall strategic management. It is called strategic human resource management (SHRM) and has only recently been introduced into the field of health care management (Fottler, Hernandez, and Joiner, 1988; Fottler, Phillips, Blair, and Duran, forthcoming). SHRM is very consistent with our strategic stakeholder management approach, since it increases involvement of a generally supportive internal stakeholder (employees) in furthering the strategic goals of the organization through effective and strategically linked human resource management. We will discuss both quality circles and human resource management reflecting this strategic orientation in Chapter Eight, focusing on the implementation of involvement strategies for internal stakeholders.

Strategy 3: Defend Against Nonsupportive Stakeholders. Stakeholders who pose high threat but whose potential for cooperation is low are best managed using a defensive strategy. The federal government and indigent patients are good examples of this nonsupportive stakeholder group for most health care organizations. In terms of Kotter's (1979) framework on external dependence, the defense strategy tries to reduce the dependence that forms the basis for the stakeholders' interest in the organization. In our terms, a defensive strategy involves preventing the stakeholder from imposing costs—or other disincentives—on the organization.

However, health care executives should *not* attempt to totally eliminate their dependence on nonsupportive stakeholders. Such efforts either are doomed to failure or may result in a negative image for the organization. For example, a hospital's trying to sever all ties with the federal government is counterproductive if that hospital hopes to market to older patients. A public hospital that tries to deny access to all indigent patients will almost surely be viewed negatively by the public and the local government.

Let us consider an example of this defense strategy in action, using the federal government's regulatory agencies as the stakeholder. For example, given the regulations hospitals face, their most appropriate tactic is to explore ways of complying with the demands imposed by the federal government at the least possible cost. DRGs that produce a surplus for the hospitals define their areas of distinctive competence. Hence, hospital executives might adopt a case-mix approach to the delivery of health care, modifying the services they offer based on cost and process accounting. Investment in more effective management information systems, specialized medical records "grouper" software, and recruiting and paying for more highly skilled medical records personnel are all part of this defensive strategy vis-à-vis a nonsupportive, demanding third-party payer or regulator.

Defensive strategies may be proactive. Academic medical centers by their very nature have a great deal of physician turnover in their ambulatory clinics. One result of this turnover is difficulty in keeping funded patients. A defined policy of contacting current patients, advising them of changes, and ensuring continuity of their care when their primary physician leaves can enhance the patients' loyalty to the clinic team and help the clinic retain these patients. Since these patients are very likely to become nonsupportive by no longer coming to the clinic, this proactive strategy *anticipates* that decrease in co-operation and keeps it from happening through communication to maintain their satisfaction and support.

This generic strategy can also take the form of either driving out or reducing competition. On one hand, a hospital might drive out competition by securing a monopoly over a particular market segment through PPO contracting. On the other hand, to reduce competition with urgi- or surgicenters, a hospital could build new ambulatory facilities or restructure existing facilities. In these examples of the defense strategy, the connection of stakeholder management to broader strategic management is very clear, involving many traditional marketing and strategic notions for handling competitors.

However, other nonsupportive stakeholders, such as the investigative news media and employers from other industries concerned about health care costs, are not traditionally examined in strategic management. Nonetheless, the investigative media can be defended against through careful monitoring of organizational information, providing good external relations, and training clinical managers and executives in how to talk to the media. Also, employer coalitions can be appeased through managed care programs.

Strategy 4: Monitor Marginal Stakeholders. Monitoring helps manage those marginal stakeholders whose potential for both threat and cooperation is low. For example, numerous special-interest groups are opposed to certain procedures such as abortion or artificial implants or are concerned about certain patient groups such as the aged. Typically these groups have only a marginal stake in the activities of the organization, affecting operations indirectly through advocating a moral or ethical standpoint. Taxpayers and stockholders also represent marginal stakeholders. They are unlikely to be either much help or much hindrance unless the organization takes actions that activate them.

Often patient families are considered as marginal stakeholders. Leaving this key marginal stakeholder unmonitored ignores the possibility of the development of a supportive stakeholder that can make a decisive difference in facilitating the course of patient care. However, dissatisfied patient families that go unnoticed potentially can wreak havoc on an organization. Assigning specific responsibility for monitoring this stakeholder to a member of the patient care team can avert disaster for the organization's management.

The underlying philosophy for managing these marginal stakeholders is proactively maintaining the *status quo,* but with finances and management time kept to a minimum. Executives address issues on an *ad hoc* basis. The general thrust of this approach is to "let the sleeping dogs lie." Keeping them asleep, however, may require an organization to engage in ongoing public-relations activities and to be sensitive to issues that could activate these groups to become an actual threat.

As noted at the beginning of this chapter, marginal stakeholders should—in general—be *minimally satisfied.* What it takes to keep a particular marginal stakeholder minimally satisfied may increase over time, thus necessitating greater involvement of managerial time and other organizational resources. Managers must monitor such expenditures of inducements or disinducements to determine whether they have become excessive or are perhaps inadequate—at this time—because the marginal stakeholder has become a key stakeholder, either in general or on a particular issue.

Overarching Stakeholder Management Strategy

In addition to using the four strategies specifically tailored for stakeholders classified into one of the four diagnostic categories, health care executives may also employ an overarching strategy. This overarching strategy moves the stakeholder from a less favorable category to a more favorable one. The stakeholder can then be managed using the generic strategy most appropriate for that "new" diagnostic category.

For example, rather than simply defend against the news media as a nonsupportive stakeholder, a hospital could implement an aggressive program of external relations with openness to the media. If successful, the program would change the news media to the less threatening category of marginal stakeholder, allowing it to be managed through a monitoring strategy (Fitzgerald and Wahl, 1987). If the hospital is willing to invest more time, energy, skill, and money in the effort, the media might even be coopted enough to become a supportive stakeholder. This appears to be what happened in the Hermann Hospital discussed later in this chapter.

As another example, a hospital could involve an employee union in a quality-of-work-life program of productivity enhancement combined with gain sharing to union members. Such an effort may succeed in moving the employee union from the least favorable stakeholder category—nonsupportive—to the most favorable—supportive. Such programs have been used successfully in some hospitals in New York City (Fottler and Maloney, 1979).

Of course, stakeholders generally will not just sit still and be managed. Stakeholders who are powerful and hence threatening are as likely to try to manage organizations as vice versa. Many organizations and their stakeholders continuously engage in management and countermanagement strategies, often leading to direct negotiations, which we will discuss in Chapter Five. The full range of the negotiations between organizations and their stakeholders will be discussed there. To manage these stakeholders effectively, executives should continuously identify stakeholders and match their diagnoses with appropriate strategies. In other words, we suggest periodically repeating the prior steps to ensure that key assumptions still apply.

Managing Stakeholders Strategically: Examples from the Managed Care Industry

We now look at some examples of how key HMO stakeholders discussed in Chapter Two can be managed through effective formulation and implementation of the stakeholder strategies. To remain viable in an increasingly competitive environment, the managed care industry and individual HMOs have to do a better job of identifying and assessing their key stakeholders; classifying each key stakeholder as supportive, mixed blessing, or nonsupportive (or even marginal on a particular issue); formulating generic strategies to involve the supportive stakeholder, collaborate with the mixed-blessing stakeholder, and defend against the nonsupportive stakeholder; and implementing these generic strategies through a variety of specific tactics.

Table 8 provides a convenient summary of generic strategies and specific tactics for managing key HMO stakeholders, including staff or affiliated physicians, nonaffiliated physicians, employers, and enrollees. The staff or affiliated physicians are likely to be either mixed-blessing or supportive stakeholders. Consequently, both collaborative and involvement strategies may be appropriate. Remember, since stakeholder management is inherently issue specific, executives must be careful to change diagnoses—and strategic prescriptions—as new symptoms appear.

Nonaffiliated physicians may be either marginal or mixed-blessing stakeholders. Those nonaffiliated physicians who may be hostile to HMOs need to be monitored in terms of identifying their specific needs, concerns, or problem areas. They may, on some issue, even be nonsupportive and need to be defended against. Other nonaffiliated mixed-blessing physicians may need to be managed through positive collaboration, not only by the managed care organization and its managers but also with the affiliated physicians to improve patient access and quality, correct administrative problems, and minimize paperwork.

Finally, employers are likely to be mixed-blessing stakeholders who should be managed by various collaborative tactics such as developing flexible service packages, providing requested information, and meeting their employees' needs for accessible, high-quality care. In a study conducted by Hewitt Associates, a Lincolnshire, Illinois, benefits consultant, only 5 percent of six hundred companies surveyed said their HMOs provided enough data (Shellenbarger, 1990).

We now move to another segment of the overall health care industry and examine the importance of specific issues in stakeholder management. We look at an example of how a large hospital in Houston, Texas, managed a complex and potentially very threatening issue through effective management of the key stakeholders involved in or impacted by the issue.

Table 8. Strategies and Tactics for Managing HMO Key Stakeholders.

Key Stakeholder	Strategies	Tactics
1. Staff or affiliated physicians	1. Collaborate 2. Involve	1. Ownership incentives 2. Collaboration on changes 1. Clinical autonomy 2. Minimization of paperwork 3. Feedback on performance 4. Self-regulation 5. Reward system tied to objectives 6. Orientation programs 7. Continuous education programs 8. Supportive environment 9. Open communications
2. Nonaffiliated physicians	1. Monitor 2. Collaborate	1. Identification of specific needs, concerns, or problem areas 1. Collaboration with affiliated physicians to improve patient access and quality, correct administrative problems, and minimize paperwork
3. Employers	1. Collaborate	1. Designing of flexible service packages 2. Negotiation to meet employer needs 3. Provision of educational programs for learning and exchange 4. Provision of requested data 5. Meeting of employee/patient needs for accessible, high-quality care
4. Enrollees	1. Involve	1. Sensitivity to enrollee needs 2. Monitoring and correction of problem areas 3. Educational programs 4. Minimal paperwork 5. Wide choice of providers 6. Convenient access 7. High quality 8. Continuity of care

Managing a Specific Issue Strategically: Hermann Hospital and Indigent Trauma Patients

Hermann Hospital is a nine-hundred-bed private teaching hospital in the Texas Medical Center in Houston, Texas. It was founded by George Hermann and provided with a charitable trust endowment to support the care of charity patients, who comprise 10 percent of the hospital's patients by law. The legal designation of 10 percent is the result of a major public scandal, uncovered by investigative media coverage concerning the board of trustees' management of the trust fund. The outcome of that scandal was a lawsuit brought against the hospital and various individuals by the attorney general's office of the state of Texas. The hospital's focus for charity care has been to provide care to those who are "medically indigent," that is, those individuals do *not* qualify for government programs, usually because they work yet do not have medical insurance coverage.

When the University of Texas opened its medical school in Houston in the early 1970s, Hermann Hospital underwent a large expansion and became the primary teaching facility for the school. With the collaboration of the medical school, Hermann became the base of the first "Life Flight" service for the area, a program developed under the sponsorship of Dr. "Red" Duke (known for his nationally syndicated television medical updates) that became a prototype for regional trauma transport programs across the country. In conjunction with the program, Hermann developed a level-one trauma center to augment the only burn center, the Institute for Thermal Injuries, in Houston. The only other burn center in the area is in Galveston and is associated with the University of Texas medical branch there.

Prior to this time, the only trauma center in the Texas Medical Center was at the county hospital, Ben Taub, and these two centers have remained the only level-one trauma centers (as classified by the American College of Surgeons) in Houston, even though they are separated by only a few hundred yards.

These two facilities are uniquely qualified due to their teaching mission (Ben Taub is a teaching facility for Baylor College of Medicine) and their around-the-clock availability of highly qualified personnel. As such they have become known nationwide as excellent training facilities in the area of emergency medicine. The development as a center of excellence in emergency medicine was crucial to the early development of the University of Texas as a medical school. Because of this, it was historically the policy of the emergency center at Hermann to admit all trauma patients arriving by automobile, ambulance, or the Life Flight program (which includes helicopter and fixed-wing capability) regardless of ability to pay, which in many trauma cases is difficult if not impossible to determine prior to admission.

The past few years have seen a steady increase in the cost of providing care and a decrease in the payment level of paying patients. The cost shifting that allowed Hermann to support the high level of uncompensated trauma care in the past became increasingly difficult. In June 1988 the burden became too great. Hermann found it necessary to put itself on a day-to-day "drive-by" status with the Houston Fire Department (HFD) ambulance service to limit the numbers of patients admitted. In other words, on days the Hermann emergency room was already full, the HFD was told to "drive by" the hospital to another, even if Hermann was closer. The effect of this day-to-day policy was confusion among ambulance personnel and elimination of not only nonfunded trauma patients but also patients referred by hospital staff. As a result of this policy, in April, May, and June 1989, Hermann's surgical and neurosurgical intensive care units were closed to trauma patients 49 percent of the time. This situation benefited neither the hospital, the medical school, nor the community as a whole. The board of trustees deemed it necessary to find a better solution to the problem.

The Hermann board approached the Harris County Hospital District to obtain sufficient funding ($14.5 million) for providing trauma care to the district's indigent trauma patients and to contract for compensation for care to those eligible for county programs in the future. This would allow Hermann to eliminate the necessity for the drive-by status. At the same time, the University of Texas School of Medicine offered to donate its physicians' services. The hospital district declined the proposal on the basis that it did not have the funds available and maintained that those eligible for district programs should be taken to Ben Taub.

Since it is impossible to determine program eligibility of most trauma patients, the board of trustees adopted a new policy. This policy was to clearly define, with the considerable coordinated assistance of the local media, which patients, by degree of severity and location, should be transported to Hermann for emergency or trauma treatment. The HFD ambulance service was instructed to take all level-one trauma patients (those suffering from things such as knife wounds, severe injuries from accidents, or gunshot wounds to the head) to Ben Taub as of October 1, 1989. The result of the hospital district's position and the subsequent change in policy at Hermann was that the patient load at the Ben Taub Trauma Center increased by 20 percent in an environment where it is not unusual for patients to have to wait for hours or days on a gurney before being transferred to a bed.

On Sunday, October 1, the local papers ran three items (Dalston, 1989; Hermann Hospital, 1989; Wilson, 1989). The first was a news story concerning the policy change, the second was an article written by the CEO of the hospital to the community explaining the policy change, and the third was a three-quarter-page print advertisement that also explained the change. Hermann would continue to accept burn victims, all Life Flight–transported trauma patients of any type, any patients who came by their own transportation, and less seriously injured patients transported by HFD as well as trauma patients from outside the Harris County Hospital District. This policy was designed to minimize the highest cost uncompensated care while concentrating a manageable patient load in the hospital's financial and human resource capabilities as well as to maintain the patient population and mix necessary for the teaching mission of the hospital and the medical school.

The board of trustees continued to consider future possibilities by actively participating with the Harris County Medical Society's Trauma Commission in its investigation of the advisability and feasibility of a freestanding trauma hospital in the Texas Medical Center. However, because of its cost, the likelihood of this facility actually becoming a reality is quite low.

Figure 25 provides a stakeholder map of the many entities involved *in this issue* of indigent trauma care. Obviously, the degree to which Hermann chooses to provide indigent trauma care is an issue of corporate/competitive strategy as well as of stakeholder management. The broader ethical issues associated with indigent care, as a common stakeholder management challenge, are not addressed here but are discussed in Chapter Nine along with other ethical concerns. Central to the issue is Hermann Hospital itself including its board of trustees and employees, its ongoing relationship with and commitment to the University of Texas medical school as a teaching hospital with an appropriate patient mix to support their programs, and its responsibility to maintain a financially sound institution. The Harris County Hospital District, as management of the tax-supported trauma center at Ben Taub Hospital, the only other source of trauma care in the city, is the other major stakeholder in the issue of indigent trauma care. Other key stakeholders include the various patient groups affected by the policy decisions: desired groups such as *funded* trauma, non-trauma emergency, charity patients provided for by the trust fund, and other funded patients, and undesired groups such as *indigent* trauma and nontrauma emergency patients. Also included are referring groups such as local and regional physicians and hospitals; emergency medical service (EMS) personnel at trauma sites, who determine the need for land or air transport for victims; the Harris County Medical Society; which is actively studying ways to provide trauma care to the community; and the community at large, which provides financial support for the hospital through self-referral (as patients) and donor programs. Key to the chosen strategy of the board was the support and cooperation of the media, which previously had been a key nonsupportive stakeholder.

Figure 25. Issue-Specific Map: Hermann Hospital and Indigent Trauma Patients.

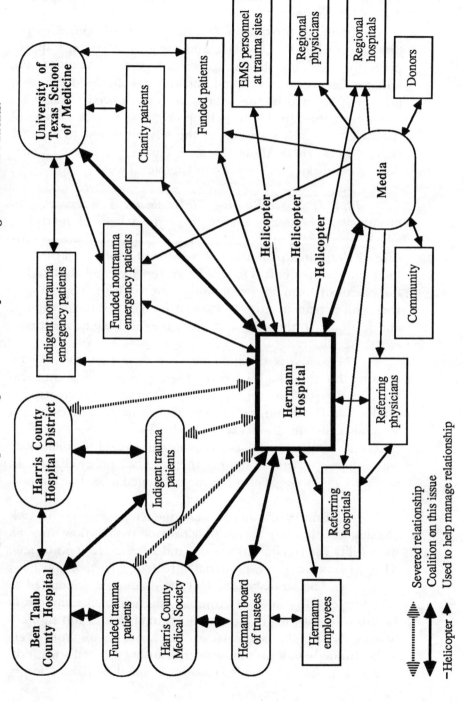

Figure 26 provides a summary of the diagnosis of the key stakeholders for this issue and the generic strategy appropriate for each. The shaded arrows in Figure 25 indicate where linkages between the hospital and the stakeholder have been effectively severed by the policy decision. Desired linkages facilitated by the Life Flight helicopter are shown. A picture of the helicopter was included in the advertisement "To Every Citizen Concerned About Trauma Care in Houston." Coalitions are indicated as they are in Chapter Two.

Type 1: Mixed-Blessing Stakeholders. The key mixed-blessing stakeholder is undoubtedly the school of medicine, which provides much of the personnel and support for the care of all trauma patients at Hermann and for which the hospital supplies patients. On this issue they have collaborated to the extent of forming a coalition to approach the hospital district with a plan to provide care to indigent trauma patients, and in doing so the school of medicine has become a supportive stakeholder.

The media is traditionally viewed, at best, as a mixed blessing due to its high potential for threat as well as cooperation. In the past the media had been a nonsupportive stakeholder for Hermann, acting as the whistle blower during a scandal earlier in the decade. On this issue the hospital diagnosed the media as a mixed blessing and sought to collaborate with it to successfully announce the hospital's policy change. In doing so, *for the purposes of this issue,* the media became supportive.

The funded trauma and emergency patients are mixed-blessing stakeholders in that they provide patient flow through the facility for teaching purposes and revenue to the hospital. They always carry the potential threat to take their business elsewhere. The strategy that Hermann adopted attempted to collaborate with these nontrauma emergency patients from Houston to opt for the Hermann Trauma Center through educating them to the policy. Heart-attack victims are more likely to be funded than are those with gunshot or knife wounds. The new policy admittedly put the hospital at risk of losing

Figure 26. Implementing Generic Stakeholder Management Strategies
for a Specific Issue: Hermann Hospital and
Indigent Trauma Patients.

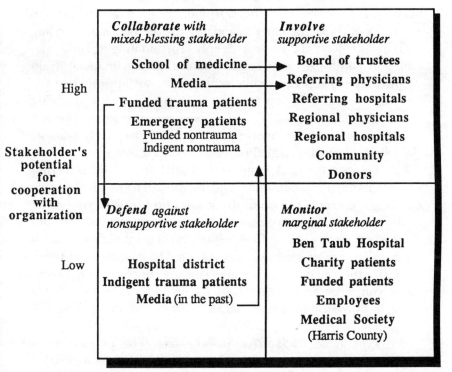

some funded trauma patients from Houston (thereby changing them from mixed blessing to nonsupportive) who would be automatically transported to Ben Taub, but Hermann would hopefully retain those funded patients, emergency as well as trauma, from outside the Harris County District.

Indigent, nontrauma emergency patients were almost borderline in terms of potential for threat and cooperation. While they contributed to the richness of the case mix, they were a fiscal threat to the hospital. However, it was difficult to effectively screen out this group without antagonizing other mixed-blessing stakeholders. Hermann chose to minimize the financial burden by screening out the higher-cost indigent trauma patients and agreeing to accept this borderline group.

Type 2: Supportive Stakeholders. The board of trustees, acting in coalition with the hospital, took an active and involved position as the chief negotiator for the hospital. In doing so they involved themselves deeply, formulating several specific and contingent strategies to minimize the financial drain of uncompensated care while maintaining an appropriate patient mix to fulfill the teaching mission. By effectively involving the media and moving it from mixed blessing to supportive, Hermann was able to involve its support to effectively manage the other supportive stakeholders.

These other stakeholders included the many referring physicians in the community and in the adjacent professional building, referring regional physicians and hospitals that often utilize the Life Fight program to transport patients whose conditions are beyond their facilities or staffing capability, and local hospitals in the same position. The media coverage did much to clarify the situation and to alleviate the concerns of the community at large and of the many donors who have historically provided physical and financial support to the hospital.

Type 3: Nonsupportive Stakeholders. The primary nonsupportive stakeholder in this issue was the hospital district. Since the district had tax support and access to funding for indigent patients, it had the capability to contract that care to hospitals other than the existing district hospitals. That is not to say that the tax support and funding was sufficient to care for all of those in need, as it appears in this case. Although the district is fiscally nonsupportive of Hermann, it also does not appear that its denial of funds will ultimately be beneficial to the hospital, since the action will further stress an already overloaded facility (Ben Taub) and the funding resources. Regardless of the district's dilemma, Hermann staked its fiscal survival on defense against the district's position and the influx of high-cost indigent trauma patients.

As noted earlier, it is important to satisfy all key stakeholders, including nonsupportive ones. Failure to satisfy them could result in possible costs (or disinducements) for the hospital. Alternatively, satisfying them, through implementing appropriate stakeholder strategies and tactics, could move them from a less supportive to a more supportive category, as in the case of the media, which eventually become supportive.

Type 4: Marginal Stakeholders. Perhaps the most surprising of the marginal stakeholders is the county hospital, Ben Taub. Although it was the facility that would take the indigent patient overflow and would suffer an overload on its physical and human resources, it actually had a very low potential for either direct threat to or cooperation with Hermann because of Ben Taub's subservient position to the hospital district. This same relationship, however, demanded monitoring for signs of developing coalitions.

Screening of charity patients must also be carefully monitored to allocate available funds and to enable the hospital to continue to deliver the level of care appropriate to the legal mandate. It was also important to Hermann not to alienate indigent as well as funded patients, who might choose Hermann in self-transport situations.

Hermann's burgeoning relationship with the Harris County Medical Society concerning the proposed stand-alone trauma center also requires close monitoring in order that Hermann remain "in the loop" as the plans and policies develop.

Last, but by no means least, the reaction and involvement of employees as a result of the policy change must be monitored to ensure their overall satisfaction and to encourage their input as the situation develops and changes. Effective use of the media in informing employees—and their neighbors—has helped keep it marginal on this issue. Its potential for threat could have been increased on a sensitive issue that clinical professionals in particular could have defined as an ethical quality-of-care and access issue.

Strategy Implementation: Who Is Responsible for Whom?

Strategic stakeholder management represents a new way of thinking for health care executives. Given the importance of the key stakeholders for an organization's overall business strategy, successful implementation of the stakeholder management concept should provide the organization with a competitive advantage. Our research indicates a definite need for emphasis on stakeholder management by health care executives. While most hospitals (75 percent) in our questionnaire study, discussed in Chapter Two, claimed to have an explicit stakeholder management strategy, the examples provided by the respondents indicated that most were ignoring the majority of their stakeholders and focusing on only one to three whom they deemed of critical importance. The most common stakeholders mentioned in terms of explicit management strategies included the corporate office, the medical staff, and the board of trustees. At best, hospital executives' stakeholder management perspectives are incomplete, and their approaches to stakeholder assessment are underdeveloped and haphazard. At worst, they display a total lack of explicit awareness of, and involvement in, a systematic and effective stakeholder management approach.

In this book we focus on further developing *systematic* and *strategic* stakeholder approaches integrated with still broader strategic management issues. A key issue in all strategic action is the implementation of the planned and articulated strategy. Now we turn from conceptual plan to organized action through assignment of responsibility to the organization's managers.

It is important to identify managerial responsibility for different stakeholders. While the previous sections have shown the variety of stakeholders with an interest in today's health care organization, it would be a mistake to assume that the CEO or any other single individual manages all stakeholders. Instead, the evolution of some organizations has seen the development of management specialists whose major purpose is to manage particular stakeholders. For example, in some organizations a medical staff director, or vice-president for medical affairs (VPMA), has the major responsibility for managing

Table 9. Hospital Executives Responsible for Particular
Key Stakeholders.

Key Stakeholder	Responsible Managers
1. Medical staff	CEO, COO, associate administrator, medical staff director
2. Patients	Director of marketing, director of guest relations
3. Hospital department managers	COO, associate administrator, assistant administrator, product or service line manager
4. Professional staff	CEO, COO, associate administrator, human resources director, VP nursing, clinical department heads
5. Board of trustees	CEO, COO, associate administrator
6. Federal government	Depends on issue
7. Corporate office	CEO, COO, VP marketing, CFO
8. Nonprofessional staff	Human resources director
9. Third-party payers	VP finance, reimbursement manager, VP marketing
10. Elected public officials	CEO, director of government relations, director of public relations
11. Political pressure groups	CEO, director of government relations, director of public relations, director of community relations
12. Local business/industry	CEO
13. Accrediting/licensing agencies	VP for risk management, director of quality assurance, appropriate department head
14. Other hospitals	CEO, COO, VP marketing
15. Media	Director of public relations, director of marketing
16. Labor unions	Director of human resources

the medical staff. Others, including the CEO, are also available to help handle nonroutine problems.

Table 9 again reflects our qualitative and quantitative data and provides examples of management personnel who might have *primary* responsibility for managing particular stakeholders. These examples of health executive titles may vary widely from organization to organization. Not only titles but also the particular functional areas and the managers who are primarily responsible for particular stakeholders vary. Table 9 furnishes some common titles for those managers who are often responsible for particular stakeholders.

In the following section we look at one executive who typically devotes much of his or her time to managing several key stakeholders. This role was chosen as one example—but not the only one, as shown by Table 9—of managers who have responsibilities for several stakeholders.

Vice-President of Marketing as One of Many Stakeholder Managers

In this section we focus on a specific executive role—that of the hospital marketing vice-president (VP) or marketing director—to illustrate the assignment of managerial responsibility in implementating stakeholder management strategies. The marketing VP is a hospital manager (as are others in the administration) in the traditional sense of planning, organizing, staffing, directing, budgeting, and controlling.

In addition, the marketing VP is expected to be a significant leader in helping the organization in its overall responses to the changing health care environment, including changing expectations and actions of key stakeholders. "Patient acquisition" is a key part of the marketing VP's role, as are the overall coordination, monitoring, and evaluation of the marketing process. The marketing VP also has considerable responsibility for protecting the organization from competitors with similar product or service lines. He or she is involved in the development of external linkages with community groups as well as other health care institutions (for example, rural hospitals as referral sources). The marketing VP is expected to further the establishment and maintenance of linkages with community physicians, particularly those on the hospital's medical/professional staff. If the hospital has a full-time paid VPMA or medical director, this may be a secondary role for the marketer, with primary management responsibility assigned to the VPMA.

Marketing Vice-President's Stakeholder Seesaw. The marketing VP may often feel that she or he is standing in the center of a circle of people, all of whom are making demands of time, attention, decisions, and actions. Many of those around the circle are from in the organization. They are fellow administrators, nurses, physicians, departments heads, and patients. Others are external to the organization and represent regulatory agencies, medical societies, practice groups, other hospitals, news media, third-party payers, and the public, all of which can exert considerable pressure on the institution generally and on the marketing VP in particular. The stakeholder seesaw facing the marketing VP can be seen more clearly in Figure 27. This figure presents the hypothetical *key external and interface stakeholder map* for the multiunit religious hospital discussed in Chapter Two.

Figure 27 does not simply identify the hospital's key external and interface stakeholders. Some of the rectangles representing different stakeholders are lightly shaded. These represent the hospital stakeholders for which the marketing VP has *primary responsibility*. In other words, one essential part of his or her role is to "manage" these stakeholders. The marketing VP also has *secondary responsibility* to manage certain other stakeholders, as indicated by vertical lines in other rectangles. In these cases, the marketing VP is expected to help manage these stakeholders, but participates equally in a joint effort to do so or supports some other manager who is primarily responsible. The marketing VP has quite limited responsibility in managing the remaining stakeholders (those with no shading). In other words, these last stakeholders may be key stakeholders *for the hospital* but not for this executive.

Figure 27. Key External and Interface Stakeholders for Marketing
Vice-President and Other Managers in Multiunit Religious
Hospital System.

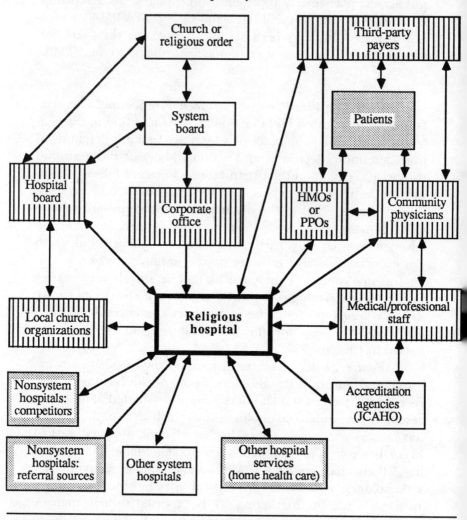

Stakeholder = Marketing VP has primary responsibility for managing this stakeholder

Stakeholder = Marketing VP has secondary responsibility for managing this stakeholder

Stakeholder = Marketing VP has minimal responsibility for managing this stakeholder

Key Internal Stakeholders. One might imagine that the seesaw would be more than full already. However, the marketing VP also has internal stakeholders to deal with. In Figure 28 we present a hypothetical *internal* stakeholder map with some of the key stakeholders a marketing VP would confront. Shown are other members of the administration. In particular, the CEO has a key stake in the behavior and effectiveness of the marketing VP. Indeed, he or she will serve to a greater or lesser extent exclusively at the pleasure of the CEO.

Other key administrative stakeholders are the chief operating officer (COO) and chief financial officer (CFO). The marketing VP will be very concerned with the ongoing operations of the hospital, and the COO will be equally concerned about the effectiveness of the marketing VP in ensuring the contribution of the marketing staff in making those operations effective—especially by their impact on hospital census and the reimbursement mix of inpatients. The CFO may be the pri-

Figure 28. Key Internal Stakeholders for Hospital Marketing Vice-President.

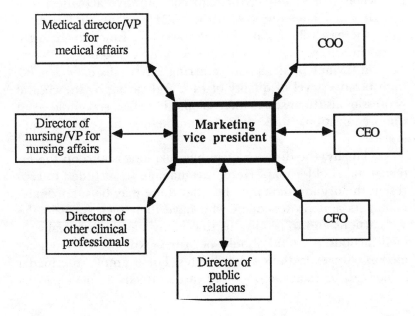

mary force for cost containment in the hospital and may provide a clear alternative perspective to the VPMA/medical director's and the VP nursing/nursing director's presumably primary focus on quality of care. Understanding these different perspectives and priorities and managing relationships with these key internal stakeholders is crucial for the marketing VP.

Other individuals also have a key stake in the activities and decisions of the marketing VP, especially with regard to her or his primary external stakeholder—past, current, and potential patients. The directors of nursing and various other clinical professions such as pharmacy, medical technology, radiology, and social work will have a stake in the marketing VP's orientation to cooperation with their clinical concerns. The VPMA will be concerned on an ongoing basis with the accuracy, completeness, and timeliness of the medical/professional staff's charting and documentation and will be equally concerned with the efficient use of resources and the quality of medical care delivered by that medical/professional staff—issues important to several other key organizational stakeholders.

The marketing VP's ability to influence medical staff physicians (for example, through collaborative activities) in a way that facilitates the jobs of the VPMA or the clinical managers increases their stake in the marketing function. In turn, these clinical managers are essential to the marketing VP's job. Having former patients and referring physicians experience a high positive level of quality of care and caring by the clinical professionals (themselves internal and interface stakeholders in the organization) is necessary for marketing the organization's services.

Finally, the director of public relations is also on the internal stakeholder map. Here, this manager is included to represent the organizational reality that there may be subordinate managers and professionals who have their own stake in the VP's actions and to remind us that many stakeholder management actions are (and should be) further delegated from senior executives to their subordinates. For example, the media is likely to be more actively and more effectively managed by the director of public relations (and her or his staff) than directly by the marketing VP.

Stakeholder responsibility and coordination maps, such as Figures 27 and 28, could be prepared for any executive position. This technique provides a way to go from a general stakeholder map developed during stakeholder assessment to incorporating stakeholder management into an executive's job description. This is an aid in clarifying and communicating unique and overlapping managerial roles and responsibilities. Obviously, development of these maps requires some agreement among the various managers concerning *who* (singular or plural) will manage *which stakeholders* on *which issues*. This process typically involves internal negotiations and the development of organizational policies and procedures. The usefulness of the stakeholder map is to help *clarify* relationships and responsibilities.

Summary and Managerial Implications

To survive the turbulent and revolutionary changes facing the health care industry, health care executives must better manage their internal, external, and interface stakeholders. Organizations have to rethink their strategies and operations as they face increasing and potentially conflictful demands for effectiveness and efficiency from these stakeholders. Executives must minimally satisfy the needs of marginal stakeholders while they maximally satisfy the needs of key stakeholders. To satisfy key stakeholders, managers must first seek those stakeholders likely to influence the organization's decisions. Managers must then make two critical assessments about the stakeholders' potential to threaten the organization and potential to cooperate with it.

When determining the stakeholders' orientation, managers should account for such factors as control of resources, relative power, likelihood and supportiveness of potential stakeholder action, and coalition formation. These factors should be interpreted in the context of the specific context and history of the organization's relations, the stakeholder and other key stakeholders' influencing the organization as well as that stakeholder. The stakeholder's orientation discloses whether it is supportive, marginal, nonsupportive, or a mixed blessing.

As an overarching strategy, managers should try to change their organization's relationships with the stakeholder from a less favorable category to a more favorable one. The stakeholder can then be managed using the generic strategy most appropriate for its new diagnostic category. In other words, health care managers should involve supportive stakeholders, monitor marginal stakeholders, defend against nonsupportive stakeholders, and collaborate with mixed-blessing stakeholders.

Executives need to do more than merely identify stakeholders or react to their demands. Executives must *proactively* develop or enhance their organizations' capacity for strategic stakeholder management rather than concentrate only on effectively dealing with a particular stakeholder on a specific issue. This means they need to satisfy their key stakeholders by offering appropriate inducements in exchange for essential contributions. Executives also should monitor their marginal stakeholders so that they do not become key nonsupportive stakeholders who confront the organization with undesired discontributions.

To survive in the future, organizations should establish goals for their relationships with current and potential stakeholders as part of an effective strategic management process (see also Coddington and Moore, 1987; Shortell, Morrison, and Friedman, 1990). Such goal setting should include clear analyses and consideration of *both* the organization's *and* the stakeholders' goals.

As guidelines for formulating and implementing stakeholder strategies, we encourage practicing managers to approach the management of stakeholders systematically through a set of specific steps:

1. Integrating business and stakeholder management strategies
2. Diagnosing key stakeholders in terms of potential for threat and for cooperation

3. Mapping the different types of stakeholders
4. Formulating generic strategies for stakeholder management
5. Formulating/adapting/reformulating specific stakeholder management strategies in response to specific issues facing the organization
6. Identifying managerial responsibilities for different stakeholders
7. Monitoring stakeholder behavior and changing stakeholder diagnoses and strategies as needed

In the next chapter we examine a key issue in implementing any of the stakeholder management strategies we suggest in this chapter—negotiating with representatives of supportive, nonsupportive, mixed-blessing, and marginal stakeholders. This will return us to the micro level of analysis by looking *strategically* at a key interaction process.

Before we leave the current topics, however, we present here a hands-on toolkit for executives who wish to take on the challenge of managing their organizations' stakeholders *strategically.*

Resource: Stakeholder Diagnosis, Strategy Formulation, and Implementation Toolkit

Exhibit 7: Integrating Competitive and Stakeholder Management Strategies. Exhibit 7 provides a form for managers to use to begin linking their organization's competitive strategy to the management of key stakeholders. The obvious first step is to identify the key stakeholders for each of the ten competitive strategies specified by Coddington and Moore (1987) and drawing on Porter's approach to generic competitive strategies. Obviously, the key stakeholders (physicians) necessary for pursuing a physician bonding strategy will be different than the key stakeholders (employees and suppliers) necessary for pursuing a low-cost provider strategy.

Exhibit 8: Diagnosing Stakeholders' Potential for Threat and Cooperation. Once the key stakeholders are identified, their potential for threat or cooperation may be analyzed using Exhibit 8. There are spaces to list four key stakeholders at the top of the form. Under each stakeholder, the manager should circle the responses that best describe that particular stakeholder—on an ongoing basis or, more likely, on a specific issue. At the bottom of the form the manager should circle a *summary* evaluation (high or low) that best describes the particular stakeholder's potential for threat or cooperation.

Exhibit 9: Diagnosing and Classifying Organizational Stakeholders. Based on the analysis performed using Exhibit 8, the manager can fill in the key stakeholders in the appropriate cells in Exhibit 9. For example, if physicians are a key stakeholder, then they are most likely to be placed in the mixed-blessing cell. Remember, however, that some stakeholders may fall into more than one category.

Exhibit 10: Implementing Generic Stakeholder Management Strategies. Exhibit 10 indicates the appropriate generic stakeholder management strategy for each cell. As the classification of a stakeholder changes, the type of generic strategy used will also change. Once again, the type of generic strategy employed may depend on the specific issue.

Exhibit 11: Stakeholder Strategy Implementation. Exhibit 11 identifies the generic strategy appropriate for each category in which *a particular stakeholder* is placed. (Note that one of these forms is needed for each stakeholder diagnosed.) Then a set of diagnostic questions is provided to help the manager work through the implementation of the generic strategy. By filling out the form, a manager is able to move from a generic strategy, such as defend, to a systematic plan for implementing that strategy.

Exhibit 12: Checklist for Implementing Stakeholder Strategies. Exhibit 12 provides a checklist for implementing the generic strategies. These questions alert the manager to the many subtleties involved in implementing a given stakeholder strategy.

Exhibit 13: Organizational Executives Having Responsibility for Particular Key Stakeholders. Finally, the identification of the manager or managers responsible for managing particular key stakeholders can be recorded using Exhibit 13. The specific tactics discussed in this and later chapters need to be adequately communicated to and understood by those managers.

Exhibit 7. Integrating Competitive and Stakeholder Management Strategies.

Instructions: Circle the competitive strategy your whole organization is following (or for a particular product line). Then list key stakeholders necessary for making that strategy successful.

Competitive Strategy	*Key Stakeholder*
1. Cost leadership	
a. Being low-cost provider	1. _____
b. Downsizing	2. _____
2. Differentiation	
a. On basis of technical quality	1. _____
b. On basis of functional quality	2. _____
c. Aggressive marketing	3. _____
3. Focus	
a. Centers of excellence (service lines)	1. _____
b. Physician bonding	2. _____
4. Restructuring	
a. Diversification to new markets	1. _____
b. Vertical integration	2. _____
c. Networking	3. _____

Exhibit 8. Diagnosing Stakeholders' Potential for Threat and Cooperation.

Write the name of each of four key stakeholders in the box at the top of the column. Use as many sheets as necessary for all key stakeholders for a given issue. Under each stakeholder, circle the responses which best describe that stakeholder. At the bottom of each column, circle the summary evaluation (high or low).	Stakeholder:		Stakeholder:	
	Increases or Decreases Stakeholder's Potential for Threat?	Increases or Decreases Stakeholder's Potential for Cooperation?	Increases or Decreases Stakeholder's Potential for Threat?	Increases or Decreases Stakeholder's Potential for Cooperation?
Stakeholder controls key resources (needed by organization)	Increases	Increases	Increases	Increases
Stakeholder does not control key resources	Decreases	Either	Decreases	Either
Stakeholder more powerful than organization	Increases	Either	Increases	Either
Stakeholder as powerful as organization	Either	Either	Either	Either
Stakeholder less powerful than organization	Decreases	Increases	Decreases	Increases
Stakeholder likely to take action (supportive of organization)	Decreases	Increases	Decreases	Increases
Stakeholder likely to take nonsupportive action	Increases	Decreases	Increases	Decreases
Stakeholder unlikely to take any action	Decreases	Decreases	Decreases	Decreases
Stakeholder likely to form coalition with other stakeholders	Increases	Either	Increases	Either
Stakeholder likely to form coalition with organization	Decreases	Increases	Decreases	Increases
Stakeholder unlikely to form any coalition	Decreases	Decreases	Decreases	Decreases
Summary Stakeholder Diagnosis:	High Low	High Low	High Low	High Low
	Potential for Threat	Potential for Cooperation	Potential for Threat	Potential for Cooperation

Stakeholder:		Stakeholder:	
Increases or Decreases Stakeholder's Potential for Threat?	Increases or Decreases Stakeholder's Potential for Cooperation?	Increases or Decreases Stakeholder's Potential for Threat?	Increases or Decreases Stakeholder's Potential for Cooperation?
Increases	Increases	Increases	Increases
Decreases	Either	Decreases	Either
Increases	Either	Increases	Either
Either	Either	Either	Either
Decreases	Increases	Decreases	Increases
Decreases	Increases	Decreases	Increases
Increases	Decreases	Increases	Decreases
Decreases	Decreases	Decreases	Decreases
Increases	Either	Increases	Either
Decreases	Increases	Decreases	Increases
Decreases	Decreases	Decreases	Decreases
High Low	High Low	High Low	High Low
Potential for Threat	Potential for Cooperation	Potential for Threat	Potential for Cooperation

Exhibit 9. Diagnosing and Classifying Organizational Stakeholders.

Instructions: Basing your choices on the diagnoses in Exhibit 8, fill in all key stakeholders into the appropriate cells in Exhibit 9. This provides a "portfolio of stakeholders."

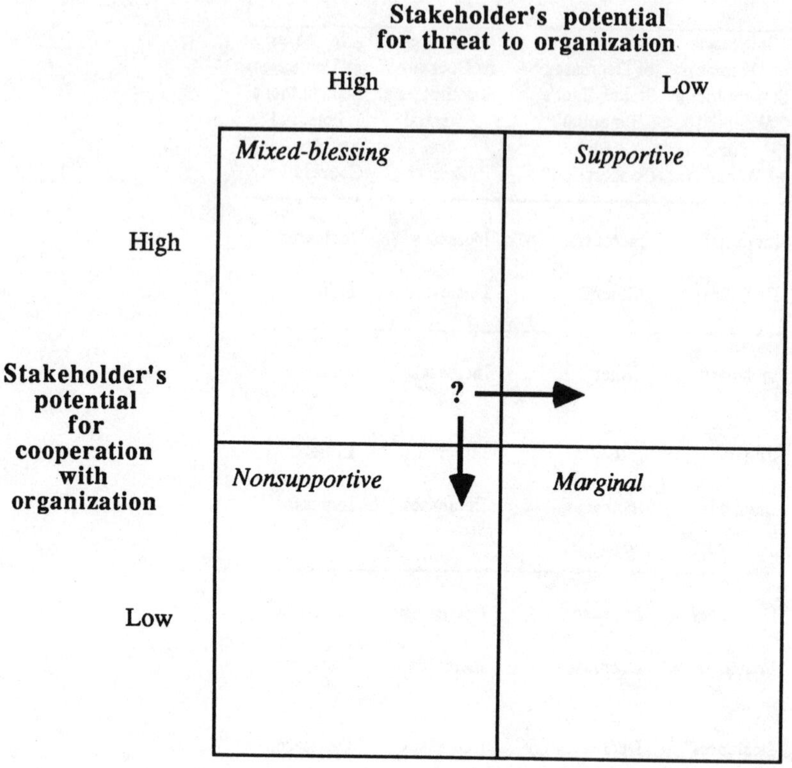

**Stakeholder's potential
for threat to organization**

High   Low

	Mixed-blessing	Supportive
Stakeholder's potential for cooperation with organization — High		
Low	Nonsupportive	Marginal

Exhibit 10. Implementing Generic Stakeholder Management Strategies.

Instructions: In each cell in Exhibit 10, write a phrase that captures how you will follow the generic strategy suggested for each stakeholder classified in Exhibit 9.

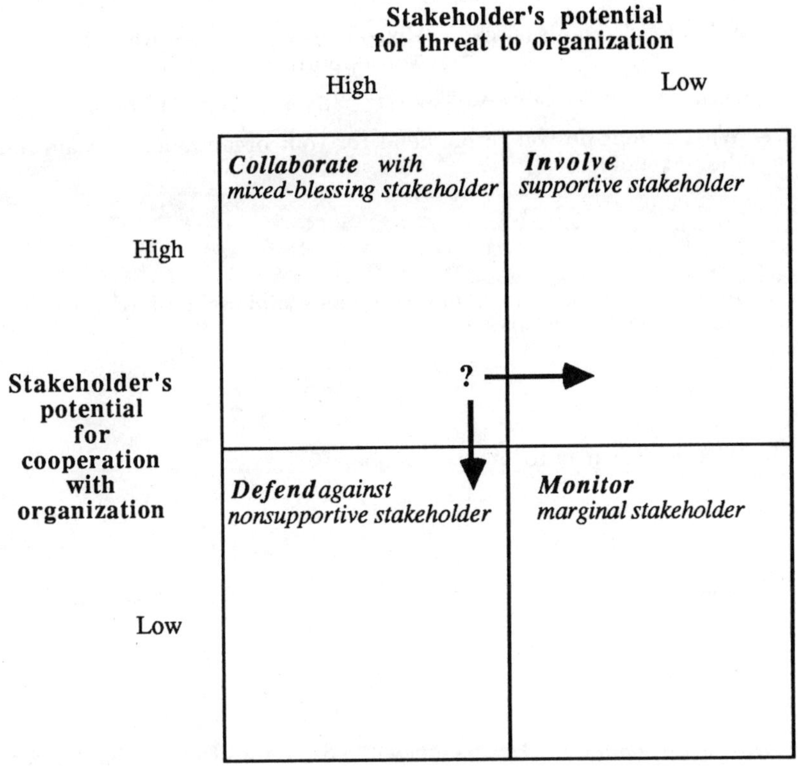

**Stakeholder's potential
for threat to organization**

    High   Low

	High	Low
High	*Collaborate with mixed-blessing stakeholder*	*Involve supportive stakeholder*
Low	*Defend against nonsupportive stakeholder*	*Monitor marginal stakeholder*

Stakeholder's potential for cooperation with organization

? → ↓

Exhibit 11. Stakeholder Strategy Implementation.

Instructions: Complete this exhibit for each key stakeholder diagnosed in order to plan the implementation of the appropriate generic strategy.

Stakeholder: _____

Stakeholder diagnosis (circle):   Mixed blessing   Supportive
                                  Nonsupportive   Marginal

Generic strategy (circle):   Collaborate   Involve   Defend   Monitor

1. What actions do you recommend for your organization in managing the stakeholder?

2. In what ways do your recommendations support the business strategies of your organization?

3. What is your plan for implementation?

4. What resources will be required for implementation, and are they available?

5. Which organizational managers will have the lead role in implementing the particular strategy?

6. What other hospital personnel should be involved as internal stakeholders in the implementation process?

7. If the implementation process does not work as planned, to what contingency approach will you go next?

Exhibit 12. Checklist for Implementing Stakeholder Strategies.

Instructions: Use this list to check the completeness and appropriateness of your implementation plan detailed in Exhibit 11 for each stakeholder.

---

1. General information for this stakeholder:
   a. How stable is the relationship with this stakeholder?
   b. How positive is the relationship with this stakeholder?
   c. Is the relationship with this stakeholder likely to shift significantly from issue to issue?
   d. How will it shift? More positive or more negative?
2. Increasing this stakeholder's potential for cooperation:
   a. What kind of cooperative behavior (action) is desired from the stakeholder?
   b. How can your organization increase cooperation from the stakeholder?
   c. How much time and other resources are appropriate to devote to increasing this stakeholder's cooperation?
3. Decreasing this stakeholder's potential for threat:
   a. What kind of threatening (or potentially threatening) behavior (action) does your organization need to minimize or avoid from the stakeholder?
   b. How can your organization avoid or reduce threatening actions from the stakeholder?
   c. How much time and other resources are appropriate to devote to decreasing this stakeholder's threat?
4. What are your proposed actions for this stakeholder?
   a. How cost effective are your recommendations? If they are not cost effective, what alternative actions can you take?
5. Key issues in implementing your proposal:
   a. What are the most significant factors that will affect the implementation process, and how can they be dealt with?
   b. Is the implementation process supportive of the appropriate generic strategy for this type of stakeholder?
   c. Is the implementation process supportive of overall hospital goals and strategies?
6. What stakeholder reactions might you face?
   a. Why will the targeted stakeholders respond as desired?
   b. Is the stakeholder level of supportiveness likely to decline during implementation? If so, how can your organization cope with it?
   c. Is the stakeholder level of threat likely to increase during the implementation stage? If so, how can your organization cope with it?
7. Assigning managerial responsibility:
   a. What other managers (or personnel) will feel they have their own stake in what you are trying to do?
   b. Does the responsible manager have the necessary ability and power to effectively implement the strategy?

**Exhibit 13. Organizational Executives Having Responsibility for
Particular Key Stakeholders.**

Instructions: Identify those executives of the organization who will be responsible for managing specific key stakeholders. List those with primary responsibility first.

Key Stakeholder	*Responsible Managers*
1. _____	1. _____
	2. _____
	3. _____
	4. _____
2. _____	1. _____
	2. _____
	3. _____
	4. _____
3. _____	1. _____
	2. _____
	3. _____
	4. _____
4. _____	1. _____
	2. _____
	3. _____
	4. _____
5. _____	1. _____
	2. _____
	3. _____
	4. _____

6. _____   1. _____
                      2. _____
                      3. _____
                      4. _____

7. _____   1. _____
                      2. _____
                      3. _____
                      4. _____

8. _____   1. _____
                      2. _____
                      3. _____
                      4. _____

9. _____   1. _____
                      2. _____
                      3. _____
                      4. _____

10. _____   1. _____
                      2. _____
                      3. _____
                      4. _____

¤¥¤¥¤¥¤¥¤¥¤¥¤¥¤¥¤¥¤¥¤¥¤¥¤¥¤¥¤¥

CHAPTER 5

The Strategic Approach
to Negotiating

In Chapter Four we examined how to carefully diagnose stakeholders of all kinds and suggested generic strategies for managing them. One important way to manage stakeholders is through negotiation tied to broader strategy. In the previous chapters we also looked at how the economic, personal, and social importance of health care organizations and the sensitivity of their mission make them particularly susceptible to stakeholder attempts to influence their direction and functioning. In Chapter Three we saw how such organizations face an exceptionally diverse set of stakeholders with varied and frequently conflicting interests and goals. The successful implementation of competitive strategies and tactics requires that the appropriate generic stakeholder management strategies and specific tactics be implemented. All of the generic stakeholder management strategies, as well as their associated specific tactics, require either explicit or implicit negotiation processes.

Indeed, a health care organization's success in steering through a turbulent environment might be as much a consequence of its negotiation strategies and the facility of its managers in negotiating as of any other factor. Every manager negotiates to resolve conflicts, to implement projects, and to create opportunities. Such negotiations strike at the heart of the fundamental inducements/contributions exchanges discussed in Chapter One. Negotiations with stakeholders often focus on what inducements the organization must give for stakeholders to make needed contributions. Whether negotiating with representatives of key stakeholder groups such as blue-collar employees, professional staff, department managers, or representatives from other organizations, managers should consider carefully how to handle these interactions. Such diverse stakeholders require a health care manager capable of successfully negotiating with individuals, groups, and other organizations.

In fact, many of the daily challenges and actions of health care managers imply some form of negotiation (Savage, Blair, and Sorenson, 1989; Savage and Blair, 1989). Hence, during this decade of strategic realignment in health care, negotiation has become a key skill for the manager. We advocate that executives approach negotiation more explicitly, that is, as a conscious decision process linked to overarching competitive strategies.

Successful stakeholder negotiation, however, goes beyond basic bargaining skills. Health care managers should also be sensitive to potential and existing coalitions of internal stakeholders as well as potential and existing coalitions among external stakeholders, such as those identified during stakeholder assessment discussed in Chapter Three, whenever they negotiate with a particular stakeholder (Blair, Savage, and Whitehead, 1989). Additionally, managers should recognize that their negotiations with stakeholders depend on the political astuteness and authority of the representatives with whom they actually bargain (Bacharach and Lawler, 1980). These concerns are compounded by the fact that stakeholder negotiations are influenced by the organization's overall business strategies *and* its stakeholder management strategies.

The following discussion provides a comprehensive approach to stakeholder negotiation that focuses on more than the slice of the pie. Most discussions of negotiations concentrate on how much one wins or loses in a negotiation—the slice of the pie. We argue that this almost exclusive concern with *substantive* outcomes is too narrow and hardly effective when negotiating (or otherwise interacting) with representatives of key stakeholders. Consequently, our approach to negotiation

will give equal consideration to the importance of other crucial, but often neglected, outcomes of negotiation processes:
the impact on *relationships*. Consistent with Chapter Two, to
make negotiation a central part of our strategic stakeholder
management approach, we combine micro and macro perspectives to integrate three key approaches from three different
literatures: strategic management, stakeholder management, and
negotiation. The result is a conceptually based diagnostic *and*
action framework for conducting stakeholder negotiations
strategically. The eight steps in our strategic approach to stakeholder negotiation are

1. Linking negotiating to business and stakeholder manage-
    ment strategies
2. Assessing the stakeholder's potential for threat and coop-
    eration
3. Diagnosing the negotiation situation by focusing on both
    relationship and *substantive* outcomes
4. Selecting an outcome-focused negotiation strategy
5. Refining the negotiation strategy based on sensitivity to key
    stakeholder contingencies
6. Implementing the negotiation strategy through appro-
    priate tactics
7. Changing the stakeholder-sensitive strategy as needed
8. Monitoring the ever-changing stakeholder negotiation
    context

Step 1: Linking Negotiating to Business and Stakeholder Management Strategies

Once an organization has determined what competitive
strategy or strategies to pursue, its managers then have to
identify and assess key stakeholders. Such an assessment leads
to the summary diagnosis discussed in Chapter Four and then
to the selection of the appropriate generic stakeholder management strategy. Several specific tactics are usually selected to
implement the generic stakeholder management strategy. Regardless of which stakeholder strategy or particular tactics are

selected, their implementation requires interaction—and usually some form of negotiation—with relevant key stakeholders.

Negotiating with stakeholders should not be an isolated act. Given that the stakeholder, as the other party to the negotiation, has a stake in the health care organization's decisions and actions, strategies for negotiating with a stakeholder need to be connected to two other types of organizational strategies: the organization's overall competitive strategy (see Chapters One and Two) and the organization's strategy for managing each stakeholder (see Chapter Four). In addition, the *stakeholder's* own implicit or explicit strategy and its likely response *to the organization's attempts* to "manage" it need to be assessed.

Here we extend the connection between competitive strategy and stakeholder management strategy by including negotiation strategy as well. These strategic linkages move away from the exclusively micro level of analysis and interpersonal focus of most negotiation research, grounding the negotiation process in broader organizational processes.

For example, a multispeciality group practice of primary care physicians may find itself at strategic risk because of the growing penetration of managed care into their local market. The result of the growth in size of many HMOs and various forms of PPAs has been a refunneling of patients to those providers that have contractual relationships with managed care organizations. Consequently, the group practice has seen a significant decrease in the number of both new and long-term patients. To gain a competitive advantage to compete successfully in this changing marketplace, the group decides to pursue the generic *low-cost provider* competitive strategy discussed in the strategic management literature (Porter, 1980, 1985; Coddington and Moore, 1987). However, prior to negotiating with the various managed care organizations (as external stakeholders), the leadership of the practice must negotiate with key internal stakeholders—the members of the practice and its staff. These negotiations will necessarily focus on the essence of how medicine is practiced by the practice members, because the low-cost provider strategy can be implemented only if they can drive their costs (not their prices) down to the level that no compet-

itors can provide care at a lower cost. These will be very deli-
cate but crucial negotiations for the strategy to succeed. If these
internal negotiations to bring down costs are not successful,
negotiations with the managed care stakeholders may put the
organization at significant financial risk because of discounted
prices that must be negotiated.

In this chapter we repeat and then extend an example
presented in Chapter One because it is a situation commonly
faced by health care managers and is central to illustrating the
nature and complexity of stakeholder negotiation. The senior
management team of a large urban hospital might face many
empty beds, perhaps because of the prospective payment system's pressure for shorter lengths of stay. Whatever the cause,
they might decide that this problem can be remedied primarily
through capturing a larger share of the tertiary care referral
market. Their thinking reflects the generic business strategy of
market penetration. That is, they plan to grow through expanding the hospital's share of an existing market (tertiary care referrals) using the same products (beds and services to provide
tertiary care). Further, they have identified the key stakeholders impacted by that strategy—and essential to its success—to
include the rural hospitals and rural primary care physicians
in the hospital's secondary market area. Both of these stakeholders are what we call mixed-blessing stakeholders because
they are high on both potential for threat and potential for
cooperation. In earlier chapters we suggest that the most appropriate management strategy for this type of stakeholder is
collaboration.

As indicated in the next step, a combination of high threat
and high cooperation represents a moderately favorable negotiating situation. The issue of assessing threat and cooperative potentials also will be elaborated in the next section.

To effectively collaborate, the hospital might set up a
department of regional services. The director of regional services would negotiate collaborative ventures with rural hospitals and members of their medical staffs. Such ventures would
be sought to reduce the stakeholders' actual threat and to increase their cooperation. During the negotiations with these

stakeholders, the strategies used by the director of regional services must further both the urban hospital's goals for effective stakeholder management and its overall business strategy.

Implementing the overall competitive strategy affects the hospital's stakeholder management strategy; carrying out the stakeholder management strategy influences the hospital's negotiation strategy. (Briefly, the four generic negotiation strategies are collaborating, subordinating, competing, and avoiding negotiations. They will be discussed in detail later in this chapter.) In turn, the success of a negotiation strategy helps reformulate the strategy for managing a stakeholder. Similarly, the success of the stakeholder management strategy provides valuable input for evaluating the original business strategy.

To continue our example, the director would negotiate with the rural hospitals through their representative, such as the administrator, and with the physicians' representative, such as the chief of the medical staff, using the appropriate strategy given certain key contingencies to be discussed below. Should the chosen negotiation strategy fail, it may call into question both the business and the stakeholder management strategies. For instance, the basic collaborative stakeholder management strategy might not be effective because the hospitals' and medical staffs' levels of actual threat or unwillingness to cooperate were underestimated. Further, the failure may indicate that a simple market penetration business strategy is not adequate. Alternatively, successful negotiation resulting in improved relationships and increased tertiary care referrals may suggest that both the stakeholder management strategy and the business strategy were well formulated.

Step 2: Assessing Stakeholders' Potential
for Threat and Cooperation

As the preceding discussion illustrates, many stakeholder negotiations occur as a hospital implements a competitive strategy *as well as* a strategy to manage particular stakeholders. By looking again at key stakeholders' potential for threat and cooperation, using the criteria discussed in Chapter Four, health care executives can determine those stakeholders with whom it would be most advantageous to negotiate. Remember that the diagnosis may be different for different issues.

Looking at the *potential for threat* of stakeholders is similar to developing a worst-case scenario and protects managers from unpleasant surprises. Carefully examining the threat potential of a stakeholder is especially important for estimating the probable substantive outcomes of negotiation.

Of equal importance is the second dimension, *potential for cooperation.* Assessing the potential for cooperation is critical because of its implications for the relationship outcomes of negotiation. Cooperation is not only a way of dealing with competitive threat but also a complement to it; competition may exist along with collaboration (Sheldon and Windham, 1984).

The cooperative potential is also similar to scenario development, here a best-case one. It may open new possibilities otherwise ignored or unseen because of fundamental assumptions and perspectives. To negotiate effectively, managers of the health care organization need to assess both its own potential to cooperate as well as the stakeholder's potential to cooperate.

As we saw in Chapters Three and Four, the stakeholders who are *relevant* to health care managers are specific to the particular issue under negotiation. If, for example, the issue concerns a collaborative effort by an insurance company and hospital administrators to negotiate with the medical staff to provide discounted services through a preferred provider arrangement that includes both the hospital and the members of its medical staff, the concerned stakeholders will be different than if the issue is one of the same hospital administrators' negotiating with another insurance company over reimbursements rates for particular procedures that are not part of managed care arrangements.

The *classification* of the relevant stakeholders along the two dimensions of potential for threat and potential for cooperation may be different for any given issue as well. Whatever the prior classification of a particular stakeholder on a particular issue (supportive, nonsupportive, marginal, or mixed blessing), managers should attempt to reclassify all relevant stakeholders prior to or during each negotiation episode. The ongoing classification process will make the managers' assumptions explicit, highlighting biases, exposing flawed assessments, and challenging erroneous assumptions.

For example, competitors are usually classified as nonsupportive stakeholders, since their potential for threat is high but their potential for cooperation is low. In some cases, however, a competitor might be a potential ally in managing another very nonsupportive competitor. To more completely implement the market penetration (of rural referral areas) strategy discussed above, the large urban hospital may need to match its main competitor's emergency helicopter service—to enter an air war, as it were, with patient acquisition, not land, as the target.

This air transport-capability has given a significant competitive advantage that can be sustained unless offset by a similar service to the competing hospital. But such a helicopter service is not financially feasible for the original hospital at this time. However, by constantly challenging their own stakeholder assumptions (Mason and Mitroff, 1981), the original hospital's managers can reconceptualize a third competing hospital as a mixed-blessing stakeholder with higher potential to cooperate *on this issue* than on most issues—hence, negotiation over a potential joint venture helicopter service that would permit both hospitals access to rural areas. Given that such a service will *not* give them the competitive advantage currently enjoyed by the first hospital with the service, it is important to offset that initial advantage at lower financial risk and cost.

Potentials for threat and for cooperativeness of stakeholders affect their willingness to negotiate, their strategy selection, and the type of outcome they seek (Blair, Savage, and Whitehead, 1989). Managers should consider what their organization and the stakeholder have at stake as well as the human and material resources available to both potential negotiators.

We suggest that the health care manager should consider negotiation with stakeholders under the following rank-ordered conditions:

1. The stakeholder's potential for threat is low and potential for cooperation is moderate to high, presenting a highly favorable negotiating situation.
2. The stakeholder's potential for both threat and cooperation is moderate to high, presenting a moderately favorable negotiating situation.
3. The stakeholder's potential for threat is high and potential for cooperation is low to moderate, presenting a highly to moderately unfavorable negotiating situation.

Because a party with low potential for threat and cooperation typically can be handled more effectively through other means than negotiation, for example, monitoring techniques that avoid direct negotiations, it is not included above.

Even though a stakeholder with high potential for threat and low potential for cooperation may not negotiate in good faith (rank order 3), a negotiated agreement may be essential for the manager of a threatened organization. For example, small hospital organizations in markets dominated by a few large providers would be well advised to negotiate with them. The larger organizations often have many ways to threaten the existence of the small providers and are unlikely to need to cooperate with the small hospitals. Managers of the threatened hospitals should creatively form and negotiate cooperative ventures of value to the larger hospitals. Alternatively, they should negotiate with other stakeholders (for example, other small hospitals) to form coalitions to offset the level of threat they are facing. For example, a hospital may want to negotiate a contract with a nursing home to place recovering hospital patients in less expensive nursing home beds, reduce case costs, and enhance relationships with a nonthreatening stakeholder.

Step 3: Diagnosing The Negotiation Situation by Focusing on Outcomes

Most of the negotiation literature focuses on the substantive issues and outcomes involved in a potential negotiation. For example, game theory emphasizes that the advantages and disadvantages of alternative actions should be weighed carefully prior to initiating any negotiation (Raiffa, 1982). Thus, just as a successful buyer at an auction should not bid beyond the market value of an item, so also should health care negotiators withdraw from any negotiation that presents a settlement worse than their "best alternative to a negotiated agreement," or BATNA (Fisher and Ury, 1981). In other words, by knowing their BATNA, managers avoid settling for suboptimal agreements.

However, assessing only substantive outcomes—such as net economic benefits from a negotiation or negotiation episode—can lead a manager to focus on short- rather than long-term costs and benefits. The game theory viewpoint encourages a health care manager to look at short-term substantive outcomes, that is, the size of the *slice* of the pie, in negotiating with stakeholders because they can be estimated more easily than long-term relationship outcomes. Hence, a manager may decide not to negotiate, even though the negotiation could establish or maintain a significant relationship with long-term benefits—which might, by the way, increase the size of the *total* pie.

In contrast, we advocate that managers should consider both the substantive *and* the relationship outcomes of any potential stakeholder negotiation. The relative importance of these two outcome factors should help managers decide whether and how to negotiate. However, before making this decision, managers should link any prospective negotiations to other strategic issues.

Health care managers, in this step, should consider the relative importance of the situation's substantive and relationship outcomes for the organization. As depicted in Figure 29, the relative importance of each of these two outcomes determines the *organization's priorities*. To the extent that the relationship outcomes are important to the organization, it needs to give greater emphasis to satisfying both the noneconomic (relationship) as well as the economic (substantive) goals of the organization. We recognize, of course, that some relationships will have economic consequences in the long run. *The point here*

Figure 29. Diagnosing the Negotiation Situation.

Is substantive outcome very important to organization?

		Yes	No
Is relationship outcome very important to organization?	**Yes**	*Situation 1* Organization's priorities are on **both outcomes**	*Situation 2* Organization's priority is on **relationship outcomes**
	No	*Situation 3* Organization's priority is on **substantive outcomes**	*Situation 4* Organization's priority is on **neither outcome**

is to look at the priorities for a particular negotiation episode (or several related episodes) with a specific stakeholder representative.

If the importance of the relationship and the substantive outcomes varies, then managers should focus on the more important outcome (situation 2 and 3). When the relationship between the organization and the stakeholder and also the substance of the negotiation are very important (situation 1), then both outcomes become a priority. Alternatively, if neither the relationship nor the substantive outcome is very important, then managers should question the value of this particular negotiation (situation 4).

Clearly, sometimes executives negotiate to secure the best possible substantive outcome. For example, if multiple venders of supplies are available, negotiations with these venders may focus on only substantive outcomes (situation 3), that is, the prices of the supplies, ease of ordering, or speed of delivery.

In contrast, consider executives of large hospitals negotiating about the price of management consulting services with rural hospitals. Recognizing that the rural hospitals serve as tertiary care referral pipelines, the executives place their priority on establishing positive relationships (situation 2), with little emphasis on the actual substantive outcome—the negotiated price for providing the management services.

Joint ventures often involve a situation 1–type negotiation. When the urban hospital we have been discussing is involved in negotiating with the third hospital over a joint helicopter service, hospital managers should be concerned both with obtaining a cost-effective service and with creating a positive working relationship with the other hospital. In this instance, the manager focuses on both substantive and relationship outcomes.

Of course, other joint venture opportunities may be offered to an organization that, from the perspective of the executive, do not provide either direct or indirect financial payoffs or improve the relationship with the other partner in the proposed joint ventures. These situation 4–type negotiations should be avoided.

The following is a medical school case in which all four negotiating situations must be faced. In considering the development of affiliation agreements between a medical school and several independent community hospitals (A–D), the dean, as the manager negotiating on behalf of the medical school, may have a different diagnosis for each of the community hospitals under consideration depending on the school's perception of relative power, levels of conflict, and its own needs. For example, Hospital A possesses a great number and variety of patients appropriate for the educational and training needs of the medical school. However, it has little potential for developing close interorganizational coordination and cooperation with the school because it is the subsidiary of a large investor-owned corporation concerned primarily with market share and cost containment. In this context, the medical school's dean may view it as a situation 3–type negotiation, with the achievement of substantive goals as the most desirable result in a negotiated agreement.

In contrast, Hospital B has a particularly renowned professional and community reputation, but its inpatient population has been inaccessible for the educational needs of the school. Under these circumstances, the dean may consider this a situation 2–type negotiation, with the establishment of a positive relationship as the most desirable outcome in a negotiated agreement. However, Hospital C possesses many of the favorable attributes of Hospital B and has an inpatient population already accessible for teaching medical students and residents. Given these conditions, the medical school dean may view it a situation 1–type negotiation, with priority placed on both substantive outcomes and maintaining already positive relationships. Because Hospital D possesses none of the favorable attributes of hospitals A, B, and C, the dean may well classify it as a situation 4–type negotiation, with the school's priority on neither outcome, even though Hospital D has asked to negotiate such an affiliation agreement.

Step 4: Selecting an Outcome-Focused Negotiation Strategy

After assessing their own priorities concerning relationship or substantive outcomes, health care managers should select an initial negotiation strategy. Figure 30 illustrates four strategies that correspond to the different negotiation situations previously discussed. Because our analysis of the strategies advocated in Figure 30 emphasizes *relationship* as well as *substantive* outcomes, our following descriptions develop the *subordinative* strategy concept explicitly as well as extend the previous discussions of competitive and collaborative (or cooperative) strategies in the negotiation literature (see, for example, Derr, 1978; Filley, 1978; Pruitt, 1983; Johnston, 1985; Lax and Sebenius, 1986). Later in this chapter we present specific tactics consistent with these strategies. The effective negotiator will be careful in both the selection of the most appropriate generic strategy and the specific tactics to implement that strategy during different phases in the negotiation process.

Figure 30. Selecting an Outcome-Focused Negotiation Strategy.

Is substantive outcome very important to organization?

	Yes	No
Yes Is relationship outcome very important to organization? **No**	*Strategy C1* **Collaborate** when both types of outcomes are very important	*Strategy S1* **Subordinate** when priority is on relationship outcomes
	Strategy P1 **Compete** when priority is on substantive outcomes	*Strategy A1* **Avoid negotiating** when neither type of outcome is very important

Collaborate: Strategy C1. A collaborative strategy helps the health care manager achieve both the relationship and the substantive outcomes important in situation 1. Here, the manager seeks a win-win, substantive outcome to sustain a positive relationship. An effective problem-solving process and a resulting win-win settlement typify the results of successful collaboration.

A variety of joint ventures and other collaborative efforts in the health care industry illustrate this strategy (Mancino, 1984; Morrisey and Brooks, 1985a; Snook and Kaye, 1986; Bettner and Collins, 1987; Coddington and Moore, 1987). For example, a hospital manager might seek a win-win outcome with members of the medical staff by offering them office facilities if they will support a certain preferred provider organization (Boland, 1985; Merz, 1986). Both the hospital manager and the medical staff assume that referrals from the PPO will be made primarily to the hospital. Although both the hospital and the physicians potentially can benefit, they also share the risk of low patient numbers or reduced profit margins. Of course, care should be taken to ensure that the negotiated settlement provides substantive outcomes for both joint venture partners. Otherwise the interdependent relationship between the two may be strained rather than strengthened. Some of these complexities were discussed in detail in Chapter Five and should be considered prior to negotiation.

Collaboration between organizations (in the limits of antitrust restrictions) can not only save money but also improve long-term strategic business relationships. In the helicopter joint venture discussed previously, the executives may wish not only to provide a mutually profitable service but also to anticipate and counter the actions of other hospitals. Each joint venture partner may also be a potentially attractive coalition partner for still another hospital, such as the one that already has the helicopter service, but may seek allies in other areas. By collaborating to form the helicopter venture, the partners may gain direct substantive outcomes *but also deny a coalition relationship to competitors.*

Compete: Strategy P1. A competitive strategy is appropriate for situation 3 because it allows managers to focus on substantive goals with little concern for the relationship with the stakeholder. The executive competes by trying to claim more favorable substantive outcomes than the other party. When competing, health care managers will often take hard positions and may become highly aggressive by bluffing, threatening, and otherwise misrepresenting their intentions. Such actions hide the organization's actual goals and needs, preventing the stakeholder representative from using that knowledge to negotiate substantive outcomes.

Not surprisingly, the credibility of the executive's aggressive tactics and thus the success of the competitive strategy often rests on the organization's power vis-à-vis the stakeholder. When following a competitive strategy, the manager seeks a win-lose substantive outcome and a neutral to negative relationship.

For example, a hospital manager might use a competitive strategy to reduce the hospital's vulnerability to medical staff members opposed to staffing an outpatient surgical center. By negotiating with a large corporate chain for a turnkey operation, the manager may induce cooperation from these reluctant medical staff members. If the staff members do not change their position, the manager still will have the option to pursue the arrangement with the corporate chain. In this case, the relationship with the medical staff should not be adversely affected since no direct threat was made to the staff's autonomy in the hospital itself. The hospital manager is not particularly concerned with the relationship between the hospital and the physicians *on this issue*. If, however, the executive were to expect strong spillover on the general relationship between the hospital and its medical staff, this kind of strategy would be inappropriate.

Another situation that may call for firm competition could occur because of recent shortages of examination gloves resulting from concern over AIDS. Some hospitals have had at least short-term difficulty obtaining gloves. However, member hospitals of Voluntary Hospitals of America (VHA) had ample supplies because of VHA-negotiated agreements with suppliers in Taiwan. If the manager in charge of supplies in the VHA hospital has a surplus, she or he may be requested to sell them to a competing hospital. If fostering a positive relationship with that hospital is not important, the manager might negotiate to get a significantly higher price than paid to VHA, that is, focus only on substantive outcomes.

Subordinate: Strategy S1. The subordinative strategy calls for health care managers to accommodate the needs of the stakeholder to establish or to sustain a relationship (situation 2). Typically, a subordinative strategy results in lose-win substantive outcomes (negative substantive outcomes for the organization) but positive to neutral relationship outcomes.

Moreover, a subordinative strategy may be used whether the manager's organization exercises more, less, or equal power to the stakeholder. A subordinative strategy is a key way to dampen hostilities, increase support, and foster more interdependent relationships.

This last point underscores the difference between subordination as a strategy and subordination in a role. Subordination *as a strategy* has as its goal making the stakeholder more dependent on the organization to increase the relationship's overall interdependence. In contrast, subordination *within a role* serves to reaffirm the one-up/one-down relationship between a superior and a subordinate or between the powerful and the less so.

For example, managers of small hospitals often are interested in establishing stronger and more positive relationships with the medical staff. In hospitals with less than a hundred beds, more than 70 percent of the admissions come from the top five physicians (Morrisey, Shortell, and Noie, 1983). The administrator might use a clearly subordinative strategy when negotiating with top physicians over substantive issues of marginal significance to the small hospital—for example, personal parking spaces and free meals when conducting rounds—but of greater significance to the top admitting physicians. Properly implemented, this strategy should enhance the supportiveness of the manager's relationship with those physicians. Thus, a subordinative strategy might be appropriate for managers when they negotiate with key stakeholders over certain substantive issues where they are willing to concede more than they gain in the negotiation itself.

As another example, a large hospital's manager might seek to foster relations with members of the medical staff by ing them subsidized office facilities if they will support a certain PPO or other managed care arrangement. The substantive outcomes of the negotiated prices on the office facilities are not what are important to the hospital. In fact, the hospital may even lose money as a result of the negotiation. By offering low-cost offices to the medical staff, the hospital manager anticipates that the medical staff will become more favorably disposed toward the hospital. This change should make medical staff members view their overall relationship with the hospital as more interdependent, encouraging these PPO medical staff members to make referrals primarily to this hospital rather than to competing hospitals with similar managed care contracts.

Moreover, if a subordinative strategy can strengthen the hospital's relationship with the medical staff, the hospital should be in a better position to negotiate with employers participating in the PPO or with the insurance companies that have set up the arrangement. Negotiations with these stakeholders, however, are likely to be quite different from those with the physicians. If the hospital managers' priority is primarily on the negotiation's substantive outcomes, then the strategy will be different, that is, a competitive one.

To build on an earlier example, a subordinative strategy for negotiating management service contracts might lead the large urban hospital to provide these services at or below cost to a rural hospital. The priority of the hospital administrator would be on the *outcome for closer relationships* (and its future potential for referrals) that could be developed as a result of the negotiated settlement. The *substantive outcomes* (the profit from the rural hospital for providing management services) of the negotiation would not be seen as very important. Such a strategy tries to enhance the manager's relationship with the stakeholder by allowing the stakeholder easy access to those substantive outcomes of slight import to the organization.

Avoid: Strategy A1. When the substance of the issue brought up by the stakeholder *and* the relationship with that stakeholder are clearly of little importance to the organization (even though perhaps very important to the stakeholder), the manager should *refuse* to negotiate. In other words, if a potential negotiation is not advantageous, as in situation 4, managers should seek alternative actions. For example, other rural hospitals or medical staffs might approach the urban hospital and want to negotiate over receiving similar management services. However, if there is little likelihood of significant referrals because of the other hospitals' particular case mixes, managers in the urban hospital may well see neither the likely substantive nor relationship outcomes as very important. Here negotiation is not likely to further the hospital's implementation of either stakeholder or business strategies.

Too many managers are confronted with one-sided issues. Many proposed joint ventures, for example, are of little benefit to the organization or are likely to become, as we will discuss in Chapter Seven, purely stakeholder-focused ventures with little potential for financial success. These ventures are not likely to improve relationships with key stakeholders and may even run the risk of hurting them because the proposed ventures are not financially sound and put both the organization and the stakeholder at financial risk. However, quickly but systematically determining which issues are a waste of time— *prior to actually starting to negotiate*—is essential if managers are to use this strategy effectively.

To avoid negotiating, managers can engage in tactics ranging from the confronting to the accommodative. Simply *refusing* to negotiate is the most direct form of avoidance. However, if the stakeholder views the negotiation as important for either a relationship or a substantive outcome, the hospital manager might *regulate* the issue. Here, rather than negotiating, the manager can either apply standard operating procedures or develop new policies.

Strategies for All Four Negotiating Situations: Medical School Case. Returning to the example of negotiating an affiliation agreement between the medical school and four community hospitals, the dean—as the manager negotiator for the medical school—should select various negotiation strategies appropriate to the diagnosed situation for each of the stakeholder hospitals. In the case of Hospital A, the medical school's top priority is on only substantive outcomes, for example, the amount the hospital will be willing to pay in salary support for residents who provide twenty-four-hour call at the hospital, with no expectation of a broader relationship. Therefore, strategy P1 (compete) is an appropriate negotiating position. For Hospital B, with which the school desires to establish a relationship and identification, strategy S1 (subordinate) is the favored approach to try to foster that relationship to eventually get educational access to a large and varied inpatient population, even if the immediate substantive outcomes are low or negative. With Hospital C, where the medical school desires both substantive and relationship outcomes, strategy C1 (collaborate) can best be applied. Because the medical school has diagnosed the status of Hospital D as unfavorable for both its substantive and relationship goals, negotiating with it is appropriately avoided by the dean (strategy A1, avoid).

Step 5: Refining Negotiation Strategy Based on Sensitivity to Key Stakeholder Contingencies

In the case of the joint venture for helicopter services, both acquiring the helicopter service and developing and then maintaining a positive relationship with the other hospital are important, so we suggested that the manager select a collaborative negotiation strategy. There may be a problem in implementing the strategy, however. It may or may not be successful depending on certain contingencies associated with the stakeholders being negotiated with. In the next section we discuss the contingencies most crucial to stakeholder negotiation.

In addition to diagnostic questions that clarify the relative importance of substantive and relationship outcomes, two other key diagnostic issues need to be resolved before implementing an outcome-focused strategy as suggested in Figure 30. The diagnostic questions the manager should ask include: Can the stakeholder representative ensure broad stakeholder acceptance of the negotiated agreement? and Will the coalitions the stakeholder is likely to form be acceptable to the hospital?

Because many internal stakeholders (and some external stakeholders) are not formally organized, the representative's ability to ensure stakeholder acceptance of a negotiated agreement should be carefully assessed. Thus, our third key diagnostic question focuses on this issue. Even when a stakeholder is formally organized, the representative's integrity and authority to commit the stakeholder to a negotiated settlement may still be problematical (Bacharach and Lawler, 1980).

Consider, for example, a negotiated agreement with an elected chief of the medical staff concerning physician sensitivity to and participation in cost-containment efforts. This agreement may not be accepted by members of the medical staff, or, even if accepted in principle, it may not change physician behavior as the hospital desires. To return to an earlier example, negotiated agreements by the director of regional services with administrators of rural hospitals may not be implemented because members of their respective boards find them unacceptable. As a result, these stakeholder hospitals cannot deliver on their part of the agreement.

Moreover, even if a representative can ensure stakeholder acceptance of an agreement, that negotiated agreement may be ill advised if the stakeholder has reasons to seek allies among other stakeholders hostile to the hospital. Thus, the acceptability of the coalitions the stakeholder is likely to form is our fourth key question.

The potential plight of the urban hospital illustrates the significance of this question. If a rural hospital that it is courting forms a coalition to get a better deal with a competing hospital, the urban hospital's subordinate negotiation strategy will be of questionable value. A similar problem arises if several rural hospitals form a coalition that collectively negotiates with each city hospital. In either of these cases, the subordinative negotiation strategy and the stakeholder management strategy designed for a mixed-blessing stakeholder would be ineffective. For each case, the potential levels of threat and cooperation were inaccurately assessed during the strategy formulation process. Rather than mixed-blessing stakeholders, in these cases the rural hospitals are more accurately seen as high-threat, low-cooperation nonsupportive stakeholders. (In Chapter Four we suggest a defensive strategy for the nonsupportive stakeholder coalition.) Moreover, even the market penetration business strategy is likely to need reassessment.

In Figure 31 we present the key set of contingencies managers may face in negotiating with stakeholders. The far left side of Figure 31 reminds us of the connections among the three levels of strategy. The left part of the tree diagram depicts the four situations and associated strategies as suggested in Figure 30. The right side of the tree diagram extends this set of situations as they are modified by the answers to the two diagnostic questions about stakeholders. This part of Figure 31 shows how stakeholder negotiation strategies may be refined based on these two stakeholder contingencies.

In short, when selecting a stakeholder-sensitive strategy, hospital managers must account for both their own priorities *and* the stakeholder's abilities and likely activities concerning the negotiation's potential relationship and substantive outcomes. Figure 31 shows how a manager's negotiation strategies are contingent on both outcome-focused priorities *and* key stakeholder contingencies.

Remember, different competitive strategies require the involvement of different key stakeholders. The organization then selects a generic strategy to manage each key stakeholder. No matter which generic stakeholder management strategy is selected, the organization has to evaluate the organizational and stakeholder contingencies to select a negotiation strategy as shown in Figure 31. Most likely, key stakeholders will require collaborative, competitive, or subordinative negotiation strategies, while marginal stakeholders will need to be avoided when they attempt to initiate negotiations.

To anticipate the stakeholder contingencies shown in Figure 31, health care managers should consider the kinds of action the stakeholder might take through its representatives. Are those actions likely to be supportive or hostile? Will those actions represent short-term reactions or long-term approaches? The answers to these questions will depend on the specific context and history of the manager's relations with the stakeholder and the key individuals and groups influencing the manager and the stakeholder.

As Figure 31 illustrates, when the answers to both contingency questions concerning the stakeholder are positive, in only two of four cases are the outcome-focused and stakeholder-sensitive strategies identical. Collaborative and subor-

Figure 31. Selecting and Refining Stakeholder Negotiation Strategies.

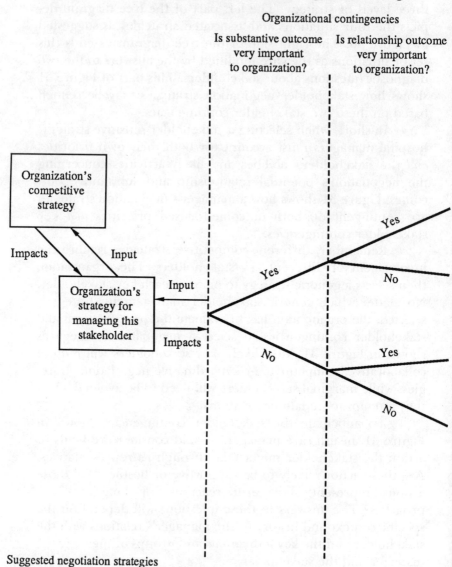

Organizational contingencies

Is substantive outcome very important to organization?   Is relationship outcome very important to organization?

Organization's competitive strategy

Impacts   Input

Organization's strategy for managing this stakeholder

Input   Yes   Yes

No

Impacts   No   Yes

No

Suggested negotiation strategies

C1: Collaborative   C2: Cautious Collaborative
P1: Competitive   P2: Respectful Competitive
S1: Subordinative   S2: Guarded Subordinative
A1: Avoidance   A2: Avoidance with Monitoring

Stakeholder contingencies

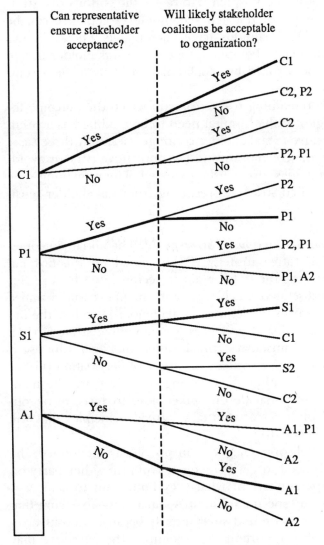

dinative strategies are continued if the stakeholder representatives can ensure stakeholder acceptance *and* if likely coalitions are acceptable to the hospital. However, the competitive strategy should be pursued when stakeholder acceptance can be ensured but likely coalitions are *not* acceptable. The avoidance strategy continues to be appropriate when stakeholder acceptance *cannot* be assured but coalitions are likely to be acceptable.

Of the remaining twelve cases in which the outcome-focused strategies of the hospital need to be modified as a result of being sensitive to stakeholder contingencies, only three cases utilize either the collaborative (C1), competitive (P1), or avoidance (A1) strategies, previously discussed. The remaining nine cases use modified strategies resulting from stakeholder-sensitive analysis.

Collaborate Cautiously: Strategy C2. The initial, outcome-focused collaborative strategy (C1) is based on the hospital manager's trusting the stakeholder to reciprocate whenever information is disclosed. Such trust and openness will victimize the manager, for example, if the stakeholder perceives the negotiation as situation 3 and uses a competitive strategy (P1). Under such circumstances, the hospital manager can use a modified collaborative strategy of *principled* negotiation (Fisher and Ury, 1981). Rather than relying on only trust, the manager attempts to persuade the stakeholder to agree to negotiations based on a set of mutually agreed principles that will benefit each negotiator.

In the helicopter negotiation previously mentioned, the executive will need to get agreement from the other party on the general parameters of what they both want to achieve—prior to resolving specific substantive outcomes—to ensure that he or she is not victimized substantively because a positive relationship is also important. For example, the executive may seek to base patient allocation between the two hospitals on the joint principles of medical specialty and reciprocity rather than on some *ad hoc* figure or percentage. By focusing on the principles that will bring the issue of patient allocation to agreement, the executive avoids taking a position and competing against a position offered by the other hospital. To continue the example, one hospital may have the facilities and medical staff specialists to handle patients with severe burns, the other can handle high-risk neonatal patients, and both have superior care units for cardiology patients. Given this situation, the executives of each hospital may agree to allocate patients with specialized needs to the hospital with the best care unit and to split the remaining patient load evenly for patients or patients' families who have not registered a specific hospital preference.

Compete Respectfully: Strategy P2. Under some circumstances the potential ruthlessness of the initial competitive strategy (C1) may need modification. For example, even though the hospital manager may place little importance on the relationship outcome, this relationship may be very important to the stakeholder. If the stakeholder is powerful and potentially threatening, the manager would be wise to use a competitive strategy that also enhances the relationship outcome to some extent. Such a modified competitive strategy calls for hard bargaining *without* the dirty tactics that might engender stakeholder hostility. For example, hospitals may compete actively for patients but might want to share certain other services now or in the future. A P2 strategy will make this more possible.

If the stakeholder involved in the negotiation is powerful and potentially threatening, the executive would be wise to use a competitive strategy that does *not* further strain the relationship, even if it cannot be enhanced. For example, if the CFO in the largest and most highly regarded hospital in a city is negotiating with the provider representative from Blue Cross over next year's reimbursement rates, the CFO should consider that although the Blue Cross representative may want to keep this hospital available to Blue Cross policy holders, that representative could also deny the hospital a large amount of money. Even if Blue Cross patients only represent 10 percent of the hospital's admissions, the lack of endorsement of the hospital's pricing structure could severely hurt the hospital, since many other private insurance companies use the Blue Cross negotiated rates as their benchmark. Here the CFO should use a modified respectful competitive strategy of bargaining *without* using highly aggressive tactics that could engender high levels of mistrust and hostility.

Subordinate Guardedly: Strategy S2. The initial, outcome-focused subordinative strategy assumes that the substantive outcome is of little importance to the manager. Sometimes, however, hospital managers care about substantive and relationship outcomes, but the stakeholder has little stake in either outcome. In this case, managers should use a modified subordinate strategy to induce the stakeholder to negotiate. By discovering and then acquiescing to as many stakeholder needs as possible, managers can still preserve some substantive outcomes for themselves while ensuring a positive relationship outcome. Here, the key modification is to conceal from the stakeholder those substantive issues that are important to the hospital so that only unimportant issues are acceded, thus enhancing the hospital-stakeholder relationship without substantively draining the hospital's resources.

For example, the vice-president for patient care services (PCS) may want to implement a collaborative strategy by increasing salaries for a key but mixed-blessing internal stakeholder—registered nurses, who are in short supply—but does not want to further strain his relationship with the vice-president for human resource management (HRM), another key internal stakeholder necessary to success in implementing the nurse stakeholder strategy. Unfortunately, in the past these two executives have been on opposite sides on many issues in the executive council of the hospital and are thus seen as members of different managerial coalitions. In addition, the VP for HRM may want to avoid any salary negotiations because she or he does not want to further complicate the compensation plan. To induce the VP for HRM to negotiate about registered nurses' salaries, the VP for PCS could volunteer to implement a pilot study of a new performance appraisal system that is being promoted by the VP for HRM, even though such a study will strain the PCS staff budget and be an additional burden to its subordinate managers.

By discovering and then acquiescing to as many key needs of the other party as feasible, organizational executives can still preserve some substantive outcomes for themselves while ensuring a relatively positive relationship outcome. Here, executives both create substantive outcomes for the other stakeholder *and* achieve substantive outcomes for themselves through building relationship outcomes.

Avoid but Monitor: Strategy A2. If the organization has little reason to negotiate, but the stakeholder can potentially form a coalition with other stakeholders hostile to the hospital, the manager should avoid negotiating *but still monitor* the stakeholder's actions. Additionally, a less confronting and more accommodative refusal might be appropriate in this situation. Monitoring, as the key modification of this strategy, protects the hospital from being blindsided by the stakeholder at a later time.

For example, the VP of PCS is approached by a representative from the emergency room (ER) staff about installing a money changer next to vending machines outside the ER. Recognizing that the money changer itself will provide no revenue and that the ER staff already receives many "perks," the VP's first reaction is to actively avoid negotiation. However, the VP realizes that the ER staff will probably view the hospital more favorably if something can be worked out. Thus, the VP passively avoids the negotiation by delegating it to his assistant director and monitors the progress without direct involvement.

Alternatively, the VP can be responsive but still avoid negotiating by applying standard operating procedures (for example, directing the ER staff to submit a request that documents the need to the assistant director) or by developing a new policy that addresses the money changer issue (for example, that all contracts with machine venders shall require that they supply money changers). This permits the VP to avoid

Table 10. Stakeholder Negotiation Tactics Across Various Negotiation Phases.

	Negotiation Tactics		
Negotiation Phase	Competitive	Collaborative	Subordinative
Search for arena and agenda formulation	• Seek to conduct negotiations on manager's home ground • Demand discussion of manager's agenda items; curtail discussions of other party's items • Ignore or discount other party's demands and requests	• Seek to conduct negotiations on neutral ground • Elicit other party's agenda items and assert manager's items; incorporate both • Consider other party's demands and requests	• Seek to conduct negotiations on other party's ground • Elicit other party's agenda items and subvert manager's items • Concede to other party's demands and requests
Statement of demands and offers	• Insist other party make initial offers or demands on all items • Respond with very low offers or very high demands • Commit to each item; exaggerate manager's position and discredit other party's	• Alternate initial offers and demands on items with other party • Respond with moderate offers or moderate demands • Indicate reasons for manager's commitments to item outcomes; probe other party's reasons	• Make initial offers or demands on all other party-relevant items • Make high offers or low demands • Accept other party's commitments to items; explain manager's commitments

Stage			
Narrowing of differences	• Demand other party make concessions; back up demand with threats • Delete, add, or yield only on low manager interest items • Magnify degree of manager's concessions; downplay other party's	• Seek equitable exchange of concessions with other party • Delete, add, or yield items if mutual interests converge • Honestly assess manager's and other party's concessions	• Concede to other party's demands • Delete, add, or yield to any other party-relevant item • Acknowledge other party's concessions; downplay manager's concessions
Final bargaining	• Seek large concessions from other party • Concede only minimally on high manager interest items • Use concessions on low manager interest items as bargaining chips	• Seek equitable exchange of concessions from other party • Seek mutually beneficial outcomes when conceding or accepting concessions on items	• Yield to other party's relevant preferences by accepting low offers and making low demands

direct negotiation but still allows monitoring of the situation that prompted desired negotiations by the ER staff.

Step 6: Implementing Negotiation Strategy Through Appropriate Tactics

To implement the appropriate stakeholder-sensitive negotiation strategy, managers need to consider the detailed tactics needed. The negotiation literature is full of ideas about how to proceed tactically while in a negotiation (Fisher and Ury, 1981; Raiffa, 1982; Greenberger, Strasser, Lewicke, and Bateman, 1988; Longest, 1990). Here we summarize how to use key tactics across different phases of the negotiation.

We view tactics in two ways: (1) as clusters of specific actions associated with implementing one or another strategy and (2) as actions that derive their strategic impact from the particular phase of the negotiation in which they are used. In Table 10, we combine these two perspectives to provide health care executives with descriptions of competitive, collaborative, and subordinative tactics across various phases of negotiation. We suggest that most negotiations go through four phases: (1) a search for an arena and agenda formulation, (2) a stating of demands and offers, (3) a narrowing of differences, and (4) final bargaining (Savage, Blair, and Sorenson, 1989). Not every negotiation will involve all of these phases. Rather, these phases characterize *typical* negotiations of the kind with which we are concerned here. Hence, a specific phase may be skipped or never attained.

For example, during the first phase, the search for an arena in which to carry out discussions may be unnecessary in some ongoing negotiations. However, most negotiations will initially involve some interactions about the items to be discussed. During the second phase, both the health care executive and the stakeholder representative express their preferences and establish their commitments to specific issues and outcomes. Although the third phase may be skipped, it usually occurs if the executive and the stakeholder representative are far apart in their preferences and commitments. Here both sides may add or debate bargaining items or shift preferences to avoid an impasse. The fourth phase completes the negotiation. In it the manager and the representative reduce their alternatives, making joint decisions about each item until a final agreement is reached.

Table 10 should help health care managers recognize how tactics during various phases of a negotiation are essential to implement their strategy and how the tactics of the other party reflect a particular strategic intent. Thus, after implementing their stakeholder-sensitive strategy, health care executives should monitor the stakeholder representative's tactics. Next we discuss what managers should do in step 7 if new information that emerges during the multiple phases of negotiation suggests reassessment.

Step 7: Changing Stakeholder-Sensitive Strategy as Needed

The diagnostic process involved in choosing a stakeholder-sensitive strategy is a continuing one. Negotiation strategies should change as circumstances change. To determine if a stakeholder-sensitive strategy should be changed, hospital managers must monitor the actions and responses of the stakeholder. These stakeholder reactions will help the executive determine whether strategically relevant elements are undergoing unanticipated changes.

How the stakeholder representative acts and responds will signal the stakeholder's perceptions of and strategy for the negotiation. An unanticipated stakeholder strategy may indicate that the manager inaccurately assessed the levels of threat or cooperation, under- or overestimated the representative's ability to ensure acceptance by the stakeholder, or failed to anticipate possible unacceptable coalitions. Hence, once the actual stakeholder strategy is known, health care managers should reassess the negotiation, repeating the sequence described above, to check the appropriateness of the generic stakeholder management and stakeholder-sensitive negotiation strategies they have selected.

Sometimes, however, the stakeholder's use of an unanticipated strategy does *not* mean the manager's assessment of the negotiation context and its contingencies was inaccurate. In Figure 31 some contingencies result in the listing of two strategies. Hospital managers should normally use the primary strategies in these listings when facing the contingencies on which they are based. The secondary strategies are suggested as countermoves if the stakeholder uses a strategy different from that expected, *but* the negotiation contingencies remain unchanged.

Take, for example, the urban hospital manager whose organizational priorities suggest a competitive (P1) strategy but whose anticipated stakeholder contingencies suggest a cautiously collaborative (C2) strategy when offering management services. Here the manager expects that the stakeholder (the rural hospital) will probably choose to collaborate. However, the rural hospital actually tries to compete. Assuming that the manager's assessment of the stakeholder's priorities is correct, the manager might be well advised to match the competitive strategy of the rural hospital with a P2 (compete respectfully) strategy. Such a strategy by the urban hospital denies the stakeholder *inexpensive* management services but does not deny the rural hospital such services at slightly above cost. (We list the P2 strategy as preferred because it is less likely to escalate the conflict between the manager and the stakeholder to the same degree as the more direct, and potentially ruthless, P1 strategy.)

Another example of a changed strategy is a hospital facilities executive negotiating with the representative of a vender of hospital supplies. Her priorities suggest a competitive (P1) strategy, but she also anticipates the representative may want to build the relationship with her hospital further through providing some additional inventory and other information management services. In essence, the representative has hinted that these services will not be provided to any direct competitors as are other services provided currently—that is, likely stakeholder coalitions will be acceptable to the organization. The manager further is confident that whatever she negotiates with the representative will be agreed to and implemented by the vender. Thus, her diagnosis of the situation must change since it is sensitive to stakeholder contingencies that have changed. Assuming that further interactions prior to actual negotiations confirm the correctness of the full and changed diagnosis, she might be well advised to change her P1 strategy to a respectfully competitive one (P2) during the current or next negotiation episode. Here the P2 strategy is preferred because it is less likely to escalate conflict between the executive and the stakeholder. If these negotiations result in some of the anticipated outcomes, in still future negotiations relationship outcomes with the vender may also become a priority, and more collaborative strategies may be necessary.

Step 8: Monitoring Ever-Changing Stakeholder Negotiation Context

Figure 32 summarizes steps 2 through 7 and illustrates the ever-changing negotiation context, showing those aspects of the situation and of the negotiation episode that shape relationship and substantive outcomes. Existing levels of threat and cooperation influence the negotiation strategies chosen by the organizational manager and the target stakeholder (as well as other possible stakeholders involved in a particular issue). The stakeholder representatives involved in the actual negotiation episode may or may not be able to fully represent the stakeholder and ensure that the negotiated agreement will be accepted and implemented by the stakeholder. Both the hospital's and the stakeholder's strategies may also be influenced by possible coalitions between the target stakeholder and other stakeholders that may or may not be acceptable to the organization.

These strategies, in turn, are not to be put in a formal plan and set on a shelf but are to be used during actual negotiation episodes—for example, a one-on-one encounter, a telephone call, a meeting with a representative of a key stakeholder. During the episode, the strategies guide the manager's actions and help to interpret what is happening for the negotiation to establish certain substantive and relationship out-

Figure 32. Changing Stakeholder Negotiation Context.

Favorableness based on stakeholder's potential for threat and cooperation

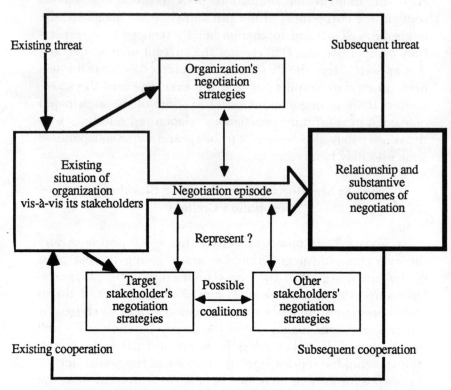

comes. Each episode, no matter what its duration, influences future negotiation episodes by changing the relative threat of and degree of cooperation between the manager's organization and the stakeholder. We advocate, therefore, that after each episode and prior to the next episode the manager reassess the context, the stakeholders involved, and what the organization's negotiation strategy should be.

Summary and Managerial Implications

Much of the negotiation literature focuses on either interpersonal and group negotiations or labor-management negotiations (Walton and McKersie, 1965; Raiffa, 1982; Dunlop, 1984). The stakeholder negotiation approach presented here provides an organizational level of analysis that meshes both of these micro and macro levels; moreover, it has the potential to be applied to a broad spectrum of hospital-stakeholder relationships.

Our approach links negotiation to the hospital's overarching strategic context and decision making. It is not uncommon for hospital managers to face a large and diverse group of stakeholders who are frequently confrontational, high in threat, and low in cooperation.

Without a guiding managerial framework that links ongoing pressures to negotiate with broader strategic issues, undesirable, conflicting, or compromising outcomes are likely. These undesirable results occur because of *ad hoc* responses to particular negotiation episodes.

We have highlighted two problematical aspects of stakeholder negotiation that differentiate it from other, better understood, forms of negotiation. These are the representativeness and authority of the stakeholder negotiator and the propensity for stakeholders to form coalitions.

The diagnostic and action-oriented approach presented here conceptually integrates the micro and macro approaches found in the negotiation literature. As an integral part of the analysis, we have used the concepts of *relationship* outcomes as well as *substantive* outcomes. This approach provides a framework for determining and focusing on desired outcomes and anticipating likely stakeholder actions.

We suggest managers look at negotiation strategically and follow eight essential steps for effective stakeholder negotiation. Of course, as with other activities in stakeholder management, these steps are often overlapping and occur simultaneously as executives integrate their many organizational concerns and plan their multitude of managerial activities. Such an approach minimizes the potential negative results from developing strategy through *ad hoc* responses to a particular negotiation episode. In summary, these steps are

1. Linking negotiating to business and stakeholder management strategies
2. Assessing the stakeholder's potential for threat and cooperation
3. Diagnosing the negotiation situation by focusing on both relationship and substantive outcomes
4. Selecting an outcome-focused negotiation strategy
5. Refining the negotiation strategy based on sensitivity to key stakeholder contingencies
6. Implementing the negotiation strategy through appropriate tactics
7. Changing the stakeholder-sensitive strategy as needed
8. Monitoring the ever-changing stakeholder negotiation context

Health care executives should integrate their negotiation, stakeholder, and business strategies.

Other researchers should further test and extend through both empirical and conceptual research the strategic approach presented in this study. The notion of stakeholder negotiation promises to extend negotiation theory and at the same time to provide better advice to health care executives who must manage their way through this muddled ground of negotiating with the multitude who have a stake in their organizations.

This chapter finishes laying out the general stakeholder management process from *identification* to *assessment* to *diagnosis* to *strategy formulation* and finally to *strategy implementation,* including the use of stakeholder-sensitive *negotiation strategies.*

In the final chapters of this book, we look in some detail at how organizations manage key health care stakeholders. We start by looking at collaborative strategies for physician stakeholders in Chapters Six and Seven. Then we examine involvement strategies for internal stakeholders in Chapter Eight. Finally in Chapter Nine, we consider some thorny issues facing health care executives as they manage key stakeholders today and tomorrow.

Resource: Stakeholder Negotiation Strategy Formulation and Implementation Toolkit

Exhibit 14: Diagnosing Organizational Contingencies for Negotiation Situations with Different Stakeholders. Once the key stakeholders are identified, the organization's priorities in any negotiation with their representatives may be analyzed using Exhibit 14. The manager is able to enter different key stakeholders into the appropriate cells in the form. For example, if the organization's priorities in negotiation with physicians are on both relationship and substantive outcomes, then they are most likely to be placed in the "both outcomes" cell. Remember, however, that in different negotiations on other issues the organization's priorities could be on relationship outcomes, in others on substantive outcomes, and in others on neither outcome.

Exhibit 15: Diagnosing Stakeholder Contingencies for Negotiation Situations with Different Stakeholders. Once the organization's priorities have been diagnosed, further guidance prior to the negotiation may be provided using Exhibit 15. Again, the manager enters different key stakeholders into the appropriate cells in the form. For example, if during a negotiation with physicians their representative can ensure that physician stakeholders will accept whatever agreement made in the negotiation *and* any likely coalitions made by physicians (for example, with other health care organizations) are acceptable to the organization, then the organization can most likely let its negotiation strategy remain "basically the same" based on its own priorities, and physicians would be put in that cell. Remember, however, that in different negotiations on other issues the stakeholder representative's ability to ensure stakeholder acceptance may be low, or the likely coalitions could be unacceptable, therefore, the negotiation strategy should become somewhat more cautious, and in yet others the strategy should become much more cautious.

Exhibit 16: Selecting Stakeholder-Sensitive Negotiation Strategies Consistent with Competitive and Stakeholder Strategies. Once the organization's priorities and stakeholder contingencies have been diagnosed, further guidance prior to the negotiation may be provided using Exhibit 16. Three black outlined boxes are provided to write in (1) the organization's *competitive strategy* (for example, "achieve and sustain competitive advantage through a focused differentiation strategy in critical care") (2) the organization's *strategy for managing this stakeholder* (for example, "defend against the nonsupportive stakeholder"), and (3) the *suggested negotiation strategy* (for example, "compete respectfully") to be used with this stakeholder representative during the next negotiation episode. This last box should be filled in after the manager has used the decision tree to locate the answers to questions in Exhibits 14 and 15 and to identify the most appropriate stakeholder-sensitive strategy as indicated on the right side of Exhibit 16.

Exhibit 17: Stakeholder Negotiation Strategy Implementation. Exhibit 17 identifies the stakeholder representative's name and then provides a systematic way (consistent with Exhibits 14 through 16) to arrive at the generic negotiation strategy appropriate *for each episode* with *a particular stakeholder representative.* (Note that one of these forms will be needed for each stakeholder negotiation episode diagnosed.) Then a set of diagnostic questions are provided to help the manager work through the tactical implementation of the generic negotiation strategy. By filling out the form, a manager is able to move from a generic strategy, such as "S2: subordinate guardedly," to a systematic plan for implementing that strategy.

Exhibit 18: Checklist for Stakeholder Negotiation Tactics. Exhibit 18 provides a checklist for tactics necessary to implement the three basic generic strategies at different phases in the negotiation process. These questions alert the manager to the many *tactical* subtleties involved in implementing a given negotiation strategy.

Exhibit 14. Diagnosing *Organizational Contingencies* for Negotiation Situations with Different Stakeholders.

Instructions: Fill in Exhibit 14 with the stakeholder names (and issues) in preparing for negotiations with representatives of different key stakeholders—or the same stakeholders on different issues.

Is substantive outcome very important to the organization?

	Yes	No
Yes	*Organization's priorities are on* **both outcomes**	*Organization's priority is on* **relationship outcomes**
relationship outcome very important to organization? No	*Organization's priority is on* **substantive outcomes**	*Organization's priority is on* **neither outcome**

Exhibit 15. Diagnosing *Stakeholder Contingencies* for Negotiation Situations with Different Stakeholders.

Instructions: Fill in Exhibit 15 with the stakeholder names (and issues) identified in Exhibit 14—but place them according to the two stakeholder contingencies. Exhibit 15 will indicate whether (and how) negotiation strategy based initially on organizational priorities should change.

Can representative ensure stakeholder acceptance?

	Yes	No
Yes	*Negotiation strategy should remain* **basically the same**	*Negotiation strategy should become* **somewhat more cautious**
Will likely stakeholder coalitions be acceptable to organization? No	*Negotiation strategy should become* **somewhat more cautious**	*Negotiation strategy should become* **much more cautious**

**Exhibit 16. Selecting Stakeholder-Sensitive Negotiation Strategies
Consistent with Competitive and Stakeholder Strategies.**

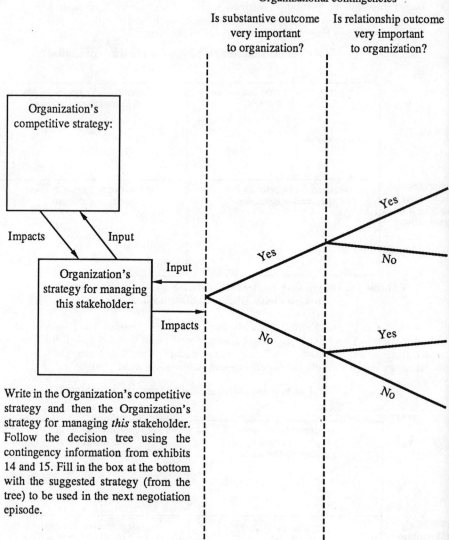

Organizational contingencies

Is substantive outcome very important to organization?   Is relationship outcome very important to organization?

Organization's competitive strategy:

Impacts   Input

Organization's strategy for managing this stakeholder: Input

Impacts

Yes   Yes   No

No   Yes   No

Write in the Organization's competitive strategy and then the Organization's strategy for managing *this* stakeholder. Follow the decision tree using the contingency information from exhibits 14 and 15. Fill in the box at the bottom with the suggested strategy (from the tree) to be used in the next negotiation episode.

Generic negotiation strategies

C1: Collaborative   C2: Cautious Collaborative
P1: Competitive   P2: Respectful Competitive
S1: Subordinative   S2: Guarded Subordinative
A1: Avoidance   A2: Avoidance with Monitoring

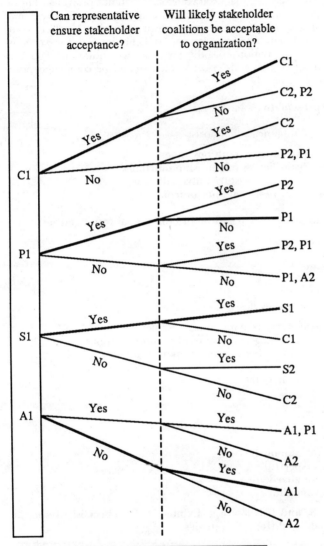

Stakeholder contingencies

Suggested negotiation strategy to be used with this
stakeholder representative during next episode:

Exhibit 17. Stakeholder Negotiation Strategy Implementation.

Instructions: First, identify the representative of the stakeholder you will be negotiating with. Second, diagnose your organization's priorities. Third, circle initial negotiation strategy you should consider. Fourth, assess and circle how the stakeholder contingencies shown in Exhibit 15 affect your initial strategy. Fifth, circle the appropriate stakeholder-sensitive strategy for the upcoming negotiation episode. Sixth, answer questions 1–9. To plan negotiations effectively, this entire exhibit should be completed prior to each episode.

Stakeholder representative's name: _____

Organizational contingencies diagnosis:

   Organization's priorities = both outcomes
   Organization's priorities = relationship outcomes
   Organization's priorities = substantive outcomes
   Organization's priorities = neither outcome

Generic negotiation strategy based on organizational contingencies:

   C1: Collaborate
   P1: Compete
   S1: Subordinate
   A1: Avoid

Stakeholder contingencies diagnosis:

   Negotiation strategy = remain basically same
   Negotiation strategy = become somewhat more cautious
   Negotiation strategy = become much more cautious

Stakeholder-sensitive negotiation strategy:

   C1: Collaborate
   P1: Compete
   S1: Subordinate
   A1: Avoid
   C2: Collaborate cautiously
   P2: Compete respectfully
   S2: Subordinate guardedly
   A2: Avoid but monitor

Note: For 1, 2, 8, and 9 below, see Exhibit 18 for checklist of specific tactics appropriate to different strategies.

1. What specific tactics do you recommend for your organization in negotiating with the stakeholder representative during the next episode?

2. In what ways do these tactics help implement the generic negotiation strategy for this stakeholder?

3. What is your specific plan to prepare for the negotiation?

4. What resources will be required for you to follow through on any negotiated agreement, and are they available?

5. Which organizational managers will have the lead role in negotiating during the next episode?

6. What other organizational personnel (as internal stakeholders) should be involved in the negotiation process with this stakeholder?

7. If the negotiation process does not work as planned, to what contingency negotiation strategy will you go next?

8. What do the specific tactics being used by the stakeholder representative indicate about the negotiation strategy he or she is trying to use?

9. If your strategy seems correct but the specific tactics do not work as planned, to what contingency tactics consistent with your negotiation strategy will you go next?

Exhibit 18. Checklist for Stakeholder Negotiation Tactics.

Instructions: Check this list for appropriate tactics involved in negotiating using generic strategies. These tactics change as the negotiation progresses. Also, use this list to check on what strategy the stakeholder representative is using as indicated by his or her tactics.

	Negotiation Tactics		
Negotiation Phase	*Competitive*	*Collaborative*	*Subordinative*
Search for arena and agenda formulation	— Seeks to conduct negotiations on manager's home ground — Demands discussion of manager's agenda items; curtails discussions of other party's items — Ignores or discounts other party's demands and requests	— Seeks to conduct negotiations on neutral ground — Elicits other party's agenda items and asserts manager's items; incorporates both — Considers other party's demands and requests	— Seeks to conduct negotiations on other party's ground — Elicits other party's agenda items and subverts manager's items — Concedes to other party's demands and requests
Statement of demands and offers	— Insists other party make initial offers or demands on all items	— Alternates initial offers and demands on items with other party	— Makes initial offers or demands on all other party-relevant items

	— Responds with very low offers or very high demands — Commits to each item; exaggerates manager's position and discredits other party's	— Responds with moderate offers or moderate demands — Indicates reasons for manager's commitments to item outcomes; probes other party's reasons	— Makes high offers or low demands — Accepts other party's commitments to items; explains manager's commitments
Narrowing of differences	— Demands other party make concessions; backs up demand with threats — Deletes, adds, or yields only on low manager interest items — Magnifies degree of manager's concessions; downplays other party's	— Seeks equitable exchange of concessions with other party — Deletes, adds, or yields items if mutual interests converge — Honestly assesses manager's and other party's concessions	— Concedes to other party's demands — Deletes, adds, or yields to any other party-relevant item — Acknowledges other party's concessions; downplays manager's concessions
Final bargaining	— Seeks large concessions from other party — Concedes only minimally on high manager interest items — Uses concessions on low manager interest items as bargaining chips	— Seeks equitable exchange of concessions from other party — Seeks mutually beneficial outcomes when conceding or accepting concessions on items	— Yields to other party's relevant preferences by accepting low offers and making low demands

❦❦❦❦❦❦❦❦❦❦❦❦❦❦❦❦❦❦❦❦❦❦❦❦

CHAPTER 6

Using Collaborative Strategies with Physician Stakeholders

Since the early part of the twentieth century, hospitals and physicians have pursued complementary goals. Now the current turbulent environment, with its increased competition, cost constraints, and rapid technological change, has reduced profit margins, created excess capacity, and opened up new opportunities.

Yet most physicians and hospitals still relate to each other in a pattern that took shape during a period of abundant resources and minimal competition. Rosenfield (1988) has characterized that pattern in terms of the following characteristics: no sharing of capital risk; conflicting economic interests; overlapping market share; severe excess capacity in terms of both physician manpower and hospital beds; no loyalty to the institutions; physician control of costs, admissions, and discharges; and a limited ability to reward or penalize physician behavior.

As a result of the macro environmental factors noted above, these conditions will have to change in the future. They have already begun to change in most places as physicians and hospitals struggle to redefine their relationship.

In Chapter Four, physicians were classified as most likely to be mixed-blessing stakeholders for health care organizations since they can do much for the hospital and can also threaten it because of their control over admissions, utilization, and quality of care. There is a high potential for both threat and cooperation. Of course, on a given issue they may be supportive, nonsupportive, or even marginal. We suggested that mixed-blessing stakeholders such as physicians are best managed through a general collaborative strategy. If hospital executives seek to collaborate with physicians, they may find it more difficult to oppose the hospital and could even become consistently supportive. Alternatively, if physicians are not well managed using a collaborative strategy, they could become nonsupportive stakeholders.

In Chapters Three through Five, we looked at the overall strategic stakeholder management process. The remaining chapters focus on a series of specific issues, challenges, and possibilities facing health care executives as they try to manage their organizations' stakeholders in a strategic manner.

In this chapter we examine the range of ways to *implement* collaboration strategies using a variety of physician bonding activities and tactics. In Chapter Seven we look in depth at a particular implementation of collaboration—the hospital-physican joint venture. We address in detail how to manage this particular form of collaboration. Then in Chapter Eight we move our detailed focus from *collaboration* with key *interface* stakeholders (physicians) to *involvement* of *internal* stakeholders (employees).

Specifically, this chapter will

- Examine reasons why hospitals and physicians need to emphasize collaborative relationships
- Identify and discuss specific collaborative strategies that link day-to-day management activities to the organization's strategic goals
- Examine the physician-hospital relationship, collaboration, and stakeholder management from the physician perspective.

Collaboration: The Necessary Imperative

In Chapter Three we identified physicians as the most powerful of the key stakeholders of health care organizations.

This power was based on physicians' ability to admit patients, control the patient care process, control the use of resources, and provide necessary services. Some writers have described the medical staff as "guests" of the institution and the hospital itself as a "doctor's workshop." Physicians have traditionally utilized hospital facilities to treat their private patients and advance their professional interests, but they have had relatively little involvement in and commitment to the institution itself. The physician's desire to maximize the care and treatment of each of his or her patients was viewed as in conflict with a broader hospital perspective that emphasized both the organizational requirements of all patients and the need for practice patterns that enhance institutional viability and profitability. Since hospitals depended on physicians for patient admissions, many writers have viewed them as being in a weak position to exercise control of medical staff behavior.

While Chapter Three indicated the physician was the most powerful hospital stakeholder, it also showed a split among hospital executives in our pilot study in terms of whether physicians were increasing in power relative to that of the hospital. Only a minority (40 percent) of those executives thought physicians were increasing in power.

A more realistic view is that while physicians *are* increasing their power vis-à-vis hospitals, hospitals are also increasing their power vis-à-vis physicians. In other words, there has been an increase in *mutual dependence*.

Why Should Physicians Collaborate? Several recent trends have increased the dependence of physicians on the hospital (Morlock, Nathanson, and Alexander, 1988). First, rapid advances in medical technology have resulted in increasingly complex and costly facilities, machinery, and equipment for diagnosis and treatment. Since purchase of this equipment is beyond the means of most physicians, the hospital has become the central source of access to such technology.

Second, there has been increased competition resulting from the rapid growth in the number of physicians. Increasing numbers of physicians desiring hospital privileges have placed hospitals in a stronger bargaining position, which has enabled them to demand greater institutional loyalty on the part of medical staff members (Shortell, 1982). A recent study found that the greater the number of physicians per capita, the more likely hospital-based physicians were to be salaried (Alexander, Morrisey, and Shortell, 1986). This suggests that as physicians become more plentiful, hospitals gain greater leverage in the negotiation process.

Third, as a result of the increase in physicians, as well as other factors, there has been significant growth in salaried and other types of contractual relationships between physicians and hospitals. Currently there are several types of contractual arrangements in use that determine methods of revenue and cost allocation between hospitals and physicians. Such relationships increase physician dependence on and commitment to the institution (Roemer and Friedman, 1971).

Fourth, medical staff administrative positions have become increasingly formalized. While only 4 percent of hospitals reported compensating physicians for hospital administrative activities in 1973, 41 percent provided full- or part-time compensation to physicians for administrative duties by the mid 1980s (Morrisey and Brooks, 1985b). Chiefs of the medical staff and clinical department heads are particularly likely to occupy full-time positions. Physicians in these positions are better able to influence physician behavior when they are salaried and appointed by management rather than elected by medical staff members (Williams, 1978).

Fifth, the growing movement toward multiinstitutional systems has reduced the influence of physicians and increased their dependence on management. Multihospital systems tend to have lower levels of physician participation in organizational decision making (at both the hospital and the system level) and more integrated relationships between medical staff and management (Morlock, Alexander, and Hunter, 1985).

While all five of these developments have occurred nationwide, their speed and extent have varied signficantly by hospital size, ownership, location, and control (public, nonprofit, religious nonprofit, and so on). In general, however, these developments have tended to weaken the potential power of physicians in relation to hospital management and the board of trustees. They have also strengthened the hospital's system of influence over physicians based on formal authority and have made physicians more open to collaborative arrangements.

Physicians are also finding themselves in increasingly competitive markets where employers and patients have more alternatives. Maintaining or enhancing patient volume often depends on the physician's having a contractual arrangement with a managed care organization (HMO or PPO). Volume is becoming more important because price is coming under increasing pressure from the federal government, state governments, and managed care programs. Physicians who wish to maintain or enhance their incomes need to engage in various collaborative arrangements with other physicians and with hospitals.

The most important incentive for collaboration is that physicians need hospitals as they attempt to position themselves to prosper in extremely competitive markets. There is growing anecdotal evidence that physician-sponsored joint ventures do not have strong track records (Rosenfield, 1988). Such activities take substantial effort and experience to plan and successfully implement. Many physician-sponsored projects have been undercapitalized and poorly conceived. Hospitals have far greater staying power than physicians and often develop competitive services. Finally, physician sponsorship without hospital involvement tends to exacerbate tensions between primary care and specialist physicians.

Physician services offered without any hospital linkage may also raise questions of quality and conflict of interest. While *hospital-sponsored* joint ventures bring with them continued oversight by the medical staff, *physician-sponsored* joint ventures do not. Free of medical staff oversight, physicians participating in such joint ventures may be tempted to reduce costs to the detriment of patients (particularly if those physicians are primarily economic actors). As a result of a growing public concern about physician willingness to sacrifice patient welfare in pursuit of dollars, physicians have become more concerned about the appearance of impropriety in sending patients to facilities they may own. This concern is lessened if a hospital's name is attached to such facilities.

Why Should Health Care Organizations Collaborate? The increasingly competitive market of recent years has put more pressure on hospitals and hospital systems to reduce their inpatient census and provide as many services as possible on an outpatient basis. While developing these alternative services for increasingly competitive markets, hospitals are also attempting to increase patient referrals to their institution. These trends increase hospital dependence on physicians and the willingness of hospital executives to participate in collaborative strategies with physicians.

Changes in the industry are also creating conflict between physicians and hospitals. Reducing such conflict requires collaborative strategies.

A survey of 753 hospital CEOs was conducted in October 1987 for *Hospitals* magazine by Hamilton/KSA, an Atlanta-based consulting firm (Grayson, 1988). Results indicate that competition for outpatients and managed care were the two most important causes of such conflict, while purchasing physician practices and physician recruitment schemes were third and fourth on the list. Despite these concerns, 54 percent of the CEOs indicated that their relationships with medical staff members had improved in 1987, compared to the 36 percent who felt it had remained the same and the 10 percent who felt it had deteriorated. The West seems to have more conflict problems due to the higher degree of competition, higher physician-to-population ratio, higher degree of HMO penetration, higher degree of hospital acquisition activity, and strong entrepreneurial spirit.

Cleverley and Stetson (1985) found that "excellent" hospitals (based on financial performance) were more likely than their "nonexcellent" counterparts to define the physician as the hospital's primary customer. Excellent hospitals were also more likely to collect more data on revenue per physician than were nonexcellent hospitals. In *The Well Managed Community Hospi-*

tal, John Griffith (1987) notes that the business of a hospital is medical care and that doctors must be the hospital's allies. This means attracting good doctors, treating them well, and allowing them to participate in the organization's decisions.

The degree of responsiveness of hospitals to their physician stakeholders seems to be related to the competitiveness of the local market. Hospitals in the most competitive market areas vie with one another for physicians and their patients through such nonprice competition as offering new technologies, services, and amenities (Robinson and Luft, 1987). There is also a strong positive association between the number of hospital competitors in the local market and the average length of stay in U.S. hospitals (Robinson, Luft, McPhee, and Hunt, 1988). Longer lengths of stay respond to the preferences of both physicians (internists and surgeons) and patients for longer length of stays. (Thus, lengths of stay tend to be longer in more competitive markets where physicians and patients have more alternatives.)

The implication is that as more health care markets become more competitive, the significance of effective physician stakeholder management for achieving competitive advantage will increase. A study by the Health Care Advisory Board of Washington, D.C., found that physicians control over 70 percent of hospital admissions and continue to represent the single most important hospital distribution channel (Koska, 1988). Physicians operating in highly competitive markets have more alternative sites for practicing their craft. Thus, their dependence on any particular site is less than that of a rural physician with few options. Hospitals in highly competitive markets, therefore, have to offer more inducements to elicit the desired physician contributions. Physician bonding is more difficult and more complicated.

Collaborative Strategies

Before examining the specific collaborative strategies currently being used to bond physicians to hospitals, we need to consider physician objectives and concerns.

Physician Objectives and Concerns: Bases for Inducements/Disinducements. As noted earlier, physicians are not homogeneous and need to be segmented on the basis of several variables. Nevertheless, many share certain common values that affect their objectives and concerns. The following is a list of some such values.

Personal benefits
  Salary
  Patient care fees
  Other fees
  Return on personal investment
  Fringe benefits
  Advancement potential
Work satisfaction
  Physician experience in facility
  Perceived quality of care
  Adequacy of facilities and equipment
  Medical training opportunities
  Research opportunities
  Teaching opportunities
  Adequacy of support services
  Working relationships with other physicians, other professionals, and administrative personnel
  Acceptable work scheduling
  Physician autonomy
  Support for moral and ethical values
Patient satisfaction
  Patient access
  Minimal patient out-of-pocket costs
  Adequate length of stay
  Service amenities

These concerns and objectives provide health care executives with the motivational bases for selecting effective inducements to enhance physician contributions. They also provide the bases for selecting disinducements to forestall physician discontributions.

Not all of these concerns and objectives apply to all physicians. Therefore, a health care executive needs to consider which subgroup of physicians will be impacted by a particular business strategy or bonding strategy. A series of questions could be formulated and used to screen proposed actions in terms of their likely impact on physician stakeholders.

The following list contains useful examples of potential screening questions.

- Which particular physician stakeholders are likely to be impacted by the particular business strategy or physician bonding strategy?
- Will they be benefited or harmed in terms of the factors listed above?
- If they will be harmed, what benefit or compensation can be offered to them to reduce their threat?
- Do the projected economic and noneconomic benefits of the strategy outweigh its associated negative reaction on the part of some physician stakeholders?
- Are incentives and inducements for supporting the proposal known to those physicians affected by the proposed changes?
- Are physician stakeholders willing to accept the risk associated with the proposed actions?

Such screening questions force health care executives to examine the attitudes that major physician stakeholders (and other key stakeholders) will have toward proposed overall business strategies or particular physician bonding tactics. An acceptable proposal is one in which the major physician stakeholders are either neutral or favorable. In some cases, the negative attitudes of only a few key physician stakeholders will make the proposal unacceptable.

Physician Bonding Tactics. Figure 33 outlines some of the major physician bonding tactics currently being pursued by hospitals and hospital systems. It should be kept in mind that successful organizations select physician bonding tactics that

Figure 33. Physician Bonding Tactics by Degree of Physician and
Organization Commitment Required.

Organization commitment of time and resources

	More significant	Less significant
More significant (Physician commitment of time and resources)	*High mutual commitment* 1. Physician involvement in policy-making 2. Attracting or creating "superstars" 3. Hospital purchase of physician practices 4. Hospital-physician joint ventures	*High physician commitment* 1. Physician equity in hospitals 2. Financial and nonfinancial incentives for high-admitting physicians 3. Physician education offerings and subsidies
Less significant	*High organization commitment* 1. Physician life-cycle support: office setup, practice management, and preretirement planning 2. Computer link network 3. Physician recruitment/ retention programs: video recruitment tapes, training program for physicians, purchase of technology, and recreation facilities	*Low commitment for both* 1. Staff appointment with admitting privileges 2. Physician liaison or office of physician relations 3. Physician marketing: needs assessment, communication program, physician directories, geographic outreach, data analysis and feedback, and preferential admitting privileges 4. Other benefits: group purchasing, group malpractice, fee collection, and loan programs

Physician commitment of time and resources

reinforce their corporate, business, and general stakeholder strategies (as discussed in Chapters One and Two). The tactics in Figure 33 are classified on the basis of the commitment of time and resources required of both the hospitals and the physicians with whom they are attempting to bond. These strategies are classified in terms of the *typical* amount of commitment required for successful implementation. Obviously, any one of these strategies could be implemented with greater or lesser degrees of commitment than shown in Figure 33.

Three other caveats must be mentioned. First, the collaborative strategies outlined often require the health care organization to modify its *goals and strategies* to better accommodate the concerns and desires of its physician stakeholders. Second, the physician stakeholders are not homogeneous but can be segmented by factors such as affiliation or nonaffiliation, specialty, age, administrative role, geographic location, and so on. Obviously, the most appropriate bonding tactics will be contingent on such factors. Third, while the emphasis here is on cooperation and collaboration, the hospital may be simultaneously competing head to head with these same physician stakeholders in some market segments. Obviously, such a situation complicates the hospital-physician relationship and provides significant challenges to health care executives.

Five steps are involved in selecting among the various physician bonding tactics listed in Figure 33:

1. Clarify your philosophy regarding physicians. Do you view them as competitors; as customers whose needs you meet to gain business; as distributors whom you help make more successful; or as partners who share the equity, liability, risks, and profits?
2. Define the particular medical, ethical, and economic goals of the particular subgroup of physicians with which you wish to bond. (See the preceding list on physician concerns and objectives).
3. Define the problems these physicians are experiencing *from the physician's viewpoint.*
4. Identify and implement bonding tactics that best respond

to these problems and reflect the degree of commitment desired by both parties.

5. Monitor, evaluate, and modify the selected bonding strategies after implementation.

Low-Commitment Tactics. The physician bonding strategies that require a low level of commitment on the part of both the hospital and the physician are detailed in the lower-right quadrant of Figure 33. Most of these have been used by most hospitals for many years. Of course, the degree to which they are successfully implemented and managed varies widely between hospitals.

The development and implementation of a physician marketing plan is a major but low-risk bonding tactic. Such a plan must relate to and reinforce the strategic plan of the institution. This ensures that time and energy are being invested in achieving goals consistent with the institution's long-term goals.

Another key to physician marketing is hiring a high-level individual, a physician liaison representative, who is in charge of meeting the needs of physicians on an ongoing basis. This person goes to physicians and identifies their needs, evaluation of the hospital, and view of the appropriate role of the hospital in assisting them. Immediate responsiveness to physician requests (usually in thirty-six to forty-eight hours) is often a part of the program. Some hospitals establish an office of physician relations under the physician liaison. Centralizing all physician services in one office under the physician liaison gives bonding efforts credibility in physician eyes. Late in this chapter we discuss the role of the medical director as such a liaison.

As noted earlier, what physicians want varies by physician subgroup. The key is to determine what will help the particular medical staff the most. One recent survey of ten thousand physicians by Professional Research Consultants of Omaha, Nebraska, found that physicians want patient referral programs, continuing medical education for their office nurses, and training of all their personnel in guest relations to enhance their private practices (Droste, 1988).

According to an informal survey of more than one hundred physicians conducted by Omega Research Consultants and *Hospitals* magazine, the quality of the nursing staff would influence the hospital affiliation decision of 94 percent, while 91 percent would be influenced by the hospital's reputation for quality care (Powills, 1987). Other important factors included the accessibility of consulting physicians, availability of programs for special patient needs, and existence of special practice-related equipment. The bottom line is that hospitals need to pay particular attention to the quality of care they provide to patients as they develop physician marketing programs. In the same survey (Powills, 1987) physicians also indicated an interest in the hospital's maintaining a medical library for physician use, professional development programs for physicians, reduced-rate group malpractice insurance, and legal counsel for physicians.

Formalized physician bonding programs were being offered in 86 percent of the nation's hospitals in 1989, according to a telephone survey of 450 CEOs by National Research Corporation of Lincoln, Nebraska (Jensen, 1989b). The most common programs currently being offered are the following (Jensen, 1989b, p. 36):

Program	*Percentage of Hospitals*
Market research survey to determine physicians needs	72
Physician directories	70
Office setup	60
Physician referral	60
Physician orientation	59
Physician-to-physician referral	49
Joint ventures	48
Medical staff advertising	45
Physician marketing education	40
Marketing plans	35

Physician liaison representatives	34
Group practices	27
Computer linkages	19
Physician retirement programs	14

In light of our previous discussion of physician desires, it appears that efforts to enhance quality are underrepresented here. About 77 percent of the CEOs said their hospitals were planning new programs for the future.

One method of determining exactly what a particular subgroup of physicians wants is the development of formalized communication programs. The Hamilton/KSA survey of 753 CEOs cited earlier found that multihospital systems are beginning to listen more attentively to their medical staffs (Sandrick, 1988). One system has established biennial leadership forums as well as an open-door communication policy so that the medical staff leadership can speak directly with system management about physicians' particular concerns. Another system is encouraging high-level hospital executives in their system to spend time with physicians to learn individually what their concerns are. They are also more directly involving their medical staff in policy-making. A third system has created a physician advisory council to identify areas of common concern.

Health care executives who lack formal communication programs with their physicians often exacerbate relationships with their medical staff, which are already strained by economic and competitive pressures. At one hospital, the medical staff passed a resolution calling for the resignation of the hospital administrator after the hospital opened three outpatient clinics "that compete with the current medical staff" (Larkin, 1988). The medical staff complained that, contrary to hospital claims, they had *not* been consulted before the hospital opened the clinics. Several physicians have severed their referral relationships with the hospital. Such conflicts result from poor communications and can cause hospitals to lose admissions, create image problems, raise conflict-of-interest questions, and erupt in costly legal battles.

Communication with medical staff is particularly important during the process of merger or acquisition. Physicians are very concerned about a new owner's responsiveness in areas such as facility maintenance, purchase of new equipment, community needs, and possible standardization of physician clinical practices (Shahoda, 1987). For these reasons, it is important for the new owners to meet with the medical staff in both group and individual sessions as early as possible in the negotiation stage.

One of the most sensitive areas of communication is the analysis of data and feedback on physician clinical practices. While this has been done successfully in some cases (Smith and Fottler, 1985, pp. 185–187), recent research has shown that hospital administrators in New Jersey and South Carolina were reluctant to use reports on physician utilization to change physician behavior (Weiner and others, 1987; Gay, Kronenfeld, Baker, and Amidon, 1989). Hospitals are reluctant to meddle openly with physician practices because "physicians were the source of patient admissions, and hence of revenue" (Gay, Kronenfeld, Baker, and Amidon, 1989, p. 47). However, hospitals were willing to influence results such as length of stay. It appears that while hospitals are reluctant to directly impact physician clinical practice to better reflect hospital objectives, they have become more willing to push for particular outcomes.

In addition to compiling data on their own medical staff, some hospitals are also providing data concerning their medical staff to primary care physicians in particular geographical areas to enhance referrals to the hospital. One academic medical center significantly raised its admissions after the introduction of prospective payment through development and marketing of a *Directory for Referring Physicians* to primary care physicians in a four-state region (Eudes, Divis, Vaughan, and Fottler, 1987).

Some urban hospitals have developed referral agreements with rural hospitals for technology-intensive services such as high-risk obstetrics and neonatal services (Robinson, 1987). The rural hospital agrees to transfer patients who require specialized care to the urban tertiary care center, and the urban hospital reciprocates by transferring these patients back to the rural hospital for follow-up care. Both hospitals increase volume, and their physicians are better able to meet the needs of their patients. This example illustrates collaborative strategies for both rural hospitals and rural physician stakeholders.

Other low-commitment hospital tactics include group purchasing agreements, physician loan programs, group malpractice insurance, and preferential admitting privileges. Group purchasing agreements help physicians enhance their purchasing power through volume discounts. VHA Physician Services, established by Voluntary Hospitals of America, offers several services including supply purchasing and hospital-sponsored physician malpractice insurance to physicians affiliated with VHA hospitals. Participation in such programs is often predicated on a physician's credentials and privileging history, malpractice claims and losses, and willingness to do a "significant" amount of their business at the sponsoring hospital.

High-Commitment Physician Tactics. The upper-right quadrant of Figure 33 shows low-commitment hospital bonding tactics that require a greater commitment on the part of physicians. Recently, several for-profit chains have been selling a stake in their hospital to their medical staffs (Perry, 1989). They are betting that once physicians are owners, they will be more likely to admit patients and maximize their use of hospital resources. The physician limited partners generally buy a stake of less than 50 percent in the facility, allowing the hospital company to retain the majority interest.

Those favoring physician ownership of hospitals claim that it not only boosts patient volume but also encourages physician investors to use hospital resources more judiciously and to submit clinical information to payers in an accurate and timely fashion (Perry, 1989). When physicians practice medicine more efficiently, the hospital's cash flow and the probability the facility will survive are improved. The American Medical Association (AMA) also claims that physicians' willingness to invest in hospitals is prompted by their desire to have a voice in how the hospital provides care. There is an ongoing debate in Washington, D.C., concerning the possible abuses of physician ownership and joint ventures. Some members of Congress believe that if physicians own facilities to which they refer patients, physicians may order more tests and procedures than necessary, yet there is little agreement on what should be considered legal and what should not.

Other low-commitment hospital bonding programs requiring significant physician commitment include educational offerings and subsidies for physicians and incentive programs for high-admitting physicians. An example of the latter would be the provision of office space at the hospital for the physicians' private practice, either free or at a reduced rent.

High-Commitment Hospital Tactics. The lower-left corner of Figure 33 outlines high-commitment hospital strategies that do not require equally high commitment on the part of physicians. One of the most interesting new approaches is physician life-cycle support (Droste, 1987). This calls for a hospital to get directly involved in helping physicians in their private practices. The first phase is practice setup for new physicians. The hospital assists in several ways, including helping physicians find offices, hire and train office personnel, and select office information systems.

Since federal regulations forbid formal agreements on admissions of Medicare and Medicaid patients, hospitals are extremely nervous about any suggestion that they consciously seek referrals in exchange for office support. The following quotation illustrates that phenomenon: "One vice president of a West Coast hospital described to me his search for a physician who would set up practice in an area of town from which the hospital wasn't getting referrals. The administrator traveled to career-counseling sessions at teaching hospitals telling how his hospital would help the right person get started. By this he meant low-interest loans and similar favors. Everything was done in code, he explained. I would be in trouble if I just said "We give you a practice, you give us referrals" " (Easterbrook, 1987, pp. 83–84).

The second phase is to help proven, loyal admitters to increase their practices. In such medical practice management programs, physicians receive help from the hospital in assessing internal problems, generating marketing plans for their practices, setting up satellite offices, and adding medical residents to existing practices.

The third phase is preretirement planning in which the hospital assesses both the individual needs of retiring physicians and the future needs of their practices. This phase may involve financial planning for physicians as well as financial assessment of their practices. An associate should be recruited at least three years before the key physician's retirement to maintain the existing patient base.

Such a comprehensive physician life-cycle program should cost the hospital from $200,000 to $300,000 per year (Droste, 1987). To determine whether the investment is paying off in terms of referrals, admission trends should be monitored every three months to help identify the top admitters as well as those to whom additional attention should be given.

Computer link networks are another high-commitment bonding tactic for the hospital that requires less physician commitment. Generally the hospital supplies the linked physician offices with personal computers and software, allowing physicians to obtain their patients' data from the hospital's information system. The hospital often hires a coordinator to train the physician's office staff in computer use.

Little Company of Mary Hospital of Evergreen Park, Illinois, installed a computer link system in 1983 (Powills, 1987). Between 1984 and 1987, fifty physicians' offices consisting of about one hundred physicians with hospital admitting privileges began accessing the hospital's integrated information system from their offices to obtain data about their patients. A study was then conducted to compare linked physicians with three control groups including physicians from a variety of practices, physicians with stable practices, and physicians with loyalties to the hospital similar to physicians in the linked group. The linked group's increase in revenue was 14 percent greater than that of any of the nonlinked group's. Results also indicated that 72 percent of the physicians increased revenue in their practices, 92 percent experienced improved cash flow, 81 percent believe the system improves the quality of care, 92 percent are more likely to send patients to the hospital, and 95 percent would recommend the system to nonlinked physicians. In the future the system will link physicians with images from computerized axial tomography (CT) and magnetic resonance scanners; physician-to-physician linkages; and linkage to providers, insurers, and employers.

The third high-hospital commitment, low-physician commitment bonding tactic is the development and implementation of physician recruitment/retention systems. These often include video recruitment tapes, training programs for physician office staff members, purchase of technology desired by physicians, and provision of recreational facilities/opportunities for physicians.

One Texas hospital purchased hunting land for the use of its affiliated physicians, high-level executives, and board members. The medical staff are provided with transportation, lodging, meals, and equipment for deer-hunting expeditions. One administrator described the benefits as follows: "Back at the hospital, there is a lot of tension between the administrative staff and certain members of the medical staff. Around the campfire, we see a lot of the tension and antagonisms vanish. There is a lot of male bonding, and everyone is on a first-name basis. Physicians and administrators often become personal friends, and the goodwill usually carries over into the workplace."

High-Mutual-Commitment Tactics. The upper-left quadrant of Figure 33 outlines bonding tactics that require a significant commitment on the part of both hospitals and physicians. Physician involvement in strategy and policy-making is a major trend today. This involvement can be accomplished by employing physicians in administrative positions, increasing physician involvement in hospital governance, increasing physician involvement in strategic planning, placing physicians on boards of particular projects, establishing a physician advisory council, and offering medical staff development opportunities that reinforce the strategic plan of the hospital (Morrisey and Brooks, 1985b; Sandrick, 1988). Failure to provide such mechanisms for physician input into strategy has often resulted in the failure of proposed mergers due to "medical policies" (Cherskov, 1987).

Executives at Hillcrest Medical Center in Tulsa, Oklahoma, try to forestall hospital–medical staff conflicts by involving *all* of the medical staff (not just the officers) in formal strategic planning (Larkin, 1988). Special effort is made to involve rank-and-file physicians who may not be involved in hospital affairs but would be affected by hospital projects. The hospital executives also seek physician input on an informal basis. While these approaches do not eliminate all conflict (since some physicians may continue to have different goals than the hospital), they do tend to minimize it.

One note of caution is in order. Integration of physicians into the hospital management and policy-making structure may do little to reduce hospital costs (Alexander and Morrisey, 1988). In fact, certain integration attempts are actually associated with higher costs. When the consequences of physician integration are virtually costless and a reasonable case can be made that such actions will increase revenues, improve quality, or enhance hospital–medical staff relations, there is little risk in implementing them. Alternatively, they would not be appropriate for a hospital pursuing a cost-leadership strategy of being the low-cost provider in general or in certain submarkets (Porter, 1980).

The bonding tactic of attracting and creating superstars is very similar to the strategy of physician recruitment/retention discussed earlier except the focus is on nonaffiliated high admitters with outstanding reputations or high-potential younger physician staff members. However, the superstar approach requires a greater commitment of time, effort, and resources. It works best in profitable specialties (Koska, 1988).

Recently, hospitals have been buying physician practices, retaining ownership, and building primary care solo practices into larger primary care group practices. The goals are to stabilize referrals when physicians move or retire and then to increase referrals over time. Richmond (Virginia) Memorial Hospital began purchasing physicians' practices in 1974 and owned four major practices and several minor ones involving forty physicians in 1988 (Grayson, 1988). The hospital now obtains over 20 percent of its inpatient referrals from its own practices.

In addition to a more predictable relationship with medical staff based on more than goodwill, owning physician practices enables a hospital to expand referrals in new markets faster. By placing a group practice in a particular geographical area, the hospital can generate quicker, more predictable referral patterns. Ownership of a multispecialty practice also puts the hospital in a better position to market a complete package as part of a managed care contract. However, some hospitals pay more than the practice is worth, do not know how to operate it, and generate more ill will in the physician community than the referrals are worth (Grayson, 1988).

The final mutual high-commitment bonding tactic is hospital-physician joint venture. These tend to be more complicated and more controversial than most of the other bonding tactics we have discussed. Consequently, they are discussed in detail in the next chapter.

Where the goals, objectives, and commitment levels of physicians and health care organizations converge, we have the greatest potential for mutual gain. The implication for health care executives is to look for such opportunities, carefully evaluate them based on *both* financial and stakeholder collaboration goals, and carefully structure them to be *mutually* beneficial.

As we look to the future, the relative importance of the various physician bonding tactics is unclear. On one hand, the relative importance of tactics requiring high mutual commitment has increased. However, recent concerns in Congress and the Antitrust Division of the Department of Justice concerning kickbacks, conflict of interest, and antitrust violations have had a freezing effect on mutual high-commitment tactics such as hospital purchases of physician practices and joint ventures. Those concerns may also negatively impact other tactics requiring high commitment on the part of either physicians or the organization such as physician life-cycle support, computer link networks, physician recruitment/retention programs, physician investment in hospitals, and financial incentives for high-admitting physicians.

The most likely scenario is that the above tactics will continue to increase in terms of their relative degree of importance, although more slowly than would otherwise be the case. The reason is that the mutual low-commitment tactics have little payoff for either the organization or the physician. However, the above high-commitment tactics will be more carefully structured in the future to avoid the appearance and reality of conflict of interest or antitrust violations.

Physician Perspectives on Stakeholder Management: Two Roles and Two Views

To this point, the chapter has focused on the management of collaborative relationships with physicians as stakeholders of a hospital or hospital system. A contribution of the stakeholder management perspective is to allow managers to see the world in general, and the focal organization in particular, from the stakeholder's viewpoint.

The perspective will vary, however, depending on the role of the physician stakeholder. In this section, we first view the health care organization as the stakeholder in the physicians' practice, and then we look at a specific physician role that has potentially great role conflict associated with it: the hospital medical director or vice-president for medical affairs. In this situation the physician may at the same time represent a key stakeholder (the medical staff) and be an agent of the organization (manager of stakeholders).

Health Care Organizations as Stakeholders in Physician Practices. Figure 34 shows a simplified key stakeholder map for a physician in a primary care group practice. As in previous diagrams, the two-way arrows indicate *mutual dependence* and likely influence between the physician practice and each key stakeholder. The reasons for the practice's dependence on each key stakeholder should be obvious from our previous discussion of hospital stakeholder maps in Chapter Two.

Any key stakeholder who wishes to collaborate with the practice needs to keep in mind what the physician owners want in their relationship to each stakeholder. While there will be some variation from physician to physician and from issue to issue, the items listed earlier in this chapter are relevant. For example, most of them would apply to physicians' expectations concerning what they want from their affiliated hospital. The hospitals that best meet their affiliated physicians' needs will be most successful in implementing collaborative strategies. In meeting these needs, the hospital needs to be aware of the practice's other key stakeholders and what pressures these stakeholders are placing on the physician owners.

For example, any collaborative activity that may be viewed negatively by the physicians' peers (for competitive reasons) or professional medical organizations (for ethical reasons) may be rejected by those physicians. The objections and concerns of the physicians' other key stakeholders, as well as those of the physician herself or himself, need to be anticipated and overcome before a particular collaborative proposal is made. Collaboration can only be successfully implemented when those things that physicians value (either for themselves or for meeting the expectations of *their* key stakeholders) are maintained or enhanced.

Physicians as Stakeholder Managers. Physicians also serve as managers of stakeholders, including other physicians. For example, a hospital medical director is a physician executive employed by the hospital and reporting (in most cases) directly to the chief executive officer of the hospital. This position includes titles such as director of medical affairs, chief of profes-

Figure 34. Key Stakeholder Map for Physician in Primary Care
Group Practice.

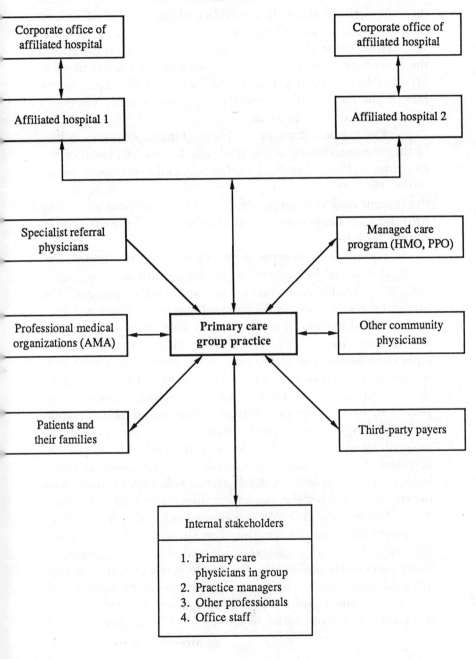

sional services, or (in keeping with the current shift to corporate titles) vice-president for medical affairs. The medical director is simultaneously a member of the *hospital administration* and also, in most instances, of the *medical or professional staff.* Thus, he or she is a so-called marginal person caught on the boundary between two groups with commitments to each. Membership in each group carries with it role expectations. Hence, the medical director often experiences conflict between managerial and professional roles.

The medical director is a hospital manager (as are others in the administration) in the traditional sense of planning, organizing, staffing, directing, budgeting, and controlling. In addition, the medical director is expected to be the integrator of the patient care processes and to assist the hospital in dealing with the total health care environment—as a physician and executive liaison.

The medical director is usually involved in the development of external linkages with regulatory and licensing agencies, other health care institutions, and patient groups. The medical director also has considerable responsibility for the acquisition and optimal internal organization of health care personnel into effective and efficient health care teams. Capital equipment acquisition is also part of the medical director's role, as are the overall coordination, monitoring, and evaluation of the care process. Most importantly, the medical director is expected to further the establishment and maintenance of linkages with physicians, particularly those on the hospital's medical/professional staff. The medical director has important responsibilities in managing several key organizational stakeholders. Here we look in detail at this role and examine it in depth, as we did for the marketing director in Chapter Four.

The medical director as a physician leader must explore the forces affecting change, the likely direction of those forces, and the relative effectiveness of various strategic responses to those forces. Thus, the role of the physician executive is rapidly evolving as one of the most important positions in the health care system and requires specialized managerial skills that are quite different from those of clinicians. The degree to which physician managers are able to exhibit this type of leadership will determine their role boundaries. Physician managers can be instrumental in improving the internal management of the organization and in forming policies that will guide the health care system.

The physician manager may often feel that he or she is standing in the center of a circle of people, all of whom are making demands of time, attention, decisions, and actions. Many of those around the circle are from in the organization. They are fellow physicians, nurses, administrators, department heads, and patients. Others are external to the organization and represent regulatory agencies, medical societies, practice groups, other hospitals, news media, third-party payers, and the public, all of which can exert considerable pressure on the institution generally and on the medical director in particular. Internal and external demands and pressures between and among these stakeholders create a dilemma for the physician manager.

For example, the public—an external stakeholder—increasingly sees health care as a right. It expects both the quality of and access to medical care to increase, irrespective of an individual's ability to pay for services. Many health care professionals support the public's expectations. Physicians, nurses, therapists, and other internal stakeholders believe they should do everything possible to improve the health of as many people as possible using every available means. However, external stakeholders such as federal and state governments, insurance companies, employers, and patients whose deductibles and co-payments are increasing expect hospital administrators to contain the costs of providing this health care.

Many stakeholders occupy a fluid position with mixed loyalties. Medical/professional staff members, for example, engaging in external independent or joint ventures may pose threats to the quality and quantity of work performed at the medical director's hospital. This stakeholder perspective is analogous to a seesaw with too many people on it, all of whom want to push off independently; medical directors must continuously attempt to balance conflicting stakeholder demands and pressures to keep the mechanism running smoothly.

The stakeholder seesaw facing the medical director can be seen more clearly in Figure 35, which provides a hypothetical key external, interface, and internal stakeholder map for this position in a multiunit hospital. Since it is in a multiunit system, the corporate office is a major stakeholder for the medical director and approves budgets, strategic plans, and key executive appointments and holds individual hospitals accountable for achieving particular corporate goals and objectives.

Patients are referred to the individual hospital by both the medical staff and other community physicians as well as through HMOs or PPOs. Third-party payers pay most of the bills and sometimes question the amount or quality of services provided. The individual hospital cooperates with other system hospitals through such mechanisms as joint purchasing agreements. The medical director also spends significant time and effort dealing with external clinical accreditation agencies such as the Joint Commission for the Accreditation of Health Care Organizations (JCAHO).

One might imagine that the seesaw would be more than full already. However, the medical director also has internal stakeholders with which to deal. In particular, the CEO has a key stake in the behavior and effectiveness of the medical director. Indeed, the medical director will serve to a greater or lesser extent exclusively at the pleasure of the CEO. Other key administrative stakeholders are the COO and CFO. The medical director will be very concerned with the ongoing operations of the hospital, and the COO will be equally concerned about the effectiveness of the medical director in ensuring the contribution of the medical staff (and perhaps other clinical professionals) in making those operations effective. The CFO may be the primary force for cost containment in the hospital and may provide a clear alternative to the medical director's primary focus on quality of care. Managing relationships with these key stakeholders is crucial for the medical director.

In addition to her or his primary interface stakeholder, the medical staff, other key internal stakeholders include clinical department heads (physicians and nonphysicians) who look to the medical director to protect clinical quality as they define

Figure 35. Key Stakeholder Map for Hospital Medical Director.

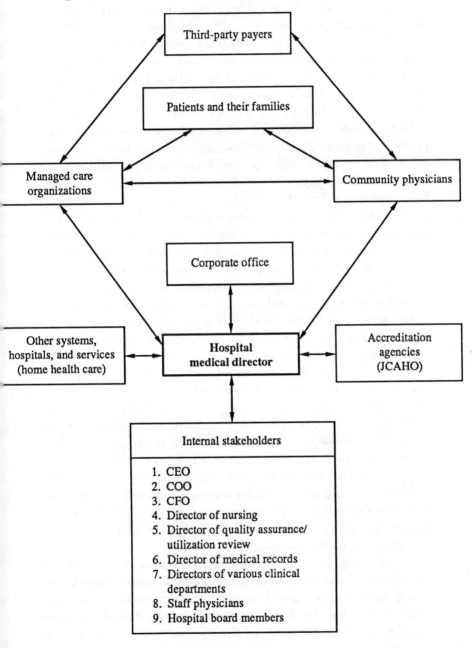

it. The director of medical records will be concerned on an ongoing basis with the accuracy, completeness, and timeliness of the medical/professional staff's charting and documentation. The director of quality assurance/utilization review will be equally concerned with efficient resource use and the quality of medical care delivery by that medical/professional staff. Medical directors will need to rethink their strategies and operations as they face increasing, and potentially conflicting, demands for effectiveness and efficiency from these and perhaps other internal, external, and interface stakeholders.

Not everyone will agree with the set of stakeholders we have used as examples for each type. There is good reason to be uncomfortable with such global classifications of particular stakeholders. Of all the possible stakeholders for a medical director, the ones who will be relevant depend on the particular issue. If the issue is cost containment, the concerned stakeholders will be different than if the issue is access to health care. The diagnosis of the medical director's relevant stakeholders in terms of the four stakeholder types and the most appropriate strategy will also be different on separate issues. Stakeholder characteristics, especially potential for threat and cooperation, may change depending on the issue.

To illustrate how stakeholder diagnosis is issue specific, take the case of a medical director's perceived need for increasing the managerial efficiency and effectiveness of the clinical department of nursing by computerizing its administrative records. By involving the director of the nursing department in the evaluation and discussion as a part of the decision-making process, the medical director might not only secure the director of nursing as a generally supportive stakeholder but also heighten that support to strong cooperation while reducing his or her threat because of possible resentment of having a system imposed on the nursing department.

In a similar way, the medical director may seek the collaboration of the medical/professional staff stakeholder in defining the need for and benefits of a computerized management system for the department of nursing, thus shifting the usual mixed-blessing status of the medical/professional staff to a supportive posture. Because acquiring a computerized management system is costly, the issue may be sufficient to cause the medical director to diagnose the usually supportive CFO, another member of the hospital's management team, as being potentially nonsupportive. To prevent the CFO from becoming nonsupportive on this issue, the medical director might properly involve the CFO in the decision-making process along with the supportive director of nursing and members of the medical/professional staff.

This issue specificity suggests that stakeholder diagnosis is an ongoing, iterative activity. Medical directors cannot assume that a stakeholder who is supportive on one issue will be so on every issue or that a stakeholder who is nonsupportive on one issue will be so on another. Stakeholders are sources of both opportunity and danger, especially those of the mixed-blessing type. Moreover, other health care executives need to understand the conflicting pressures under which medical directors operate so that they can anticipate likely reactions to collaborative proposals.

Up to this point, this section has focused on the physician as a manager of other stakeholders. How can the insights provided in this section be used to help health care executives better manage their physician stakeholders?

First, an understanding of the physician's, physician manager's, or practice's stakeholder map and the manager's relative position on it provide the manager with a powerful tool for understanding and anticipating the physician's likely behavior. For example, a key stakeholder of the physician may be exerting pressure for the physician *not* to undertake an action that might otherwise be mutually beneficial to both the physician and the organization represented by the executive. Second, as a result of that understanding and anticipation, the health care executive is better able to articulate strategies and tactics for managing physicians that are more likely to be successful because they consider physician concerns.

Summary and Managerial Implications

Collaboration between hospitals and physicians has become necessary for the survival of each in today's extremely competitive and rapidly changing environment. Each is becoming increasingly dependent on the other. The steps involved in implementing a collaborative strategy with physician stakeholders include defining a philosophy regarding physicians; defining goals of the particular physicians' subgroup; defining physicians' problems from their perspective; identifying and implementing bonding tactics that best respond to these problems; and monitoring, evaluating, and modifying these bonding tactics after implementation.

This chapter has illustrated in detail a major theme of this book—that stakeholder management concepts, generic strategies, and tactics allow executives to link strategic concerns over organizationwide competitive relationships in the organization's external environment (macro level) with the daily activities of managers (micro and macro levels). In implementing specific physician bonding programs, these micro-level activities serve as tactics to implement the generic stakeholder management strategy of collaboration (meso level). In turn, such collaboration facilitates implementation of a competitive business strategy for the organization as a whole. The success or failure of these micro activities will greatly impact the success of the organization's business strategy.

Physician bonding tactics requiring only a mutually low commitment of time and resources include physician marketing programs, physician liaisons, communication programs, and other low-cost benefits such as group purchasing, group malpractice insurance, physician fee collection, and loan programs. Others requiring a more significant physician commitment include physician equity investments in the facility, financial and nonfinancial incentives for high-admitting physicians, and physician education offerings and subsidies.

Bonding tactics requiring a more significant hospital commitment include physician life-cycle support, computer link networks, and physician recruitment/retention programs such as the use of video, training programs for physician staff members, purchase of technology, and recreation facilities for physicians. Bonding tactics requiring a significant mutual commitment from both hospital and physicians include physician involvement in strategy and policy-making, attracting and creating superstars, hospital purchase of physician practices, and hospital-physician joint ventures.

All of these bonding tactics designed to implement a generic collaborative stakeholder strategy (including joint ventures) need to be evaluated on the basis of their potential for actual financial and collaborative success. Collaborative success means the development and maintenance of a mutually satisfactory relationship, as noted in Chapter Five. We examine these two quite different definitions of success in the next chapter, on hospital-physician joint ventures. Health care executives attempting to bond with a particular group of physicians also need to see these proposals from the physician's perspective. This requires gaining an understanding of the physicians' needs, their key stakeholders, and the pressures these stakeholders exert on the physicians.

CHAPTER 7

ⵊⵊⵊⵊⵊⵊⵊⵊⵊⵊⵊⵊⵊⵊⵊⵊⵊⵊⵊⵊⵊⵊ

Approaching
Joint Ventures Strategically

As indicated throughout this book, hospital physician medical staff members can be categorized as one of the stakeholder groups that, under most circumstances, have the highest potential for both threat and cooperation. This potential is primarily realized through the power that the medical staff has in referring patients. Without these referrals, the hospital would not be able to survive. In Chapter Four we describe physicians as mixed-blessing stakeholders. Health care organizations should (and many do) attempt to manage their mixed-blessing stakeholders by attempting to increase their potential for cooperation and through collaboration to decrease their potential for threat. By collaborating, the hospital attempts to move the physician closer to the organization and into a more supportive and less threatening posture.

Although there are many hospital-physician collaboration possibilities (as we discussed in Chapter Six one major device is the hospital-physician joint venture (Mancino, 1984; Rosenfield, Mancino, and Miller, 1987; Snook and Kaye, 1987). Given the growing importance and frequency of hospital-physician joint ventures, we examine them in detail here as a specific example of stakeholder management strategy implementation. By entering into a collaborative joint venture with medical staff *as a stakeholder management technique,* the hospital creates *new* stakeholder management considerations. In addition, the organization may put itself at risk financially if it focuses exclusively on the physician bonding aspects of the venture and not its overall business potential. In this chapter we develop a strategic approach for *both* financial and collaborative success in such ventures.

Since the early 1980s many hospitals have seen the establishment of joint ventures with physicians as a panacea for market share and referral problems. Thus, hospitals have entered into many joint ventures with physicians such as physician practice purchase, surgicenters, urgicenters, managed care arrangements (HMOs and PPOs), medical office buildings, outpatient diagnostic centers, imaging centers, fertility institutes, clinical testing labs, jointly owned medical corporations, and many others. While Morrisey and Brooks (1985a) reported that only 12 percent of American hospitals had a functioning joint venture in 1984, that percentage had quadrupled to 48 percent by 1988 (Jensen, 1989b).

However, hospital-physician joint venture activity has recently slowed considerably. First-generation physician-hospital joint ventures have produced some remarkable wins—and some equally remarkable disasters (Shorr, 1987b). In a recent survey for *Hospitals* magazine of two thousand hospital CEOs, Hamilton/KSA reported that 21 percent of the respondents had established joint venture imaging centers, and 9 percent had established outpatient joint venture surgery centers (Grayson, 1988). The same survey disclosed that only 25 percent of the same respondents were actively considering entering such joint ventures; moreover, joint ventures have not generally achieved the objective of bonding physicians to the hospital and sometimes, in situations where the venture failed, have had the opposite effect (Grayson, 1988). Another indicator of problems in joint ventures is the evolution of "salvage" firms whose strategy is to purchase failing joint venture imaging and surgical centers. Moreover, trade journals targeted for those types of joint venture centers now discuss turnaround strategies (for example, Kaufman, 1988).

Although recently under attack from critics who cite the potential for abuse, at this time proposed regulatory actions such as the bill proposed by Congressman Stark (HR 5198) have experienced substantial dilution as they have moved through the legislative process. However, recent draft safe-harbor regulations are harsher than predicted (Perry, 1989). Because of the level of uncertainty facing potential hospital-physician joint ventures, innovations in legal arrangements are emerging. For example, some ventures are structured as collapsible transactions that permit physician limited partners to be bought out at a later time if the venture is deemed illegal. With the exception of patently abusive ventures and regardless of the specific restrictions eventually emerging from these legislative efforts, the hospital-physician joint venture model will continue to be embraced by the health care industry. To establish these ventures, hospitals have adapted a vehicle utilized in many other industries: the limited partnership joint venture.

The limited partnership in health care is an adaptation of a legal partnership structure that has been used for many years in other industries, particularly real estate, oil and gas, and motion pictures (Snook and Kaye, 1987). Traditionally, the limited partnership has been used to raise capital and pass tax benefits to limited partners. (Until recently, many limited partnerships were structured to establish tax shelters. The investors obtained leveraged tax write-offs, and the general partner obtained investment capital. However, the 1986 restructuring of the IRS tax code, which disallows using passive losses to offset active income and has eliminated the investment tax credit, has affected the financial feasibility of these joint ventures.) Most limited partnerships are structured similarly, with slight variations from state to state. In any case, the parties involved in the limited partnership joint venture are one or more general partners and a number of limited partners.

The health care industry has structured limited partnership joint ventures (Coddington and Moore, 1987) for a multitude of purposes. A few of the more important are

- Acquiring new sources of capital
- Achieving economies of scale
- Introducing new patient markets

- Securing and extending market reach
- Increasing revenue bases
- Acquiring state-of-the-art technology
- Warding off threats from competition
- Increasing physician alliances and collaboration

Each of these objectives has provided justification for hospitals to enter into joint ventures with physicians (Snook and Kaye, 1987; Blair and Whitehead, 1988; Shorr, 1987a, 1987b, 1987c; Smith and Reid, 1986; Shortell, Wickizer, and Wheeler, 1984; Blair, Slaton, and Savage, 1990). Perhaps the most important motivation has been to collaborate with physicians to influence referral patterns and physician-hospital linkage, or bonding.

Generally, the parent hospital of the joint venture limited partnership serves as *the* general partner or one of the general partners. The hospital may engage a management firm to act as a managing general partner. The group of physicians become limited partners, contributing a portion of the capital necessary to start up the venture. Being in a partnership relationship with a group of physicians who have the capacity to direct their referrals either to or from the parent hospital results in a new and different relationship between the physician and the general partner hospital. This new relationship with physicians *as business partners* has not only the potential to affect the affairs of the venture itself but also the potential to substantially change the relationship between the physician and the sponsoring parent hospital either positively or negatively.

As an example, a hospital might wish to enter a joint venture limited partnership with a group of neurologists and orthopedic surgeons to establish a magnetic resonance imaging (MRI) center. Although the capital requirements of such a venture are extensive, the primary motivation of the parent hospital could be less to make money from the *outpatient* venture than to collaborate with this group of physicians to attract their admissions for *inpatients* at the hospital.

In a related but negative example, a large metropolitan hospital recently solicited physician limited partners to enter in a joint venture involving an on-campus medical office building.

Many of the hospital's referring physicians became angry that the hospital attempted to initiate the project. Many of the physicians owned their own office buildings in the medical center area, which suffered from a soft market. Others also owned rental medical office space that they leased to young physicians. The physicians felt that the hospital, by building a large amount of subsidized office space, would further harm an already weak market and further devalue their properties. The hospital quickly backed out of the project.

Experiences with joint venturing vary widely. Among the more successful ventures are diagnostic imaging centers, lithotripters, independent practice associations, freestanding cancer centers, and physical rehabilitation centers (Coile, 1990, pp. 220–222). Among the losers have been a medical hotel project where demand failed to materialize at projected levels, ambulatory centers established without adequate market research, and a medical practice acquisition that generated opposition from the hospital's medical staff due to lack of communication and perceived competition (Coile, 1990, pp. 221–223).

Creating venture capital companies is one of the hottest trends in hospital-physician joint venturing. These new-wave joint ventures go well beyond one-deal-at-a-time venturing by the average medical staff and hospital. In these new ventures, the concept of a venture capital firm is used as a vehicle to align and expand several outpatient activities established by the hospital in conjunction with its physicians. One model is a master limited partnership with 65 percent of the partnership held by the hospital and 35 percent by the clinic (Coile, 1990). One goal of this joint venture was to expand the hospital and clinic's market referral area. An existing remote clinic is being expanded, and a new one is being built. The venture capital company will lease the facility from the hospital, from which it will obtain management and support services via a service contract. Other projects such as a retail pharmacy company and a home health care agency are being planned. Percentages of ownership in these businesses will vary, and the profit distributions, if any, will reflect such differences.

To understand the reasons for joint venture success and

failure, we develop here a series of conceptually based diagnostic and strategic models and analyze sources of stakeholder conflict. The models presented help capture the often conflicting goals in hospital-physician joint ventures. They draw on the stakeholder management literature to provide new diagnostic and strategic perspectives on such ventures and their potential benefits (see, for example, Blair and Whitehead, 1988). Then we use the models presented to suggest generic strategy prescriptions for different types of ventures. Finally, we look at some approaches to transform limited success ventures. In short, the strategic approach to joint venture success we present here includes the following steps:

1. Identify *key* stakeholders and linkages among them
2. Surface stakeholder conflict using issue-specific maps
3. Diagnose the venture on *both* dimensions of success
4. Classify the venture using *both* dimensions of success
5. Select a strategy to optimize the venture's current potential for success
6. Select an approach to transform the venture with limited potential for success

The logic of these steps is the same as the logic of the steps involved in stakeholder management in general. Stakeholders must first be identified and assessed, then diagnosed and classified. Finally, strategy and implementing tactics are selected to maximize success.

Step 1: Identify
Key Stakeholders and Linkages Among Them

As mentioned above, by entering into a collaborative joint venture with medical staff *as a stakeholder management technique,* the hospital creates new stakeholder management considerations. The hospital retains the physician primarily as a mixed-blessing stakeholder. The joint venture gains a new mixed-blessing stakeholder—the physician limited partner. This limited partner not only retains a power base in the hospital

Figure 36. Typical Key Stakeholders for Physician-Hospital Joint Venture.

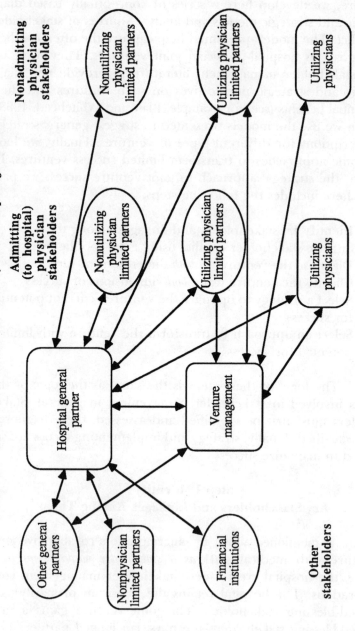

but also becomes an extremely powerful stakeholder for the venture itself. Moreover, once a hospital enters into a joint venture with physicians, it typically must also involve other stakeholders.

The key stakeholders *of a joint venture* are not all the physicians who are key stakeholders *of the hospital organization* as a whole. Only those physicians who are actual or potential joint venture partners are key stakeholders for the joint venture. The specific physicians who are potential partners will vary with the nature of the joint venture and the specific specialties required to successfully implement it. Other key stakeholders might be the general or other nonphysician limited partners, the venture management, and physicians who utilize the services provided by the venture but who are not investors. Figure 36 displays the typical array of key stakeholders in a hospital-physician joint venture. Likely linkages among them are also shown as in the stakeholder maps illustrated in Chapter Three. Although not shown in Figure 36, potential coalitions could also be anticipated and portrayed.

If all goes well with the joint venture, then the hospital can expect increased referrals and closer linkages with the physician limited partners. However, if for some reason the venture does not meet the expectations of these limited partners, the hospital may in fact suffer an increasingly difficult relationship with physicians *as hospital stakeholders*. Moreover, the joint venture may also encounter conflicts with other key stakeholders.

Step 2: Surface Stakeholder Conflicts Using Issue-Specific Maps

At the time the joint venture becomes an entity, it develops its own goals. In traditional terms, the primary goal of any organization is to maximize the wealth of its shareholders. Management of the venture would lack investor support if it did not attempt to achieve this goal. However, limited partner physicians may have goals for the venture that are inconsistent with this objective, such as convenient access to surgery facilities or favorable schedules. The parent hospital may have another set of goals, for example, increasing physician stakeholder collaboration or establishing financial stability through diversification. And the banks backing the venture may apply pressure to achieve financial goals through strategies that conflict with the goals of other stakeholders.

To help surface potential conflicts or to understand current conflicts, the hospital executive overseeing the joint venture should draft issue-specific or problem-oriented stakeholder maps. These maps help the hospital understand how the interests of the hospital and those of its key stakeholders may vary on different issues. They also disclose the relationships affected by conflicts among joint venture stakeholders. As in the previous chapters, health care executives need to identify the interests and concerns of *all* key stakeholders. Otherwise, in attempting to satisfy one key stakeholder, the venture management might offend and lose the support of other key stakeholders.

Ideally, one might assume that the parent hospital, the management of the venture, the physician limited partners, and the financial institutions would all have identical aspirations for the joint venture. Yet, as the following four cases illustrate, this is not often so. In fact, there are many specific issues that emerge that can make the stakeholder management technique itself problematical.

Issue 1: Between a Rock and a Hard Place. It is not uncommon for hospitals to contract the development of joint ventures to some outside firm that specializes in putting in such specialty ventures. Most often, the contract firm has set up many similar ventures, has access to specialized contractors for construction, has long-term relationships with venders, and has available specialized legal counsel. In many instances, the contract firm may continue to manage the venture after it begins operations. The chance to avoid pitfalls of inexperience makes this arrangement attractive.

However, the contract management general partner does not share the same relationship with the physician limited partners as does the hospital. Consider the case of a limited partner orthopedic physician who sends only a few patients per month to the surgicenter joint venture but seeks priority for scheduling use of the facilities. This physician, however, admits many patients to the parent hospital. In other words, in terms of venture profitability the orthopedic physician is not a *key* stakeholder but is very much a *key* stakeholder for the parent hospital. Figure 37 (issue 1) displays the relationships affected by these differing interests.

The dilemma facing the hospital is one brought about by the joint venture. If the hospital allows the contract management general partner to ignore the concerns of the orthopedic physician, it may alienate this important stakeholder. Yet if the hospital intervenes too forcibly, it may jeopardize the trust and support of the contract management general partners.

Issue 2: Determining The Hospital's Priorities. Circumstances may also arise in which the goals of the venture may become inconsistent with the goals of the hospital. For example, a psychiatric hospital has just entered into a joint venture with some of the physicians on its medical staff to start up a freestanding residential treatment center. The psychiatrists on the hospital's medical staff refer most of the *inpatients* admitted to the hospital. About 25 percent of these psychiatrists are limited partners who utilize the center. Another 20 percent are nonutilizing limited partners. Hence, 55 percent, or a majority of the medical staff psychiatrists, are not partners in the venture and do not utilize the center.

A clinical psychologist has just requested admitting privileges at the *residential* center. (Such facilities typically experience heavy utilization by clinical psychologists.) However, the psychiatric unit at the parent hospital has blocked privileges for clinical psychologists at the hospital. The venture management has the support of the utilizing limited partners to go ahead, but it checks with the hospital general partner before approving the request. Following the guidelines in Chapter Three for assessing key stakeholders, the hospital's executive con-

Figure 37. Issue-Specific Stakeholder Maps.

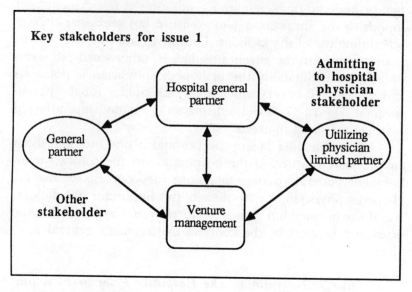

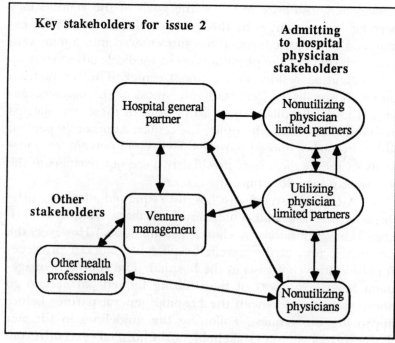

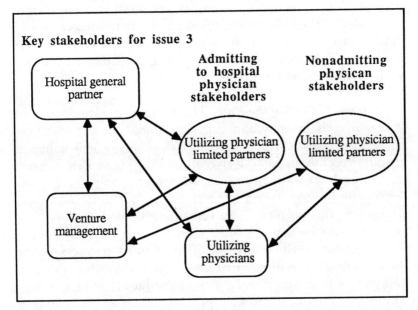

Key stakeholders for issue 3

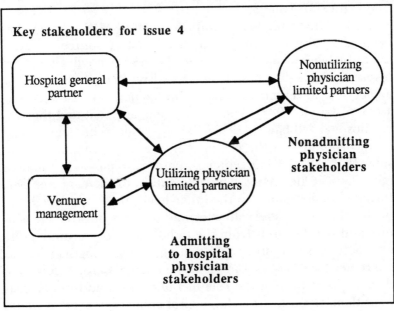

Key stakeholders for issue 4

structs the stakeholder map shown in Figure 37 (issue 2) in an attempt to understand the complex relationships, which may be strained if the venture approves admitting privileges for the clinical psychologists. At the same time, the executive recognizes that if privileges are not extended, the financial viability of the venture may be threatened.

Issue 3: Cutting the Knot. The hospital and the joint venture management may also experience goal conflict with certain limited partners and utilizing physicians. For instance, a hospital recently initiated a diagnostic imaging center containing both a MRI scanner and a CT scanner. About three-quarters of the limited partners are radiologists who do *not* admit patients to the hospital. The remaining limited partners are cardiologists who account for a large number of cardiac inpatient admissions. Currently, all of the limited partners utilize the center, as do a number of oncologists who, while not limited partners, make extensive use of the facility. As the center continues to grow, it will face problems such as the following (see Figure 37, issue 3):

1. The technological improvement of MRI scanners has been increasing extremely rapidly. Industry sources forecast the availability of modifications to the MRI that will allow noninvasive cardiac imaging, which could replace invasive cardiac angiograms in certain applications, in the next few years (Pearce, 1988; Carswell, 1988). The venture management and the parent hospital will have to decide whether this technology should be incorporated in the center. On one hand, they must consider that the imaging center contains cardiologists as limited partners who derive a sizable percentage of their income performing angiograms. On the other hand, they must weigh the profits that using alternative technologies might offer the venture and the demands from the radiologists for maximum dividends from the venture. In addition, the oncologists who use the center have become caught in the middle. Cardiologists want their support to limit the role of radiologists, and radiologists want them to push for technological enhancements that would simultaneously enhance the role of the radiologists.

2. Generally, radiologists advocate that many invasive

radiological procedures currently being performed by other specialties should be done by radiology. If the cardiologists want to perform invasive radiological procedures at the center, both the management of the venture and the parent hospital will have to decide how to handle these conflicting stakeholders. Because the cardiologists admit patients to the hospital but the radiologists do not, the hospital executive does not face an easy choice. Furthermore, *some* radiologist limited partners are likely to support the cardiologists' request since it will add revenue to the imaging center. In addition, the oncologists, who are also key stakeholders for the hospital, again will be open to influence attempts by both the cardiologists and the radiologists.

Issue 4: The Best Laid Plans . . . Other problems occur when some physician limited partners do not utilize the venture's facility and do not admit patients into the parent hospital. Although such limited partners help the hospital general partner raise enough capital to launch the joint venture, they often place demands on the hospital that conflict with the demands of other physician limited partners who *do* utilize the venture facilities and admit patients.

For instance, as illustrated in Figure 37 (issue 4), a hospital deliberately involved surgeons—who were not affiliated with the hospital—as limited partners in a surgicenter. These surgeons represent specialties not currently on the hospital's medical staff, and the joint venture is viewed by hospital executives as a means to entice the surgeons to admit patients. At the same time, these surgeons are not able to utilize the surgicenter for their invasive operations. Other surgeons affiliated with the hospital, however, are also limited partners. These surgeons do use the surgicenter *and* admit many patients to the hospital. After the first year, the venture management and the hospital face a dilemma: Do they fulfill the expectations of the nonutilizing nonadmitting physician limited partners for large dividends, or do they reinvest profits by purchasing new equipment that will satisfy the needs of the utilizing admitting physician limited partners?

Each of these issue-specific cases shows that the hospital

must make certain strategic choices as it and the venture management handle the requests, demands, and expectations of various stakeholders. The issue-specific stakeholder maps highlight the potential ramifications of any action taken by the hospital. However, to determine what choice should be made in each of these cases, hospital managers need to assess the *type of success* in the joint venture that has the highest potential benefit for the hospital, that is, is most consistent with its overall competitive strategy.

Step 3: Diagnose Venture in Terms of *Both* Dimensions of Success

Traditionally, joint ventures have been judged to be successful only in financial terms. First, if the venture is able to generate profits, raise new capital, provide a satisfactory return on investment, or provide quality care or products, then it can be judged as *financially successful* in comparison to any other business enterprise or investment. Second, when the primary goal of the venture is to provide a tax shelter for its investors, if leveraged tax losses generated are equal to or greater than those from other available tax shelters, then the venture can also be declared *financially successful*. However, the tax law changes caused by the Tax Reform Act of 1986 have diminished certain of the tax shelter benefits of joint ventures. As a result, tax shelter–oriented venture activity has decreased. In any case, financial success is an important indicator of the successful implementation of whatever competitive strategy the joint venture's management has chosen to pursue—*for the joint venture*. The broader strategic issue is the impact on the success *of the hospital's* competitive strategy.

Thus, in a joint venture between hospitals and physicians, a new definition of success can be added. Does the venture induce or increase collaboration between the physician limited partner and the hospital? Even more important, from a stakeholder perspective, is whether this collaboration reduces threat and increases cooperation from the stakeholder.

It is important to remember that in Chapter Four we

recommended collaboration to manage mixed-blessing stakeholders. Physicians on the medical staff of the hospital are clear examples of this type of stakeholder not only because they are high in their potential for cooperation but also because they have a high potential for threat. Their mixed-blessing status is particularly true given the current environment, where physicians have limited loyalty to any single health care organization. Reducing that potential threat with regard to lost referrals or opposition to hospital initiatives is another benefit of successful cooperation.

Thus, by definition, *collaborative success* is based on effectively implementing a collaborative stakeholder management strategy with a clear impact on either reducing a mixed-blessing stakeholder's potential for threat or increasing potential for cooperation. This stakeholder strategy should be linked to and consistent with hospital competitive strategy and its implementation.

One would look for examples where referrals increased due to the partnership or other signs that physicians have been bonded more closely to the hospital, such as increased cooperativeness with the director of medical records and timeliness in documenting medical records, as indicators of collaborative success. One assesses whether the partnership has made relations more difficult between the physician and the hospital as an indicator of collaborative failure. Collaborative success is likely to facilitate longer-term financial success *of the hospital* in an indirect way. However, it may require postponement of immediate financial returns to build the collaborative relationship. Thus, the venture could aid long-term financial success of the hospital while itself being a financial disaster—at least in the short term.

In any case, executives should also ask whether involving the hospital in the partnership has resulted in another set of potential problems that will undermine physician collaboration and bonding. Therein lies the potential conflicting logic that we believe has negatively affected many hospital-physician joint ventures since their inception. Many joint ventures have been implemented on the basis of traditional financial feasibility or for the purpose of acquiring new capital. Stakeholder management considerations in entering a venture have not been addressed carefully or systematically. Physicians are strategically important *hospital,* not just *venture,* stakeholders. The hospital-physician joint venture differs significantly from those in other industries and should not be judged solely on financial criteria.

Thus, health care executives need to ask themselves: "How important is financial success versus collaborative success in this particular joint venture?" The answer to this question will partly depend on another question: "How important are the particular physician stakeholders (or how important could they become) in terms of achieving other organizational objectives (often stated in the organizational mission and goals statement of the competitive strategic plan)?" The more important these physician stakeholders are for achieving these other short-term or long-term *hospital* goals, the more likely the *venture* management will be expected to emphasize collaborative outcomes. Alternatively, if the venture management is focused on short-term financial outcomes (that is, they feel that the venture should pay for itself), the more likely collaborative outcomes will have a lower priority.

In this chapter we focus on these two key dimensions of success, which we believe are most crucial for evaluating joint ventures as a stakeholder management technique. Of course, there are other potential success criteria for ventures besides financial and collaborative success. Another possible criterion might be support from nonparticipating physicians, the board of trustees, and patients who use the facility. In fact, given the current regulatory and legislative uncertainty, simple legality of the joint venture might be a particularly important criterion. In other words, additional stakeholders and satisfaction of their goals may also be important.

Step 4: Classify Venture Using *Both* Dimensions of Success

Hospital executives are exposed to a number of potential joint ventures. Ordinarily, traditional feasibility studies, break-even analysis, and other financial measurements would be performed to determine the financial considerations of entering the project. Unfortunately, many executives do not approach the analysis of stakeholder management considerations in the systematical manner argued for in this book. In examining the feasibility of a potential collaborative joint venture, health care managers should evaluate the proposed venture not only in terms of its potential to achieve financial success but also in terms of its potential to achieve collaborative success by enhancing an important stakeholder relationship.

To facilitate the analysis of ventures from both financial and stakeholder management perspectives, we have developed the following diagnostic model (see Figure 38). Health care executives should classify not only *potential ventures* but also *existing ventures* as to their potential to achieve financial *and* collaborative success.

Figure 38. Diagnosing and Classifying Hospital-Physician Joint Ventures.

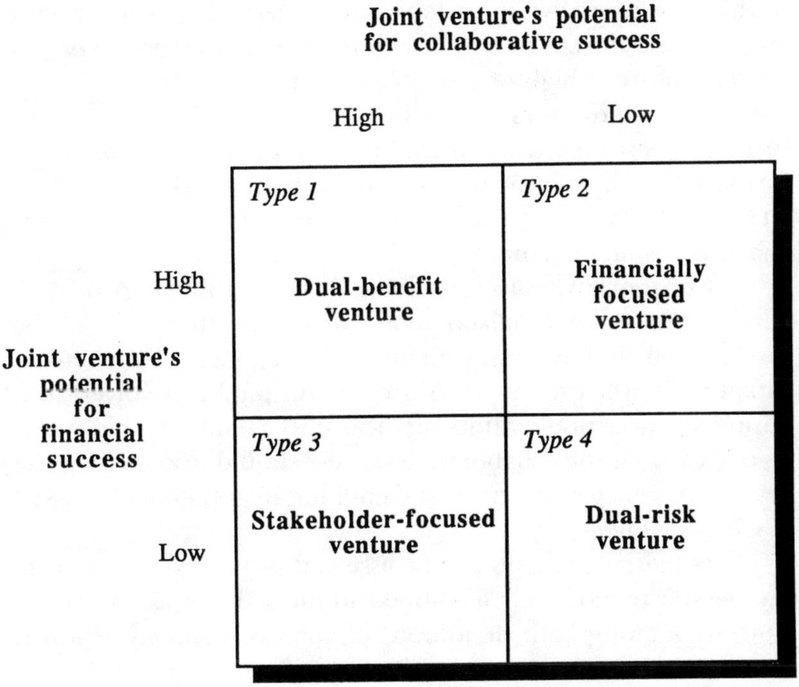

Joint venture's potential
for collaborative success

	High	Low
High	*Type 1* Dual-benefit venture	*Type 2* Financially focused venture
Low	*Type 3* Stakeholder-focused venture	*Type 4* Dual-risk venture

Joint venture's
potential
for
financial
success

One value of the stakeholder management approach is that it can erode the almost exclusive emphasis on financial outcomes (usually short term) that permeates management thought. The stakeholder management approach serves as a basis for translating financial concerns into human and, hence, collaborative concerns. However, all management activities (including joint ventures) have to at least concern financial implications. Some will by necessity need to give a greater emphasis to these considerations, while others can afford to give a greater emphasis to collaborative considerations. The critical factor distinguishing the two is the concept of available organizational "slack," which allows the organization to give a greater consideration to collaborative and long-term outcomes. Hence, distinguishing these two quite different criteria for success is analytically useful in assessing and managing a joint venture.

By systematically diagnosing potential as well as existing ventures in terms of the two dimensions of the model, potential problems can be avoided and current ones reassessed. The health care executive must look at a variety of specific criteria and information sources to determine whether an actual or potential venture is high or low on each dimension. Some of these criteria and indicators were discussed earlier. Likely financial success is best measured in traditional ways (for example, pro formas) but with a clear perspective on both the short and long term that balances the financial interest of both the venture and the hospital partner.

Collaborative success should be determined through a parallel "stakeholder collaboration pro forma" that includes the careful stakeholder assessment and diagnosis discussed in Chapters Three and Four. Since the hospital is involved in a business transaction with its medical staff members, this analysis of potential for collaborative success should also include the key contingencies affecting stakeholder negotiation discussed in Chapter Five.

Potential ventures can be assessed using Figure 38, from the perspective of their likelihood to meet the goals of the organization along both definitions of success. Planned ventures can be strategically positioned in a specific category, and existing ventures may be reexamined as to their current or desired position. Thus, the model can be used *proactively* for potential ventures or to diagnose existing ventures that have not yet experienced severe problems and *reactively* to diagnose ventures that are having problems in either financial or stakeholder terms.

Type 1: Dual-Benefit Venture. The dual-benefit venture has high potential to accomplish both financial and collaborative success. This type of venture is, of course, the "winner" that hospital executives seek. Most health care joint ventures that are thought by *both the hospital and the physician limited partners* to be successful fall into this category.

The dual-benefit venture has very different kinds of benefits resulting from the two kinds of success. Financial success, if realized, provides income to sustain the venture. Moreover, financial success may be sufficient to also provide capital to expand the hospital-physician collaborative activity or to enter into still other hospital-physician ventures.

It may not be so obvious what the dual-benefit venture's collaborative success provides in terms of benefits in addition to the expected stability or even increase in hospital referrals and admissions from the physician partners. The additional benefits are goodwill and trust. We see these kinds of benefits to hospital management as similar to the goodwill that production managers often find results from collaborative quality-of-work-life programs with unions. The goodwill these programs generate permits managers to have more freedom of action in changing work rules or operating procedures. Further, trust by key members of the medical staff involved in the joint venture may be extremely valuable in gaining their cooperation when hospital executives institute new policies or initiate new programs. Such cooperation has an effect parallel to that resulting from an electorate with high levels of trust in its elected officials. These officials have latitude to lead without having every proposal questioned.

Type 2: Financially Focused Venture. The financially focused joint venture is similar to those in other industries such as oil and gas or real estate. There appears to be potential for financial success, yet there is low potential for collaboration. An example might be a joint venture with a group of ophthalmologists in developing an ophthalmology supercenter. Although the supercenter may have great potential for financial success, opthalmologists do not have the potential to admit large numbers of hospital inpatients. Therefore, although the venture itself may have high potential for collaborative success with ophthalmologists, this may not translate into hospital admissions because the collaboration is not with a key hospital stakeholder.

Indeed, this type of venture usually is not structured to take advantage of or enhance the goodwill of the limited partner. The partner provides the capital to establish the project but is not expected to have any direct involvement on a day-to-day basis in the general partner's parent organization. This is quite unlike the physician limited partner's activity in the parent hospital.

This type of venture might be set up as a tax shelter designed to generate passive tax losses, as opposed to one with expected profits, if it were going to be done with physicians already involved in profitable passive investments. Moreover, as part of a diversification strategy, a traditional joint venture prospect would be appropriate for the hospital to enter into with other investment groups that are not as involved in the hospital.

The financially focused venture represents the model used outside of health care. Applying the traditional venture approach without consideration of the stakeholder management issues involved in venturing with physicians is, in our opinion, one of the major sources of problems with hospital-physician joint ventures.

Type 3: Stakeholder-Focused Venture. The stakeholder-focused venture will maximize collaborative efforts yet will fail to meet financial success. Here, the hospital values collaboration with the mixed-blessing physician stakeholders more than generating a profit from the joint venture. At best, this form of venture meets expenses but does not generate profits. At worst, the hospital may find it necessary to lose money to protect the physician limited partners, who are also the hospital's stakeholders.

In some circumstances, an established joint venture that is financially unsuccessful will begin to affect the collaborative goals of the hospital. If the physician limited partners are important hospital stakeholders, and the venture is threatening to financially damage the physician limited partners, then the hospital may intentionally move the venture into this classification.

For example, at times financial requirements may conflict with the collaborative goals of the joint venture. If a venture is losing money during its start-up phase, financial institutions providing loans to the venture typically suggest that the general partner supplement the venture's working capital. The normal procedure is for the general partner to call on the limited partners to contribute additional monies on a percentage-of-ownership basis. However, the parent hospital as a general partner may feel that greater damage would be done by subjecting the physician limited partners to an additional demand for investment than by simply covering the cash needs of the struggling venture itself.

As another example, to ensure collaborative success, the hospital as the general partner may reduce the initial capital investment of the physician limited partner to a small percentage of the required total investment. In doing so, the hospital decides the venture is distinctly a stakeholder-focused one emphasizing collaborative success—even at the expense of immediate financial success. The danger, of course, is that an exclusive focus on collaborative success may lead the venture into Chapter 11 bankruptcy.

Type 4: Dual-Risk Venture. The dual-risk venture is one that has little or no potential for financial or collaborative success. Obviously, the hospital would be building a predestined set of stakeholder problems by entering this type of venture, and it should avoid doing so. Given the faddishness of hospital-physician joint ventures and the pressure on the hospital from many physician groups to start one, this type is, nevertheless, far from an exception. Hospitals have rushed into ventures that were not carefully examined in financial terms and have, as a result, angered physician partners who had expected attractive financial returns and who then became increasingly uncooperative.

By systematically diagnosing *potential* ventures as well as *existing* ventures in terms of the two dimensions of the model, potential problems can be avoided and current ones reassessed. Potential ventures can be assessed from the perspective of their likelihood to meet the organizational goals along both definitions of success. Planned ventures can be strategically positioned into a specific category, and existing ventures may be reexamined as to their current or desired positioning.

The diagnostic and classification model can be used *proactively* to diagnose ventures that can be anticipated to have severe problems. Along with the key stakeholder- and problem-oriented maps, it can also be applied *reactively*. This flexibility permits executives to diagnose ventures that are already having problems in either financial or stakeholder terms and allows them to surface underlying stakeholder conflicts. We advocate a proactive approach to both diagnosing ventures and looking at how to best proceed given that diagnosis. Next, we examine proactive strategies to optimize venture success.

Step 5: Select Strategy to Optimize Venture's Current Potential for Success

What does the hospital executive need to do to ensure the kinds of success shown in Figure 38? In this section we discuss what we believe to be the most appropriate generic strategies to deal with the different types of joint ventures. We are taking what is essentially a static, although still proactive, approach to ensure that the venture's current potential for success is realized and not lost. Figure 39 shows strategies to ensure that the venture's current potential for success is realized and not lost. Later, in step 6, we discuss how ventures with limited success might be transformed.

Figure 39. Generic Strategies for Hospital-Physician Joint Venture.

Joint venture's potential
for collaborative success

	High	Low
High Joint venture's potential for financial success **Low**	*Strategy 1* **Nurture** dual-benefit venture *Strategy 3* **Subordinate** in stakeholder-focused venture	*Strategy 2* **Maintain** financially focused venture *Strategy 4* **Avoid or** **withdraw** from dual-risk venture

Strategy 1: Nurture Dual-Benefit Venture. For existing ventures that can be categorized as dual benefit, ongoing monitoring and particularly *nurturing* of the venture's accomplishment of financial and collaborative success should be performed on a continuous basis. For example, to allow the venture to continue performing at such a level, explicit stakeholder management activities (such as participative involvement of physician partners in joint strategic decision making) may be necessary to ensure that the collaborative parameters continue to be met. Any major change in the venture may result in a different set of key stakeholders and resulting conflicts such as discussed in steps 1 and 2 above. In addition to ongoing stakeholder assessment and monitoring, prudent business practices need to be followed to ensure continuing financial success. A dual-benefit venture is the ideal and should be continually nur-

tured, not taken for granted because there are no immediate problems.

  Strategy 2: Maintain Financially Focused Venture. The financially focused joint venture is similar to traditional joint ventures in other industries, and the hospital should take advantage of the financial success of this type of venture. Although the financially focused venture is not structured to take advantage of or even enhance the goodwill of the limited partner, the hospital should *maintain* it and not sell it off or withdraw from it for several reasons. First, it may provide important income to the hospital as a general partner, and that income may become more important as hospital profit margins continue to fall. Second, the income from the venture may serve as capital that can be used to start other joint ventures that are targeted as dual benefit. Third, the costs of withdrawing from the project may be high in terms of community prestige, resentment from the physician limited partners, and resistance from other physicians to enter into other collaborative efforts with the hospital given the perceived failure of this one. That is, although there are not likely to be any *positive collaborative* effects of the joint venture, a high potential for *negative collaborative* outcomes may occur if it is shut down.

  Strategy 3: Subordinate in Stakeholder-Focused Venture. Some joint ventures are strategically designed as stakeholder-focused ventures with the primary goal being to enhance hospital-stakeholder collaboration and with an explicit hospital strategy to subordinate its own financial interests to maintain or enhance the collaborative relationship. Subordination, in its general usage, often implies weakness and having to give in to a powerful other party. Here, subordination does not imply any lack of power on the part of the hospital but instead reflects an explicit strategy. Subordination of the hospital's immediate substantive interests to enhance the relationship with a key stakeholder has been described as an explicit negotiation strategy by Blair, Savage, and Whitehead (1989). Indeed, using an explicit stakeholder perspective leading to a subordinative strategy is a way to guarantee one type of success—effective stakeholder management through collaboration. Nevertheless, ongoing lack of financial success can undermine such a venture unless the hospital is very committed to such a subordinative approach or can gain financial rewards indirectly through the venture (for example, through increased inpatient referrals from or increased hospital cost-containment cooperation by physician partners).

In another example, if the venture is financially unsound and by normal business judgment is insolvent, then prudent management would dissolve the partnership and sell the assets, and each partner, general and limited, would make up the balance of any deficits owed to lenders. In the case of dissolution, each limited partner would be responsible for the difference between the value of the assets of the partnership and the remaining bank debt. Although making good financial sense, the dissolution of the partnership may cause considerable stakeholder management problems—especially if the hospital originally approached the physicians with the concept and enticed them into the joint venture.

In summary, often the general partner hospital finds itself forced to subordinate its financial position to save its collaborative position. The hospital general partner may decide it has to meet the physician limited partners' cash calls when operating funds are needed. In the event of dissolution of an unsuccessful venture, the hospital may have to absorb major financial losses to prevent damaging the physician limited partners, who are its own key stakeholders. Executives using subordination as an explicit strategy should not, however, lose sight of the venture's realistic potential for bankruptcy. A total financial collapse may also undermine the collaborative potential of the venture and result in a dual-risk venture.

Note that the subordinative approach has the focal organization (usually the hospital as general partner) subordinating its own short-term financial interest while satisfying (or at least not dissatisfying) a key stakeholder's short-term financial and nonfinancial interests. As noted in previous chapters, in the long run, the focal organization hopes to receive contributions from the key stakeholders that will balance the inducements it has been providing. *These contributions will probably be to the hospital, not necessarily to the venture, since collaboration is the hospital's stakeholder strategy.*

Strategy 4: Avoid or Withdraw from Dual-Risk Venture. Hospitals should avoid ventures that are likely to fall in the dual-risk category. Should an existing venture threaten to become an "ugly duckling," the hospital has several options. The hospital can deliberately subordinate its financial position to protect its physician limited partners and become or remain an explicitly stakeholder-focused venture through unequal absorption of losses. The hospital may be able to buy out the limited partners (another version of subordinating) to eliminate the collaborative factor involved in the partnership. This buyout might be done to prevent collaborative problems for the hospital through ill will resulting from physician stakeholders' financial losses. This buyout is, nevertheless, still a form of withdrawal from the venture but not from the ongoing hospital relationship with the physicians. Finally, the hospital may decide that it cannot afford the ongoing financial losses and that the collaborative problems being created make the venture not worth continuing and the hospital may therefore withdraw by dissolving the venture and cutting its losses.

This approach is consistent with our earlier stated view that organizations should strive for *mutual satisfaction* of their own interests as well as those of their key stakeholders. This produces stakeholder equilibrium. The dual-risk venture is a situation that offers a potential for *neither* collaborative *nor* financial success. In fact, in the dual-risk venture, the hospital runs the risk of inadvertently providing *disinducements* rather than inducements to key stakeholders. Given the obvious resource constraints of time, energy, and money, health care executives cannot (and should not) be expected to satisfy the needs of nonkey stakeholders.

The hospital may be able to find alternative collaborative techniques to offset these problems and still manage the mixed-blessing physicians. In any case, the probability that a venture may end up as this type should be carefully considered prior to and periodically during the life of a venture to ensure that this most unattractive situation does not emerge.

Step 6: Select Approach to Transform Venture with Limited Potential for Success

What can the hospital executive do to improve the overall success of the joint venture? That is, even if the strategies discussed above are successful in maintaining the level of success of the current joint venture, what can be done to further enhance that success? In this section we discuss how ventures with limited success might be transformed into more successful undertakings.

In our discussion of generic strategies we took essentially a static, although still proactive, approach. In other words, we wanted to ensure that the venture's current potential for success is realized. Here, we go beyond those optimizing—but static—strategies to suggest ways that limited success ventures (except the dual-benefit venture) could not only have their current success potential realized but also be transformed into even more successful ones.

In Figure 40 we display several transformational approaches for ventures with limited success. We do not discuss specific strategies because those depend on too many other factors. Instead, we provide broad approaches that can be applied to transform one kind of venture into another kind.

Three basic kinds of approaches will accomplish what we are suggesting: (1) the strategic management approach, (2) the stakeholder management approach, and (3) the leapfrog approach. Each approach may need several quite different specific strategies to make it work.

The *strategic management approach* is well known and has an extensive literature both in the generic strategic management literature (for example, Porter, 1980, 1985) and in the health care strategy literature (for example, Coddington and Moore, 1987). The basic idea here is that if a hospital has a stakeholder-focused venture that has been successful in achiev-

Figure 40. Transformational Approaches for Limited Success Joint Venture.

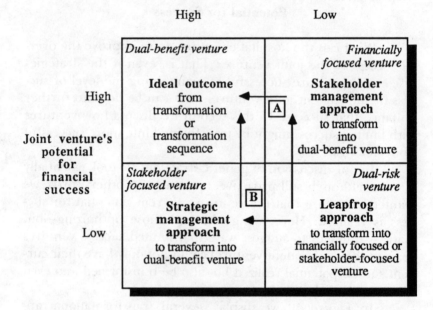

Joint venture's potential
for collaborative success

	High	Low
	Dual-benefit venture	*Financially focused venture*
High	**Ideal outcome** from transformation or transformation sequence	**Stakeholder management approach** to transform into dual-benefit venture
	Stakeholder focused venture	*Dual-risk venture*
Low	**Strategic management approach** to transform into dual-benefit venture	**Leapfrog approach** to transform into financially focused or stakeholder-focused venture

Joint venture's potential for financial success

Transformation sequences: A=Transformation of dual-risk venture first into financially focused venture and then into dual-benefit venture
B=Transformation of dual-risk venture first into stakeholder-focused venture and then into dual-benefit venture

ing collaboration with important physician stakeholders, then hospital executives can either continue to use a subordinative strategy (at some cost) to maintain collaborative success or can try to transform that venture into a dual-benefit one through systematic strategic management. For example, ventures following a subordinative strategy can be strategically repositioned into the dual-benefit venture category by increasing the potential for financial success through traditional business methods such as a more appropriate marketing mix or increased internal efficiency as part of an explicit strategic management approach. In attempting to move a joint venture from the subordinative to the dual-benefit cell, executives in the focal organization have to be careful to consider the physicians' interests and concerns, as noted in the previous chapter.

To make this change, executives may have to go back to the drawing board to identify their potential markets or reassess their product/service lines. If they are successful, they will make the venture financially successful as well. If they are not successful, then they need to continue their subordinative approach to not lose their limited success, namely, physician collaboration. In addition, they must be careful to not undo this kind of success while trying to add financial success.

If they lose their collaborative success, they will have lost the initial purpose of most hospital-physician joint ventures, namely, collaboration to enhance physician bonding. Under that scenario, they will have gone from one kind of limited success to another kind and will have a financially focused venture without collaborative success. In terms of the hospital's overall physician relations, the costs of destroying collaboration with key physician stakeholders (major admitters to the hospital,) may be far greater than the benefits even were it to fully achieve that collaboration with a particular subset of the medical staff.

Alternatively, if a venture is successful financially but has not achieved collaborative success, then we argue that an explicit *stakeholder management approach* of assessment, diagnosis, strategy formulation, and implementation should be used to supplement the maintenance strategy for continued financial success. Again, it is important to not lose what the hospital already has—financial success—when enhancing collaborative success.

Finally, we also suggest a broad approach to transform the dual-risk venture. Although our first advice would be to avoid a potential dual-risk venture or withdraw from an existing one, it may not always be possible to do so. If that is the case, the hospital should treat the venture as being in a serious turnaround situation. We do not think it is reasonable to expect to transform a dual-risk venture directly into a dual-benefit venture. Therefore we recommend what we call the *leap-frog approach*. In this approach, the turnaround attempt is focused on trying to first achieve either financial success *or* collaborative success. A subsequent step (or jump) will be to use a systematic strategic management or stakeholder management approach to make the next transformation. In Figure 40 we have labeled the leapfrog sequence of transformations from dual risk to financially focused and subsequent transformation to dual benefit as *transformation sequence A*. We have identified the sequence of transformation from dual risk to stakeholder focused and subsequent transformation to dual benefit as *transformation sequence B*.

The transformational approaches and, even more, transformational sequences represent a considerable set of challenging tasks. They do, however, point to ways to transform ventures from limited to complete, or at least more complete, success. The generic strategies discussed earlier, in contrast, represent our recommendations of how to manage ventures that are now in that state if transformation is not desired or considered possible. Before one concludes that, however, hospital executives need to carefully consider whether transformation or further transformation is possible. The transformation process itself can be considered a joint venture between the venture management, the involved physicians, and the hospital general partner.

Summary and Managerial Implications

Joint ventures between hospitals and the physicians on their medical staffs have produced successes and failures. Each joint venture has two very different dimensions of success: financial and collaborative. To ensure some form of success, we have proposed a strategic approach with a series of six steps. This approach has some clear implications for hospital managers.

First, the models and maps can be used proactively to more clearly and systematically conceptualize, analyze, and implement *proposed ventures* by permitting managers to

- Anticipate the stakeholder management implications of an action they are going to take as well as analyze the traditional financial implications
- Prevent hospitals from entering into ventures with built-in stakeholder management design problems
- Avoid ventures with built-in financial management design problems because of an attempt to work with or manage physician stakeholders

Second, the models and maps can be used either proactively or reactively to analyze *existing ventures*. For example, the diagnostic model allows managers to diagnose their existing ventures in terms of both dimensions of actual success and examine and reconcile their existing strategy in terms of maximizing their venture's present classification and benefits.

Third, these models may also be used to conceptualize strategy to reposition or transform their ventures (for example, from a dual-risk venture to a stakeholder-focused venture if collaborative success is crucial but financial success is not,) where possible by determining the transformational approach or transformational sequence that would best be applied to the venture from either a stakeholder management or a strategic management perspective.

Other issues related to hospital-physician joint ventures, not directly addressed in this chapter, should be the focus of future research. The most important of these emerging issues include the following:

- Physicians and hospitals must address the ethics of referring patients to facilities in which the hospitals and the physicians have a financial stake. Hospital executives, physician partners, and the hospital's ethics committee should establish admission guidelines, fee structures, and review processes. Without clear-cut standards, joint ventures have already encountered claims from external stakeholders that the physician limited partners are charging excessive fees and unnecessarily utilizing joint venture facilities.
- Moreover, responsible and ethical actions by the joint ven-

ture partners are essential because joint ventures face potentially significant legal and regulative constraints. For example, the proposed Health and Human Services regulations, as well as legislation proposed by Congressman Stark (HR 5198), limit the safe harbors available for hospital-physician joint ventures (Brice and Mankoff, 1988; Holthaus, 1988a; Tokarski, 1989; Perry, 1989). While the net effect of the Stark bill is unknown, its proponents claim that the bill would enforce fair utilization, fair charge structures, and explicit patient notification of physician ownership.

- The judicial system is also getting involved. Several recent court cases have handed down the broadest definition yet of a kickback under Medicare and Medicaid fraud and abuse laws. The definition now includes any payment made where the only purpose of the payment was to induce referrals. While these federal laws do not apply to patients having private insurance, the American Medical Association also considers it unethical to accept a kickback. All collaborative actions between health care organizations and their physician stakeholders will increasingly be evaluated in these terms as well.

- All of these proposals represent pressure from external legislative and bureaucratic stakeholders for hospitals and physicians to avoid business practices that raise ethical issues. Such issues will be discussed more completely in Chapter Eight.

- With the increasing shift to managed care systems, the nature and the growth of hospital-physician joint ventures may be affected. Hospitals' legal and business relationships with members of their medical staffs have already begun to change as hospitals attempt to cope with the challenges of managed care. However, although Snook and Kaye (1987) identify HMOs and PPOs as having considerable growth potential for hospital joint ventures, the actual feasibility and likely impact of hospital–managed care joint ventures are still unknown.

These emerging issues underscore the importance of a critical analysis of hospital-physician joint ventures as a collaborative stakeholder management strategy. The approach taken in this chapter can serve a crucial role in the overall strategic management of the hospital as well as of the venture itself. As we have argued throughout this book, appropriate stakeholder management remains an integral part of effective strategic management. Hospital-physician joint ventures face particular challenges to achieve both financial and collaborative success.

CHAPTER 8

꘎꘎꘎꘎꘎꘎꘎꘎꘎꘎꘎꘎꘎꘎꘎꘎꘎꘎꘎꘎꘎꘎꘎

Involving
Internal Health Care
Stakeholders

In Chapters Three and Four we identified and diagnosed the key stakeholders of health care organizations. One category of key stakeholders is the internal stakeholder, which includes upper management and middle management, including department heads, professional staff employees, and nonprofessional staff. While the significance of internal stakeholders is not universally recognized, more and more health care organizations are beginning to view their internal stakeholders as integral to the successful implementation of their business strategy.

One health care executive expressed it as follows: "When patients come into this hospital, they are going to experience it on a first-contact basis: the admitting personnel, the nurses, and the maid. We spend thousands of dollars on advertising, call this number, and if the person is not handled correctly, then we will lose that. So we look at employees as an internal audience. In order to have a cheerful outlook and promote a good feeling about their workplace and hospital, they must get along together. They must understand the workings of why things are done in a certain way, and if there is low morale, we need to find out why. If they are unhappy it is going to reflect back on the consumer. They also go out and sell this hospital every day out on the street. We are going to begin inservice for our employees on our different programs so they can go out and sell them to the church, school, or whatever they do outside work."

As we have argued throughout this book, a strategic approach to stakeholder management integrates a variety of existing or contemplated management activities. Our approach allows managers to see and manage their overall strategy for managing their key stakeholders using a variety of specific management techniques and programs.

For example, the recognition of the unique challenges facing organizations in service industries (Albrecht and Zemke, 1985; Zemke, 1989) has also had an impact on health care organizations as they struggle with influencing consumer perceptions of quality (Peterson, 1988; Zemke, 1989; Coile, 1990). Much of the focus of this approach is concentrated on various forms of guest-relations programs for patients and their families or expanded to include other customers such as physicians, co-workers, and staff in other departments. The key here is to manage one stakeholder group (employees) to help manage other key stakeholders that may be internal (for example, other departments), interface (for example, physicians), or external (for example, patient families).

Another emerging approach is that of strategic human resource management (Fottler, Hernandez, and Joiner, 1988; Fottler, Phillips, Blair, and Duran, forthcoming). This expanded perspective on managing human resources links overall strategic management and human resource management for human resource systems and practices to successfully reinforce the competitive strategy. Part of this approach has also been called internal marketing, with employees thought of as customers (MacStravic, 1989). Strategic human resource management, however, focuses only on the connection between strategy and one, albeit a key, stakeholder—employees of the organization subject to the personnel system, with its inducements and disinducements.

Other management issues have focused on various ways to improve productivity defined as either efficiency (doing the job with less resources), effectiveness (doing the job better or with higher quality), or both. These productivity-enhancing management techniques range from patient classification systems and more effective management information systems to employee involvement approaches such as quality circles. From our perspective, these are all pieces of what is needed to effectively manage internal stakeholders. In each case, managers are linking organizational and personnel issues in a way that involves employees more completely in the delivery of quality services by (1) matching their activities to where the real needs are; (2) improving the ability of managers and professionals to access, manage, and act on information; or (3) getting employees directly involved in organizational problem solving. Each of these ways enhances the staff's (including managers') potential for cooperation in dealing with other stakeholders concerned about service (for example, patients and their families), efficiency (for example, third-party payers and corporate offices), and effectiveness/quality (for example, JCAHO and the medical staff).

Strategic stakeholder management makes integrated sense of these various activities, each of which is often oversold as the only solution to the problems facing health care organizations. Stakeholder management is not an alternative program. It is an overall strategic approach that allows coordinated, purposeful selection and implementation of a variety of management perspectives, tactics, programs, and techniques. The issue is not what a program is called but what its implications are for effectively managing those key individuals, groups, and organizations with a stake in your organization whether you, as a manager, like it or not.

In this chapter we look at a variety of ways to implement the generic stakeholder management strategy of involvement. These techniques and programs we consider to be multiple tactics that support the overall strategy of enhancing current levels of cooperation among supportive internal stakeholders to optimize their overall contribution to the organization's mission and business strategy.

Involving Internal Stakeholders

Health care organizations seem to be attempting to use their internal stakeholders to manage each other as well as to manage key external stakeholders such as patients and the general public. One CEO explained the linkage between internal and external stakeholders as follows: "All of our employees should be marketing all the time. Marketing is everything you do, every interaction you have with another employee, a patient, a family member, a physician, or an employer. It is so broad; it is absolutely everything you do here. We recently had a little problem with an outside business that was wanting to come here and do some business with us. One of my managers didn't do well in the conversation, offended the person, and indicated we don't need to do business with them. Well, that implied a lot of negative things about us and was a disaster. We are trying to expand our patient base, and we are going out there and talking to these employer groups, trying to get them hooked into our system. And we have a manager right here in the hospital offending a major employer here in town."

While we might use the term *stakeholder management* instead of *marketing*, the point is that if internal stakeholders are neglected because they are not viewed as key stakeholders, negative outcomes are inevitable. Consistent with the strategic human resources management approach, competitive strategies at the corporate or business-unit level cannot be successfully implemented if they are not reinforced by involving internal stakeholders in the process (Fottler, Phillips, Blair, and Duran, forthcoming).

While most health care institutions have a personnel or human resource function, forward-thinking organizations do not expect that function alone to successfully involve employees in vecimplementing the strategic plan. One CEO expressed it as follows: "I have a VP for human resources, and his job of course is to work with or take care of those things associated with the human resources area. But the corporate image that we are trying to instill in everybody is that we are here for one reason—to serve the patient. So if an employee or group of employees have a problem, we don't just turn that over to the VP. The supervisor is involved, and I'm involved to some extent, to make sure the problem is solved. We don't just delegate that to the VP because it's so important we all need to be involved. Bad employee relations can result in bad patient and physician relations."

Involvement Tactics

The most prevalent approach to designing health care organizations calls for such features as hierarchical decision making, simple repetitive jobs at the lowest levels, professional autonomy and semiisolation, and carefully measured individual job performance. But this *control* approach appears to be losing favor, as recent literature (Lawler, 1986, 1988; Walton, 1985) has argued that we need to move toward an *involvement* or *commitment* approach to the design of work organizations. The advantages of the involvement approach are said to include higher quality services, less absenteeism and turnover, and better decision making and problem solving (Dennison, 1984).

In Chapter Three we noted that the supportive stakeholder is one who supports the institution's goals and actions and is low on potential for threat and high on potential for cooperation. Managers and staff employees (internal stakeholders) were *generally* classified as supportive. The generic strategy recommended for supportive stakeholders was to *involve* them in relevant issues to maximize their cooperative potential. Often these internal stakeholders and their cooperative potential are ignored rather than involved.

Table 11 provides an outline and overview of some possible involvement tactics for internal stakeholders. The next section discusses how these various involvement tactics might be implemented for each internal stakeholder group.

Overriding all the involvement processes described in the next section is strategic human resources management. Strategic human resources management involves linking the imple-

**Table 11. Most Appropriate Involvement Strategies for Particular
Internal Stakeholders.**

Involvement Tactic	Upper Manage- ment	Middle Manage- ment	Professional Employees	Nonpro- fessional Employees
Strategic human resources management	x	x	x	x
Role clarification	x	x	x	x
Training and development	x	x	x	x
High involvement (employees make work-unit decisions, have input to strategy decisions)		x	x	x
Job involvement (job redesign and teams)		x	x	
Recruitment/retention approaches (motivators and hygiene factors)			x	
Suggestion involvement (written suggestions and quality circles)			x	x

mentation of all human resources processes to the particular
competitive strategy being pursued (Fottler, 1990; Fottler,
Phillips, Blair, and Duran, forthcoming). Different human resource functions become more important depending on the
competitive strategy being pursued. For example, an organization pursuing a competitive strategy of differentiating itself
from the competition by providing high service or functional
quality needs a work force very aware of and responsive to
patient concerns. Such a competitive strategy would require that
all employees receive periodic training in guest relations.

Upper Management. The literature indicates that there is
a great deal of role conflict and role ambiguity among hospital
executives due to the management of interpersonal relations,
importance of the services offered, ever-changing technology,
and stakeholder groups with conflicting interests (Quick, Dalton, and Nelson, 1985; White and Wisdom, 1985). Numerous
studies across various occupations have shown role conflict and

ambiguity to be related to organizationally dysfunctional outcomes such as job dissatisfaction, unsatisfactory work group behaviors, turnover, and lower commitment to the organization (Brief, Aldag, VanSell, and Melone, 1979; Kahn and others, 1964). Previous research among health care executives shows higher levels of role conflict, role ambiguity, and job dissatisfaction in the middle level as opposed to the upper level of management (Burke, 1989; Hurka, 1980).

The major stakeholder impacting the CEO and other higher level executives and their behavior is the board of trustees. The board often recruits, approves, evaluates, rewards, and terminates individuals in these higher level positions. Their major problem seems to be the board expectation that the CEO will keep all key stakeholders satisfied; if the CEO does not, her or his job is in jeopardy. Annual hospital CEO turnover rates ranged from 17 to 24 percent nationally from 1981 to 1987 (Weil, Williams, and Carver, 1989). CEO turnover rates were higher among small hospitals, system hospitals, investor-owned hospitals, unaccredited hospitals, and hospitals with lower occupancy rates, higher costs, and lower operating margins. Not surprisingly, these executives are dissatisfied in the area of job security (Burke, 1989). Executives who are continually concerned with job security can hardly be effective long-term planners for their institutions.

There has been a recent growth of formal accountability mechanisms between the CEO and the governing board. In 1980 a majority of hospital boards (54 percent) conducted an annual performance review of their CEO, and 48 percent of those used preestablished criteria (Nigosian, 1980). Despite the growth in the formal evaluation of CEOs, only about 25 percent of governing boards conducted a formal evaluation using predetermined criteria in 1980. Thus, boards of trustees can make a major contribution to top management satisfaction and commitment by clarifying their roles and expectations concerning their performance.

Top management in health care institutions does not generally suffer from the lack of involvement often found at lower levels. However, these individuals do control mechanisms that determine the degree to which *others* do or do not feel involved in their work. How to achieve such involvement is a major challenge facing top management in health care organizations.

National Research Corporation recently conducted a telephone survey of 450 hospital CEOs across the nation (Jensen, 1989a). The four most important challenges identified by these CEOs were as follows:

1. How to work well with all types of people from doctors and nurses to food service personnel
2. How to motivate others to rally around a common vision and then get them to move toward action
3. How to grant people responsibility to make their own choices and decisions
4. How to create a core group of quality people willing to work as a team

Strategic human resources management is relevant to top management recruitment and selection, since the above challenges require a top manager to possess exceptional skills. Individuals who have demonstrated the ability or potential to meet these challenges are also more likely to be effective in attaining the organization's strategic objectives. Training and development on a periodic basis can also be used to assist managers meet the above challenges. Organizations have to decide what approaches to use to develop their top managers.

Middle Management. Middle managers include department heads, clinical managers, unit supervisors, charge nurses, and numerous other individuals having management responsibility in health care organizations. They have traditionally suffered from benign neglect vis-à-vis attention given to top executives (Kaluzny, 1989). Good programs and strategies aimed at these individuals often are not implemented or not implemented well. Turnover and absenteeism have increased. A likely explanation is that health care organizations have focused too much attention on enhancing the abilities of top management to manage strategic change and too little attention on involving middle management in the process of planning and implementing strategic change (Fottler, Phillips, Blair, and Duran, forthcoming).

In addition, most health care organizations today operate under the traditional control system that emphasizes order, control, and efficiency. The basic assumption is that the good middle manager should be able to solve any problems that come up and should be the primary (if not the only) person responsible for how the department is functioning (Bradford and Cohen, 1984). There is also mounting evidence that subordinates are less willing to follow orders on the basis of positional authority. Younger managers are less inclined to defer to authority, and they have few needs for dominance (Lawler, 1988). This is reinforced by research indicating that employees would like to have significantly more influence on a range of issues including how they do their work, work scheduling, pay raises, hiring, promotions, and organizational policy (Lawler, Renwick, and Bullock, 1981).

A common problem for middle managers in health care organizations is an inconsistency between authority and responsibility. These managers have the responsibility to achieve certain outcomes without having the authority over human and material resources to do what is necessary to achieve these outcomes. One hospital director described the dilemma as follows: "Housekeeping is critical to patient satisfaction in my unit. A lot of times the area is dirty and stays dirty for a long time. They won't tell me when they are coming or what they will do when they get here. Nor will they listen to me when I tell them what needs to be done and when. The patients complain to me, but what can I do? We should have either authority over these people or supportive supervisors who will require communication and performance."

One possible solution is to pursue a job involvement approach that involves department heads and other middle managers in working with a team of interacting professionals to redesign and restructure supervisory and nonsupervisory jobs so that authority and responsibility of supervisors are consistent, and individuals are held accountable for their own performance and that of their subordinates.

Middle management needs to redefine its roles, and executive-level managers must redefine their roles vis-à-vis middle managers (Kaluzny, 1989). A model of involvement and commitment—not control—and a new way of thinking about superior-subordinate and professional-nonprofessional relationships is needed if health care organizations are to successfully involve their internal stakeholders. Under such a system, a premium is given to adaptability, and middle- and lower-level managers are given much broader responsibility with greater involvement of all personnel in the decision-making process.

Information and decision making do not simply flow from the top to the bottom with only trivial modifications (Kaluzny, 1989). Instead, there is a great deal of emphasis on individual initiative to constantly upgrade the management system. Since a variety of skills and perspectives are necessary to adequately perform and coordinate tasks, interdisciplinary teams become the basic accountability units. Information is shared widely with full assurance that candid and open participation will not result in loss of jobs or stature in the organization. There are also a deemphasis on the control model's treatment of surveillance, inspection, and discipline and an increased emphasis on continuous improvement (Deming, 1986).

Under a system of continuous improvement, it is the job of middle managers to enhance quality by continually redesigning the patient care system to reduce variation from "common causes." The latter are random variations derived from the patient care system itself, even though it may be running strictly in accordance with its design. The involved middle manager distinguishes between common and special causes of variation from the desired standard to initiate corrective action.

The pervasive focus on quality throughout the organization and the critical role of middle management are the central themes of the emerging agenda for change in JCAHO's *Accreditation Manual for Health Care Organizations* (1989). The emphasis in this document is on quality as a function of *all* personnel in the organization and the linking of both incentives and structure to continued quality improvement.

A critical skill required of low- and middle-level managers will be the ability to build an involved and committed team. The advantage of the team approach is that it allows each individual to participate in the process, add relevant expertise, and enhance his or her commitment to the organization.

A variety of approaches can be systematically applied to build an involved and committed team. These include defining a mission and a business strategy, identifying critical success factors, identifying what has to be done to implement these success factors, and targeting those factors that will have the biggest impact on achieving the designated mission. It is crucial to involve all team members in the planning process, achieving consensus, and determining follow-through. Since some conflict is inevitable, middle managers will require skills in negotiation and conflict management.

Since the generic involvement strategy requires that individual team members have both technical and behavioral skills, the role of middle management is to develop those skills among subordinates to improve team decision making (Kaluzny, 1989). Of course, this cannot be accomplished unless the middle managers themselves possess such skills. The development of technical and behavioral skills is best achieved by an in-house developmental process (Bradford and Cohen, 1984). The process encourages task assignment to broaden subordinates' knowledge and skill with appropriate coaching and feedback by middle managers, who themselves will require monitoring and support as they engage in these activities.

Middle managers also need to infuse their respective groups with a vision of the unit relative to the total organization. This vision should unite and inspire members toward justifying extra effort, establish criteria for decision making, and help define the future. While not all individuals will have the appropriate levels of interest, motivation, and ability to benefit from an involvement approach, the role of management is to ensure that all individuals have the *opportunity* to do so.

The administrator of a mental health and substance-abuse hospital described this kind of middle-management involvement as follows:

My fundamental philosophy is that program directors are way up high in the hierarchy here. They have complete control over their programs. They are what makes this facility go; they are interwoven in all the key decisions made in this hospital. Since they know the things they should be doing, I turn all the clinical decisions over to them, let them run their programs and develop new ones. It's unbelievable the growth we have seen from just allowing them the flexibility of deciding the things they need to do as opposed to waiting for the administrator or someone else to tell them what to do. We administrators don't know enough and don't move fast enough for that. The fields of psychiatry and addiction are so specialized and have so many professional groups involved that it is impossible for one person to dictate, tell them what they need to be doing or how to accomplish a particular goal. They need autonomy to get their job done.

Professional Employees. As noted earlier, not all employees are key internal stakeholders since some have low skill levels and are easily replaced. Their stake in the organization may be very high, but they are not key *to the organization.* The major shortages today exist in professional fields such as nursing and certain allied health fields such as physical therapy, occupational therapy, medical technology, and laboratory technology. While involvement strategies are often broadly based and cover the whole work force, recruitment and retention strategies tend to focus on these critical shortage professions.

For example, day-care services for children of health care employees grew rapidly during the 1980s. One academic medical center in the Southeast recently opened a subsidized day-care center and established a priority list of personnel categories having access to the center. As one might expect, nurses and other skilled professionals had first priority. Others were eligible to receive the service only if space was available; otherwise, they would be placed on the waiting list. A Texas hospital has enhanced its recruitment and retention of nurses and other skilled personnel by offering both a day-care center and an infirmary for sick children in the same building as the day-care center. They are presently expanding both, have a waiting list, and run the facility from 7:00 A.M. to 11:00 P.M.

The executive vice-president described the motivation for development of the day-care infirmary:

> We did it for recruitment and retention of personnel, especially licensed personnel such as nurses and med techs. And it is not free. We charge a fee, and our employees pay for it. We made a tremendous effort to have the highest quality program content. It is not just a baby-sitting service; we are teaching and working with these kiddos. We also set a new higher pay standard for day-care center workers. We didn't do it totally out of benevolence. We did it to recruit and retain people, especially nurses. We are finding that almost 50 percent of our employees who have children in it are nurses. Many of them are single parents. Recently one of our competitor hospitals in town was advertising for a nursing director. We felt one of our head nurses would apply for the position, but she didn't. She later told one of our nurse directors that she couldn't face moving her three kids out of the day-care center.

Some hospitals have maintained their hospital-based diploma nursing schools to recruit and retain nurses. In most cases, the nursing school is a money loser for the hospital in terms of direct revenue and expense. However, nursing schools are kept open to facilitate nurse recruitment. One health care executive has noted, "The nursing school does not break even since tuition does not cover the costs of running the school. But if we had to recruit the nurses we get from that class in other ways, that would increase our recruitment expenses fantastically. Frankly, I don't think we could ever replace that nursing source at any expense if we didn't have the school."

Another approach to recruitment and retention of skilled professionals is job redesign. In the case of nursing, there has been a recent upgrading in the position of director of nursing services to vice-president for nursing. The change at one hospital was described as follows: "The title of vice-president of nursing was established after I got here. Prior to that there had been a number of vice-presidents, but no nursing vice-president. We felt frankly that nursing was important enough to require that level of representation on our administrative staff. We have five people whom we titled director of nursing, all of whom work for that vice-president of nursing. The vice-president is also picking up some responsibilities that are not purely nursing, and we want to encourage that. Good nursing care is the backbone of this hospital, and it has been for a long time. That is where we make our facility work and where we feel we have an edge to say to physicians, "You need to bring your patients here because we have quality nursing." We put a nurse on our senior management team, and we felt it made a statement to the nursing staff concerning how management felt about nursing."

There are also attempts in some institutions to redesign the professional nurse's role. One administrator used the term *nurse stretching* to refer to nurses' working as part of a team in a way that lets nurses perform the higher level functions while delegating the lower level functions. As another administrator noted, "Nursing is like a sponge; 40 percent of nursing functions today are nonnursing. We could improve morale and job satisfaction and reduce costs by delegating nonnursing activities."

Job involvement through redesign of the nursing role has achieved some success. For example, the vacancy rate at Beth Israel Hospital in Boston hovers around 2.5 percent, and the hospital has not raised its nurses' salaries exorbitantly (Powills, 1988). However, it has developed a primary nursing model to allow nurses to become more involved in patient management. Under the model, a primary nurse is responsible for a patient from admission to discharge, twenty-four hours a day. When that nurse is off duty, an associate nurse takes over. This method fosters a clinical ladder approach to nursing responsibility in which nurses' responsibilities directly correlate with tenure and education. According to the hospital's administrator, physicians and the administration have supported the model, and it has had a positive effect on nursing turnover and the hospital's bottom line. Similar benefits have been achieved elsewhere by collaborative practice between nurses and physicians (Cerne, 1988b).

Among both nursing and allied health personnel there has been a movement toward multiskilled health practitioners (Center for Nursing, 1989; Committee to Study the Role of Allied Health Personnel, 1989; Vaughan and Bamberg, 1989). This is basically a form of job enrichment where one or more new skills are added to the existing skills of a person already trained in one of the traditional allied health fields or nursing.

Vaughan and Bamberg (1989) found that hospitals utilizing such personnel improved their quality of care (59 percent), increased the job satisfaction of these individuals (65 percent), experienced no legal or ethical problems (96 percent), and experienced no other problems (53 percent). Other benefits mentioned included cost effectiveness, ability to recruit and retain quality employees, more efficient use of personnel, and improved employee loyalty and morale.

Another employee involvement approach used extensively with health care professionals is training and development. Many hospitals view as ends in themselves not only bonding these professionals more closely to the hospital but also managing other stakeholders such as physicians and patients. One health care executive expressed it as follows:

Our education department is geared to providing an ongoing in-service education to lots of our departments, but with particular emphasis on nursing. We think it gives us a competitive advantage in two ways. First, it is attractive for professionals to know that we have a strong educational department in house. Second, the resulting strong nursing staff attracts the physicians to want to put their patients here because they have greater confidence in the quality of nursing care. That gives us a double edge; we put a lot of resources in it, and we think we get a lot out of it. In addition, all of our training programs emphasize that patients are to be treated with kindness, dignity, and courtesy. In fact, if an employee fails to meet the standard on this one dimension of our performance appraisal, he or she is not eligible for a salary increase in that year. But we provide them with the appropriate training support through a guest-relations education program that is mandatory for all our employees. We also provide $250 for the "employee of the month" and $1,000 for the "employee of the year."

Managing patients through employees can also be done through employee attitude surveys. The assumption is that if employee attitudes are regularly monitored, suggestion involvement is provided, and adjustments are made to keep employees happy, this will be reflected in better patient care and improved patient satisfaction. One health care executive noted, "The real reason we did our employee attitude survey recently was because our employee attitudes are the starting block for our guest-relations program. We wanted to have a better feel for our employees, to understand what they want, and to allow them some direct input into decision making. We feel this is necessary for good employee relations. We want good employee relations so the employees will provide good patient relations. That was the driving force that led us to survey our employees. If our employees are happy with their employment, we believe a natural result is that they will do better in dealing with patients. If we are creating an atmosphere where they are not happy, it will come across to our patients, and we won't provide good guest relations or good quality of care.

While in-service education can attract professionals and

help the institution manage other stakeholders such as physicians and patients, it can sometimes create conflict with other stakeholders, as indicated in the following quotation:

> We are always getting new equipment, and the joint commission requires a certain amount of in-service education. So we do thirty minutes one day a month of in-service education for nurses. It seems reasonable, and three years ago we got everyone's approval to do this. Recently a couple of surgeons were setting up there and drinking coffee. They were upset that they couldn't start at 8:00 A.M. on that one morning and said the nurses should do their in-service at some other time. They didn't want to be kept waiting until 8:30 A.M. So they caused a big brouhaha over that one thirty-minute period of in-service education. They threatened to send their patients to another hospital if the in-service was not changed to another time. I talked to the director of surgery and went to a committee meeting and tried to reason with these guys. They didn't back down, and neither did we. This is a case when the hospital administrator is caught between a rock and a hard place. We have a shortage of nurses, many of whom are working mothers. If we say come in thirty minutes early for in-service education, a lot of day-care centers won't take the kiddos that early. It's just a big hassle, and so do you get the nurses and operating room people upset in order to accommodate these physicians or vice versa?

Nonprofessional Employees. One of the most common tactics for involving nonprofessional health care employees is the quality circle (QC) (Phillips and others, 1990). As a result of the publicity surrounding QC programs in industry and some service organizations, health care institutions began looking at the technique and implementing it several years ago. For example, hospitals such as Veterans Medical Center in Albany, New York; St. Joseph's in Fort Wayne, Indiana; Lakeshore Mental Health Institute of Knoxville, Tennessee; and Barnes Hospital in St. Louis, Missouri, have reported such positive results as increased employee morale and motivation and cost improvements due to QCs (Cornell, 1984; McKinney, 1984; Strader, 1987). Most of these QCs were in staff-support functions such as nursing, housekeeping, dietetics, and so on. At Central Middlesex Hospital in 1985, one QC program specific to nursing was implemented in which one of the circles reduced the incidence of pressure sores (Osborn, 1987). Foothills Provincial General Hospital in Calgary, Canada, implemented a QC program in the early 1980s that was successful in terms of human resource development (education and training), quality of care, productivity, and efficiency, although the results were not quantified (McColl, 1987). Henry Ford Hospital in Detroit, Michigan, had an extensive QC program that was said to be successful (McKinney, 1984).

In addition to the reports of successful QC programs in hospitals, there are also documentations of failures. One study of a military medical facility showed that a QC program involving 165 people reaped "little detectable improvement" in job performance and job satisfaction and concluded that if a QC program is done badly, it may actually do more harm than good (Steel, Mento, Dilla, and Lloyd, 1985). Mt. Sinai Hospital in Miami, Florida, had a QC program that included such diverse areas as work processing, housekeeping, recovery room, pharmacy, and respiratory from which actual cost savings were observed and documented. However, the Mt. Sinai QC program was later disbanded (Cornell, 1984; McKinney, 1984). Moreover, one comprehensive study of a large quality-of-work-life (QWL) program with elements similar to QCs in a hospital in the eastern United States concluded that over a three-and-a-half-year period (1974 to 1978) there were some intangible improvements in employee morale and communications but that the results did not justify the financial and human resource cost (Hanlon and Gladstein, 1984).

Considering the above examples, it is not clear whether QCs are effective. One problem in evaluating the performance of QCs in either industry or health care organizations is that measuring QC effectiveness is extremely difficult and ambiguous. Barwick and Alexander (1987) reviewed thirty-three studies that dealt with QCs in a variety of organizations (industrial, service, healthcare, and so on) in an attempt to classify these by effectiveness outcomes. Overall they found that about 49 percent showed positive results, while 51 percent showed mixed, nonsignificant, or negative results. Of the three hospitals that were included in their review, one showed positive results, and two showed mixed or nonsignificant results.

Another issue from the above examples is the length of time that QC programs are viable. Often, even the success stories do not seem to continue. Lawler and Mohrman (1985) present a life-cycle model of QCs. They explicate six phases in the life of a QC, each with its own key activities and potential threats for the QC program. These stages are as follows: (1) start-up, (2) initial problem solving, (3) approval of initial suggestions, (4) implementation, (5) expansion of problem solving, and (6) decline. The reason for the somewhat pessimistic forecast by Lawler and Mohrman is that their analysis suggests that a QC program is basically an unstable organizational structure.

Considering the many examples of successful and failed QCs (with the additional problem of how success or failure is measured), it is evident that sometimes QCs work and sometimes they do not. As discussed above, several studies showed that QCs improve quality, reduce costs, and improve morale and communications, yet there were also several studies that demonstrated QC programs failed to live up to their expectations. Obviously, whether QC programs are successful depends on the differing situations in which they are attempted and the various ways they are implemented.

A review of the quality-circle literature provides some guidelines for the design of successful quality-circle programs (Phillips and others, 1990). Obviously, the variability in QC success in both health services and general industry can be attributed to both the design and implementation of QC programs. Guidelines for a successful design and implementation of those programs are summarized in the following list.

Management supportiveness
  • Organizational diagnosis
  • Development of specific objectives
  • Estimation of costs and employee time requirements

- Support from union and management prior to program start
- Slow start, adjustments, expansion as required
- Modulated expectations of success
- Established links between QCs and upper-management levels
- Specialists made available to QCs when special expertise needed
- Acceptance of at least some proposals

Training
- Organizational hierarchy—expectations as to costs, benefits, and requirements of QCs
- QC leaders—integration of QCs into normal position requirements of supervisors and training in techniques of problem-solving and group facilitation
- QC participants—problem-solving techniques
- Other organization members—announcements and information concerning QC program

Program limits
- Voluntary participation
- Emphasis on "people building" rather than "people using"
- Emphasis on team effort rather than individual effort in QCs
- Meetings conducted during regular working hours or on paid overtime basis
- Meetings on regular basis
- Allowing QCs to choose their own problems in their immediate work area

Evaluation techniques
- Emphasis on measurable objectives
- Maintaining complete and thorough records
- Use of longitudinal design for attitudinal data
- Gathering as much cost/benefit data as possible

Management must be supportive. This is a rather broad statement with a variety of meanings and suggestions. Of course, if management is not supportive, no program will work. The basic consideration has to do with whether the organization has in place a larger participative management program, but there are other important considerations.

A very important aspect of management support is the expectations of general management. To help shape expectations as well as to determine whether a QC program is advisable, a careful diagnosis of the organization should be undertaken. Such a diagnosis ensures that a QC is appropriate and determines exactly what could be expected from such a program. A random grab for what some might consider as the latest fad to apply a quick fix to some "people problems" does not seem to hold a great deal of promise. Is a QC program an appropriate solution for the problem at hand? If so, the diagnosis should yield clear, specific objectives. Management should not introduce QCs into organizations under extreme stress; further, QCs do not appear to be a substitute for good labor-management relations and seem to work best when implemented in a stable situation. If one or more unions are involved, it is important to have the union leadership on board prior to launching the program.

A diagnosis should also include an estimate of cost and employee time requirements to minimize unpleasant surprises. Management should start a QC program slowly, allow for adjustments, then expand from a base of success. Management should also expect that some QCs will fail and not realize their objectives and should recognize the length of time it may take to effect certain improvements. Further, a QC program should not be overpromised with respect to the degree of improvement. Finally, it should be expected that some initially successful QCs will subsequently fail.

Management support also means a willingness to accept at least some proposals and implement them. In a diagnosis of a large-scale quality-of-work-life program in a large hospital, Hanlon and Gladstein (1984, p. 106) concluded: "The Parkside case suggests that the critical factor is not whether employees working in problem-solving groups are able to diagnose organizational shortcomings and offer solutions—the answer in this case is strongly affirmative. The critical factor is whether or not management is willing to provide the support necessary to implement proposals for change."

Training is necessary. Training represents the second most discussed imperative in the implementation of QCs. Training can be construed broadly—as preparing the organization to receive the QC program intervention—or narrowly—as providing instruction to individual members on problem-solving techniques. In the broader sense, the preparation of the organization to receive a QC program in at least some organizations borders on a religious conversion. There need to be pronouncements as to the good expected and assurances of the organization's support as a whole as well as in specific departments. A pilot program should be considered. QC leaders need to be trained in methods of facilitation as well as problem-solving techniques. Individual members need to have the benefits of the QC program explained and receive training in problem solving. The training of group members should emphasize that QC meetings are not complaint sessions. If supervisors are used as QC leaders, the organization should provide additional training to complement the QC-related training as part of a larger training program on good supervision.

The program needs to be voluntary. The voluntary participation principle has strong support in the literature. Five reasons for QC program failure have been noted (Herkimer, 1984). One of the five was "restricting voluntary features by goading people into joining or enforcing joining by edict."

The program needs to be conducted in certain limits. Again, a large number of articles recommend that meetings connected with a QC program occur on company time, either during normal working hours or on an overtime basis. Further, although QCs should be able to choose their own problems, they should be restricted to working on those problems affecting their immediate work area. Also, do not use a "canned" program without attempting to adapt the program to the specific organization.

Establish some sort of evaluation technique. Our review of the literature shows many missed opportunities to cite specific cost benefit estimations of large-scale QC programs. If support of management as well as of participants is important, then we suggest that evaluations go beyond short-term, attitudinal data.

In addition to the suggestion involvement offered by

quality circles and written suggestion systems, Table 11 indicates that training and development and high involvement would be appropriate involvement strategies for nonprofessional employees. In addition to the guest-relations programs discussed in the previous section, routine communication efforts aimed at two-way communication can facilitate involvement of nonprofessionals. Such efforts may take the form of retreats, informal lunches, weekly or monthly meetings, and employee attitude surveys. The important point is that employees are offered opportunities to voice dissatisfaction at the same time upper management communicates philosophy, policies, procedures, and general information.

The high-involvement approach is relatively new and tends to build on the suggestion involvement and job involvement approaches already discussed (Lawler, 1988). As noted in Table 11, it is appropriate for not only nonprofessional employees but also all employees below the level of top management. Lawler (1988, pp. 200–201) describes it as follows:

> It tends to structure an organization so that people in the lower level will have a sense of involvement not just in how they do their jobs or how effectively their group performs, but in the performance of the total organization. It goes considerably further than either of the other two approaches toward moving power, information, knowledge, and rewards to the lowest organizational level. It is based on the argument that if individuals are going to care about the performance of the organization, they need to know about it, be able to influence it, be rewarded for it, and have the knowledge and skills to contribute to it. . . . Employees are not only asked to make decisions about their work activities, they are also asked to play a role in organizational decisions having to do with strategy involvement, and other major areas. Rewards are based on the performance of the organization; hence profit sharing, gainsharing, and some type of employee ownership are appropriate.

Creating such an organization is obviously a complex task since virtually every feature of a control-oriented organization has to be redesigned. The technology to support selection, training, and compensation policies in high-involvement organizations is typically not available. This approach to management is new, and the technology has not yet been developed. There are also relatively few data available on the effectiveness of high-involvement organizations since there are so few examples to study.

The sketchy testimonial evidence that does exist on high-involvement organizations in the industrial sector generally shows superior operating results (Lawler, 1986; Peters, 1987; Schuster, 1984; Walton, 1985). There are also some supporting data indicating that companies that implement "progressive" human resource management practices achieve superior operating results (Kravetz, 1988). Of course, most of the "progressive" organizations studied would not meet our definition of a high-involvement organization, although these organizations involve employees to a greater degree than the typical organization. Finally, Luthans, Hodgetts, and Rosenkrantz's (1988) work on what differentiates *effective* managers from others indicates that those managers give a greater emphasis to communication and human resources management activities.

We know of no high-involvement organizations in the health care industry. However, a new CEO at Saint Barnabas Medical Center in Livingston, New Jersey, turned a two-year $6-million operating deficit into a $2.9-million surplus in 1987 (Cerne, 1988a). His basic philosophy was that employees drive both quality of care and financial performance. During the deficit period, when low employee morale was a severe problem, he created an operating committee to address employee concerns and provide quick solutions. He also kept employees informed concerning the financial status of the hospital on a regular basis, sharing both good news and bad. He promised that all employees would share in the financial success of the institution. The promise was kept when the surplus for 1986 was used to provide salary increases for nurses and other employees. These efforts were designed to instill employee pride and help market the hospital from within.

A high-involvement approach is not universally good for all organizations. If an organization has complex work, interdependent tasks, and managers who value employee involvement and change, it is possible to move to a high-involvement approach. Health care organizations are characterized by the first two criteria and may or may not be chacterized by the latter two.

The Internal Stakeholder Involvement Process

In a parallel fashion to the strategic implementation literature (Hrebiniak and Joyce, 1984), Figure 41 outlines a seven-step process for involving internal stakeholders in health care organizations. The first step is to formulate the organization's business strategy. This is done in the usual way through an environmental analysis consisting of an internal and external assessment. The external assessment process focuses on external environmental opportunities and threats, while internal assessment considers the organization's strengths and weaknesses. Among these strengths and weaknesses are those related to human resources. The mission of the organization is also considered.

After the business strategy is formulated, the organization needs to determine the key internal stakeholders who are most necessary to successfully implement the particular business strategy. The specific behaviors required of these internal stakeholders also need to be identified. For example, if the organization chooses to differentiate itself in terms of functional quality (patient perception of quality), then the development of sensitive, caring attitudes and behaviors among all employees is in order.

These internal stakeholder goals and the generic strategy need to be translated into specific involvement tactics and programs such as guest relations and quality circles. In the example given above, a formalized and continuing program in guest relations would be appropriate. Other possible involve-

Figure 41. Internal Stakeholder Involvement Process.

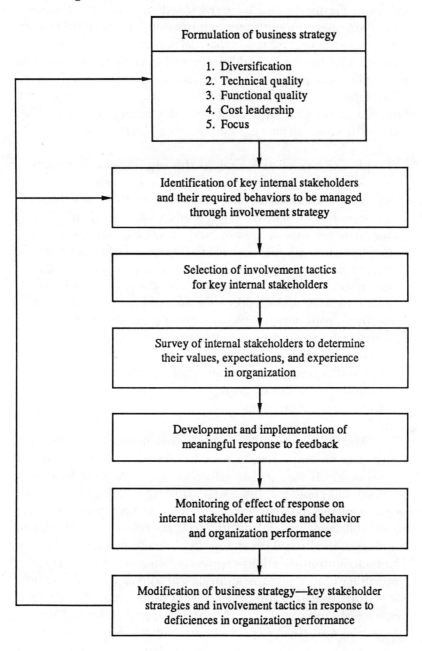

ment strategies to reinforce a functional quality strategy are shown in Figure 41 and were discussed earlier in the chapter.

Any involvement approach rests on a foundation of data concerning the organization's internal stakeholders. In fact, these internal stakeholders should be viewed as customers, similar to physicians and patients. This means internal stakeholders are viewed not only as a means of managing other stakeholders but also as an end in themselves. MacStravic (1989, p. 398) makes the case for viewing employees as customers:

> Employees are clearly vital to the organization's success and survival. They have competing choices as to whether to work in the health care field at all, or if so, which organization to work for. They daily exchange their labor for whatever mix of positive and negative experiences and benefits the organization offers. Their satisfaction is reflected not only in whether they return to work each day but also in the levels of quality, productivity, efficiency, and customer satisfaction they contribute. If thought of as loyal customers, employees are logical targets for customer relations techniques. Because their experiences with the organization occur daily, in contrast to the unpredictable and infrequent experience of patients, it is sensible to employ techniques geared to loyal frequent customers in managing employees.

MacStravic (1989) suggests gathering systematic and periodic data on employees to complement this approach. He also recommends focusing this effort on what we would call key internal stakeholders, but not excluding any employee category from the data-gathering process. Among the initial data to be collected are (1) the financial contribution potential of employees in general or any particular subcategory (the financial contribution of a 50 percent reduction in turnover), (2) a determination of what organizational and managerial factors satisfy or dissatisfy employees in general and particular subcategories of employees, and (3) employee perceptions of the organization and their experience in it in terms of each dimension identified. The latter should include probing questions concerning why a particular rating was given and what could be done to improve the rating. To protect the anonymity of employee respondents, this employee feedback should be gathered through confidential questionnaires.

Once these data have been collected and analyzed, they should be reported openly and completely, specific responses should be developed and implemented as soon as possible, and these responses should be announced to call employees' attention to them (MacStravic, 1989). The responses will probably include but not be limited to the involvement strategies discussed earlier in this chapter. This approach will demonstrate that the organization is responsive to employee concerns and action oriented.

Once feedback has been published and responses are made and announced, the employee reaction needs to be monitored. To monitor progress in addressing significant problem areas, a special survey may be used after a fairly short interval. In smaller work units, less formal monitoring of employee reaction, such as group discussions, may be used. This step may affect the employees' values, expectations, and experience in the organization so that future responses may be different than those in the original survey.

Overall organization performance also needs to be monitored to determine how successfully the business strategy is being implemented. Obviously, factors other than employee involvement could affect the success of the business strategy and the organization's performance. In any case, deficiencies in performance should lead to modifications of the strategy, key stakeholders, and involvement strategies. These modifications then become the basis for another reassessment of internal stakeholder values, expectations, and experiences. This iterative process continues, and the steps are repeated as employee involvement increases and organizational performance improves.

Employee participation in a feedback process will give employees a greater sense of control over their environment. It should also enhance the quantity and quality of employee suggestions and the employees' sense of participation, job satisfaction, commitment, retention, and productivity.

Summary and Managerial Implications

Since internal stakeholders are fundamentally supportive of the organization, the appropriate generic strategy of involvement must be implemented through a variety of specific tactics. Successful management of key external and interface stakeholders and even other internal stakeholders depends on how health care organizations involve their own internal stakeholders in the process. Indeed, these internal stakeholders should be viewed (but are sometimes not viewed) as key stakeholders in and of themselves. Involvement tactics include role clarification, training and development, high-involvement approaches (not usually found in practice), job involvement, recruitment and retention approaches, suggestion involvement, and the much publicized guest-relations programs (Peterson, 1988).

The process of involving internal stakeholders begins with formulation of the organization's business strategy. Then the key internal stakeholders and required behaviors necessary for successful business strategy implementation are identified. Next, involvement tactics and programs for these key stakeholders are selected to best match the needs of these key stakeholders and their required behaviors. Then internal stakeholders are surveyed to determine their values, expectations, and organizational experiences. Responses to this feedback are developed and implemented, and the effect of these responses on employee attitudes and behavior is monitored. The organization's overall performance is also monitored at that time. On the basis of these data, the organization's business strategy, key stakeholders, and involvement strategies are modified and the process repeated continuously.

The process of involving internal stakeholders in managing other stakeholders and as an end in itself should benefit both the organization and its internal stakeholders. The motivation, commitment, productivity, and retention of employees should be greater, resulting in improved patient satisfaction, relations with other stakeholders, and overall organization performance. Here we have discussed how known micro-management approaches and programs can be integrated into overall stakeholder management strategy at the macro level and, thereby, more explicitly connected to macro competitive strategy.

CHAPTER 9

ⵣⵎⵣⵎⵣⵎⵣⵎⵣⵎⵣⵎⵣⵎⵣⵎⵣⵎⵣⵎⵣⵎⵣⵎⵣ

Stakeholder Management Today and Tomorrow

The strategic stakeholder management approach discussed throughout this book provides both theoretical and practical advantages over previous management theory. The major advantage is an integration of macro-level (strategic) concerns and micro-level (operational) actions. This means that day-to-day management activities need to focus on key stakeholders who are crucial to the attainment of the strategic objectives under the particular manager's area of control. This approach is appropriate for a manager, an individual organization, or an entire industry.

The present chapter will step back and look at several key issues not yet fully addressed earlier by

- Contrasting economic and stakeholder approaches to managing organizations
- Discussing one fundamental challenge for executives: managing stakeholders strategically
- Examining, in depth, an equally fundamental executive challenge: managing stakeholders ethically
- Discussing possible *future* stakeholders
- Outlining scholarly challenges for researchers

Finally, this chapter will try to put the pieces all together in summarization.

Economic Versus Stakeholder Approaches to Managing Organizations

Stakeholder Model. The traditional stakeholder, and the only one of importance to scholars such as Milton Friedman, is the stockholder (Friedman, 1962). Stockholders own the corporation, and the manager of the publicly held corporation is legally and ethically bound to earn the highest rate of return on their investment. In this view, the corporation is believed to be an exclusively economic institution with no responsibilities to society other than to produce economic wealth and maximize the return on the stakeholders' investment.

This model is an extremely simplistic and narrow view of the function of the modern corporation in our society. The corporation was invented and developed primarily to meet societal needs, both economic and noneconomic. The simplistic economic model is even less relevant to the health care industry, where most institutions are still not proprietary and human service continues to exert a powerful influence on organizational behavior. Many health care organizations do not even have private stockholders.

The stakeholder management approach provides an alternative conceptual framework to the Friedman approach. The stakeholder concept broadens the groups to which the organization is responsive and responsible beyond the stockholder and considers noneconomic as well as economic concerns. Different stakeholders use different criteria to determine how well the organization is performing and judge management actions by their effects on the stakeholders' interests. Thus, management needs to be aware not only of the key stakeholders in the organization's environment but also of the criteria each stakeholder uses to judge organizational performance.

All of the health care executives whom we interviewed indicated that managing actual or likely stakeholder demands is basically what they do on a day-to-day basis. While there were some differences in which stakeholders were identified (depending on the nature of the institution and the individual's position in it), there was no disagreement that their job primarily involves balancing the various stakeholders and trying to keep them at least minimally satisfied. The latter has become a greater challenge in recent years as competition has increased and available resources for satisfying the various stakeholders have diminished.

An organization that responds to a large number of various stakeholders, many of which have noneconomic interests, is different from a purely economic institution responding to only stockholders. The organization must then be viewed as a multipurpose institution, not solely as an economic institution, since stakeholder interests range through a gamut of economic, social, and political concerns. In responding to these concerns, the organization becomes a multipurpose institution that produces economic and social betterment using its resources to deal effectively with social issues in its purview.

This view of the organization as a multipurpose institution is different from traditional economic theory. Rather than seeking only to maximize profits, the multipurpose organization seeks to balance the interests of its various stakeholders so that each receives at least some degree of satisfaction (inducements are sufficient to elicit contributions necessary to the organization). Rather than relying solely on an economic calculus to make major decisions about resource allocation, the multipurpose institution relies on compromises and negotiation to make such decisions. The key is balance among the various stakeholder interests.

In the final analysis, the stakeholder concept is political rather than economic. One important implication is that strategy formulation and implementation need to be based on both economic and political rationality. The latter requires that the interests of *all* stakeholders be considered and that the interests of key stakeholders be weighed most heavily. The stakeholder concept ties together economic, political, and social responsibilities in the framework of strategic management.

The stakeholder approach presented here goes beyond the social responsibility approach typically presented as an alternative to Friedman's neoclassical economic view. Neither of the latter two approaches provides a systematic method of analyzing all of the stakeholders, determining their power bases and needs, and managing them through maintaining an inducement:contributions equilibrium. Friedman's view is that the only stakeholder worth worrying about is the stockholder and the only inducement necessary is an economic return. The "social responsibility" approach views both stockholders and those needing various social services as appropriate stakeholders. However, there is no consideration of what kind of contributions the latter can make to the organization. Our approach considers both contributions and inducements for all stakeholders.

A statement by the Business Roundtable (1981, pp. 8–9) sums up our model of managerial behavior: "Carefully weighing the impacts of decisions and balancing different constituent interests in the context of both near-term and long-term effects must be an integral part of the corporation's decision-making and management process. Resolving the differences involves compromises and tradeoffs. It is important that all sides be heard but impossible to assure that all will be satisfied because competing claims may be mutually exclusive. Balancing the stockholder's expectations of maximum return against other priorities is one of the fundamental problems confronting corporate management. The shareholder must receive a good return but the legitimate concerns of other constituencies also must have the appropriate attention."

Implications of Stakeholder Model. This description of the stakeholder management model is of more than theoretical interest—it is of immense practical value. How you *define* the nature of an organization determines what you *do* as an organization. If a health care organization is defined purely as an economic institution, then it will behave differently and be less responsive to stakeholders not directly impacting the bottom line than will a similar organization that defines itself according to the stakeholder model. Likewise, *whom* you define as a key stakeholder determines what you *do* as an institution. For example, if a hospital does not define community leaders as key stakeholders, a decision regarding the discontinuance of a desired (but unprofitable) service is unlikely to take their concerns into account. A negative community reaction could hurt the hospital for years to come.

Long-term survivability of both the CEO and the institution is threatened if stakeholders are not managed effectively. As noted in cases cited earlier, such as the federal government's swine-flu immunization program and the case of National Healthcare, failure to consider all of the key stakeholders can threaten the organization's survival.

On a more positive note, Kaluzny and Shortell (1987, pp. 29–31) have described the significance of health care stakeholder management as follows:

> Health care involves diverse constituencies—health care professionals, employees, consumers, investors—and all have special needs. Health-care executives must sustain a balance between these groups. . . . If you want to develop a high performing organization, commit to managing strategically at all levels. Look at developing long-term, sustainable and balanced interests among the groups you serve.

The content of "managing strategically at all levels" noted above refers to three levels of strategy formulation and implementation: (1) the corporate level, where product market decisions about entering, withdrawing, or remaining in an industry are considered; (2) the business level, where the focus of strategy is how to compete in an industry; and (3) the functional level, where operational decisions are of concern (Fahey and Narayanan, 1986, p. 189).

At the corporate level a decision to eliminate a money-losing emergency department serving primarily minority patients with little or no health insurance or other means of payment may make good economic sense. Other similar de-marketing efforts directed at this segment of patients may also appear to be economically attractive. However, important political stakeholders as well as the minority community in general may be aroused and react very negatively. There may be some political repercussions in terms of reduced government funding, adverse publicity in the media, and future conflict. Reconciling these economic and political concerns with the humanitarian mission of most health care organizations requires considerable skill.

At the business level, strategy focuses on how to compete effectively in a given market selected in the corporate strategy. The way a particular institution chooses to compete in a given market niche is affected by how that organization defines its key stakeholders. One religious hospital in the Southwest decided to compete with another local hospital that was already offering helicopter service from outlying areas. Since the existing service was not overburdened and additional service was not needed, this competitive action aroused considerable negative reaction among the other three community hospitals as well as the hospital already offering the service. It was clear that since the move was designed to take patients away from the first hospital, the second hospital did not consider other competitor hospitals as key stakeholders. The long-term impact of that decision was that the other hospitals in town began to initiate and implement various joint ventures with one another, some of which have been successful. These joint ventures have limited growth of the hospital that initiated the second helicopter service. The "cutthroat" approach to competition that ignored the other hospitals and did not view them as key stakeholders failed in the long run.

At the functional or operational level, well-conceived corporate or business strategies often fail due to a failure to involve the internal stakeholders in the process. The implementation of strategy requires that the right people be available with the right skills ready to work together with other team members. If the organization does not define its own employees as key stakeholders and does nothing to build commitment to the organization, the best corporate or competitive strategies will fail.

Challenges for Executives

In this section we address two difficult challenges in managing stakeholders effectively: doing so *strategically* and doing so *ethically*.

Managing Stakeholders Strategically. One of the major gaps in both the management and the health care literature is the gap between strategic planning, on one hand, and the day-to-day operational activities of managers, on the other. The strategic level is typically concerned with macro considerations of fitting the organization to the environment. Alternatively, the manager's day-to-day activities focus on interactions with various individuals and groups both external and internal to the organization (stakeholders). The later micro orientation is not systematically connected to the macro strategic goals of the organization in either the literature or practice.

Stakeholder management relates the macro and micro levels by drawing attention to the middle (meso) level, where managers identify, assess, diagnose, classify, and otherwise manage their particular stakeholders. How well these stakeholders are managed will determine how successful the organization will be in implementing the business strategy and in achieving the organization's goals. The organization attempts to induce the key stakeholders to provide necessary contributions by offering them the necessary inducements. The types and levels of such inducements necessary will change over time as both the organization and the stakeholders adjust their expectations in response to a changing environment.

What distinguishes a more successful organization from a less successful organization is the degree to which it is able to focus its managers' attention on the strategic goals of the organization as the day-to-day activities are performed. This requires that managers

- Focus their attention on the key stakeholders necessary for successful implementation of business strategy

- Develop an explicit, systematic strategy for managing each stakeholder
- Implement the planned stakeholder management strategy by providing the appropriate inducements for key stakeholders
- Continually adjust the inducements-contributions exchange to achieve equilibrium in an ever-changing environment
- Continually monitor the stakeholders' relationship so that threats of discontributions from key stakeholders can be anticipated and then minimized through the strategic stakeholder management process
- Focus day-to-day interactions on achieving stakeholder management outcomes, which in turn are related to the organization's desired business strategy and overall outcomes

The astute health care executive will constantly monitor the environment to identify emerging key stakeholders, the management of whom will be significant for future organizational survival and performance. These emerging stakeholders need to be assessed in terms of their potential impact and then managed based on the principles discussed throughout this book.

Throughout the book we have argued for this strategic approach. Now we look at a potential down side that occurs if short-term business success becomes the *only* basis for strategic actions.

Managing Stakeholders Ethically. All of the health care executives whom we interviewed agreed that the stakeholder management concept makes good sense because it describes what health care managers actually do. Some added that an ability to understand whom the key stakeholders are, what they want, and how to meet their needs while simultaneously achieving your own is crucial to personal success as a manager.

One middle manager stated this position: "You need to develop rapport with each key stakeholder so that you have loyalty and commitment on both sides. Otherwise the stakeholder may manage you. My ability to manage stakeholders affects my viability in this institution. I don't have a lot of formal authority, so if I can't develop support for what I'm trying to do, I can't accomplish anything. I need to be continually developing a stakeholder support system. Then once I have it, I need to be continually educating them concerning our programs, what we can do for them, and what we need from them. They don't teach this stuff in school."

Another stated the role of stakeholder management in the career success of health care executives differently: "In the long run a *successful* manager in health care must also be *effective*. The "good ol' boy" politician will not survive in the present environment. People who will rise in the future will be those with operating or line experience because these individuals have to deal with many more stakeholders than do those with staff experience. The higher up in the organization an executive rises, the more likely he or she will be managing external or interface stakeholders."

Despite this general support for the stakeholder approach to health care management, there are some caveats. This approach could be used in a very cynical and manipulative manner so that the needs of the stakeholder are considered only to the degree necessary to induce their contributions.

One health care executive expressed that concern as follows: "The stakeholder management concept makes sense because it describes what we actually do. However, we all need to be careful not to use it in a cynical manner. How you manage your stakeholders should reflect your organization's core values as expressed in your mission statement. You should attempt to understand your stakeholder's interests, concerns, needs, wants, goals, and priorities. Then you need to determine how you can *simultaneously* meet their needs as well as your own. Finally, you need to follow up to make sure that your management of the stakeholder has been properly implemented and (if not) to make appropriate adjustments."

Other health care executives had additional guidelines for ethically managing stakeholders. The following were mentioned most often:

- Never lie to employees or other stakeholders.
- Don't sacrifice a long-term relationship with stakeholders for a short-term gain.
- Follow up on every promise or commitment that you make.
- Do not put people off—respond in some way to their concerns.
- Do not play one group against another.
- Provide the same information to all stakeholders.
- Always tell the patient or patient family the truth and treat them with dignity and respect.

There was a great deal of emphasis on implementation of these guidelines as a means of building a long-term relationship of trust with each stakeholder. This was expressed by one health care executive as follows: "Probably the most important strategy is to develop a relationship or an attitude of trust between the leadership of the hospital and each of the key stakeholders. When we say something, they can have confidence that we mean it. A part of that trust is that the stakeholder can feel like there is honest listening and an openness to hearing their suggestions, problems, and comments. Then we implement an active program to act on these things in a positive fashion. The goal is mutual respect and trust on both sides."

The following quotation gives an idea of the concern many health care executives have for treating each patient with dignity and respect:

The nature of health services is that it often requires certain procedures that are not particularly dignified or comfortable. We do our darnedest to maintain the individual's dignity during these procedures, to maintain a personal relationship with them and treat them like people. Sometimes we forget that hospital patients are taken from an environment where they have a lot of control and put it in a foreign environment when they have very little control. I won't say it's hostile to them, but it's one where almost all of us would choose not to have to need it if we had a choice. So we have people in a position where they would rather not be if they had a choice. What is common to us because we do it all the time is not common to them. It may be the only time in their life they have ever gone through it; most of them are a little afraid to begin with because they are sick. Treat them like people, remembering dignity, courtesy, kindness, and the importance of explaining everything very clearly.

The bottom line is that in the health care field, perhaps more than any other, management involves moral issues and moral choices (Kaluzny and Shortell, 1987). Viewing the health care industry strictly as a business destroys its basic meaning. Since we cannot ignore economic performance, we must maintain a balance between the values of business and health care, taking into account both the organization's fundamental mission and its resource limitations. Balancing these goals has become more complex as technology, economic constraints, and the number of stakeholders have increased over time.

Every stakeholder management and negotiating strategy carries ethical implications, inasmuch as each indicates a preferred way of dealing with the other persons (and groups) in ways that significantly affect them. Hence, every one of these strategies—as well as every business strategy—can be understood as an ethical position. As a consequence, *merely* having an ethical code or *merely* setting up an extensive diagnostic process begs the following questions: Are the generic stakeholder management strategies proposed in this book (involve, collaborate, defend, and monitor) or the business strategy that drives them acceptable from an ethical point of view? The answer requires a systematic assessment of which stakeholders will be helped or hurt by a particular strategy and to what degree.

The inducements:contributors equilibrium discussed throughout this book has significant ethical implications. The concept is noncoercive in the sense that it is based on free exchange of values. Neither side is forced to offer or accept an inducement or to offer or accept a contribution. However, particular inducements or contributions might be illegal, immoral, or unethical. For example, offering or accepting kickbacks for patient referrals would fall in all three categories even though the exchange of inducements and contributors was freely entered into by both parties. Thus, managers need to evaluate the ethical nature and impact of the inducements they offer to various stakeholders as well as the contributions they receive from each.

Unethical Stakeholder Management: Case of National Healthcare. The Cleveland Clinic case discussed in Chapter One reflects mismanagement of stakeholders by failing to appreciate which other groups or organizations also have stakes in the clinic's action and having no effective strategies to manage such stakeholders' likely defensive reactions. Another case provides a very different stakeholder mismanagement situation. In this case, there is a pattern of deception and unethical stakeholder management promulgated by a company over several years.

During the mid 1980s the nation's fastest growing proprietary hospital company was National Healthcare, (based at the time) in Dothan, Alabama. The company was founded in 1981 to integrate hospital and health care services to rural communities in eleven states. Its basic strategy was growth by acquisition of rural hospitals. After founding National Healthcare in 1981, Stephen L. Phelps charmed investors with pep rallies where employees would sing the company anthem. He once called his company "a cross between Amway and Herbalife" and the "Wal-Mart" of health care. While large hospital companies were avoiding rural hospitals due to the lack of economic resources in rural areas, National Healthcare went on a buying spree, confidently stating in a 1986 prospectus that it could turn around an unprofitable facility in thirty to sixty days (Beam, 1987).

At the time, about the only disbelievers were some of the company's disgruntled former employees, who alleged that the company altered the financial statements of its hospitals, played fast and loose with its bookkeeping, and stifled its creditors while home office executives had their own fleet of aircraft. Administrators who had lived in their small communities for years suddenly found themselves embarrassed by cash management policies for suppliers that one administrator described as "don't pay until they cut you off." The following is a description of National Healthcare's dishonesty (Beam, 1987, p. 2): "Bruno Santa Rosa stopped by the Elba General Hospital in Elba, AL, to make his rounds one day in June 1985 and found that he had six new patients, complete with names on their room doors and charts at the nurses station. When he asked about them, he says the hospital's administrator told him the "patients" were actually employees who were ordered into hospital beds so that visiting "investors from New York" wouldn't see so many empty rooms. The administrator said he had "orders from the top" of the hospital's operator, National Healthcare, Inc., Dr. Santa Rosa says."

In 1986 *Forbes* magazine wrote a glowing report that called the company "up and coming" and estimated earnings for the fiscal year ending June 30 at $4.3 million or 53 cents a share (Beam, 1987). While the magazine was on the newsstand, the company announced that an unexpected increase in its provision for contractual allowances would lower earnings to $3.1 million or 38 cents a share. The news got worse in January 1987, when the company first estimated an additional $7 million in pretax charges for the second quarter, most of it for bad debts and contractual allowances, but said the year would be profitable (Beam, 1987). In 1987, *INC* magazine listed the company as number five on the magazine's list of the top hundred fastest growing small public companies. Analysts fawned over the company, as did a group of bankers led by Citicorp, Inc., which extended a $150-million line of credit to fuel an acquisition binge.

In February 1987, the company said the second quarter pretax charge would be $9.1 million and there would a loss for the year. By mid 1987 the company's modern tower, once a symbol of its prosperity, had more empty desks than employees. On September 3 there was another layoff, including the vice-president, whose final act was to release the announcement about the layoff. There was also an announcement that the company expected to report a \$19.5-million loss for its fourth quarter ending June 30.

Between September and November 1987, six senior executives, essentially the men who founded the company, resigned. Three of them sat on the board of directors (Barber, 1987). Two other board members who were corporate officers also resigned. Analysts who watched the company described it as a "total housecleaning." Later there was also a class-action lawsuit, which was settled out of court. Those who knew Phelps described him as an entrepreneurial and motivational genius who did not like to hear bad news. His philosophy was not to acknowledge that something could go wrong.

A new management team headed by James T. McAfee, Jr., picked up the pieces and moved the company to Atlanta in early 1988. In January 1989, National Healthcare restructured \$133.5 million in bank debt contingent on National reaching new terms with bond holders. For the fiscal year ended June 30, 1989, the company reported a record net loss of \$37.6 million, or \$3.63 a share (Lutz, 1989). The company has since sold many money-losing rural hospitals and barely manages to survive as a significantly smaller corporation.

In this example, stakeholder mismanagement was a function more of deception than of incompetence. Stockholders, suppliers, employees, community representatives, political figures, and the financial community were all consciously deceived. The stakeholder management approach outlined in this book argues for the systematical integration and application of strategies to manage stakeholders, not to manipulate them unethically. The exchanges of inducements and contributions between the organization and its stakeholders were in disequilibrium even though the stakeholders were not initially aware of the various deceptions.

Nature of Ethical Challenge. Studies in the business corporate sector show that a significant majority of managers reported that they feel pressured to compromise their personal ethics to achieve corporate goals ("Pressure to Compromise

Personal Ethics," 1977). The amount of such pressure depended where the managers were in the corporate hierarchy. Those at lower levels felt more pressure to compromise their personal ethics than those higher up (Carroll, 1975). Relations with superiors are a major cause of ethical conflict. Supervisors often pressure middle- and lower-level managers to support incorrect views, sign false documents, overlook superiors' wrongdoing, and do business with superiors' friends (Brenner and Molander, 1977). In the National Healthcare case, however, the problem was the lack of ethical stakeholder management at the top.

These moral and ethical problems are rather obvious because they involve individual organizational participants in illegal activities. While these types of illegal activities obviously also exist in the health care industry, most ethical issues are more complex. Often there are competing courses of action, each of which has some benefits, costs, and probabilities. There are no certainties, and several stakeholders have an interest in the decision. The choice is not between good or evil but between two goods with some evils attached. The relative significance of these goods and evils depends on which stakeholders are consulted or otherwise involved in the decision. The example of indigent care is explored later in this chapter.

Obviously, typical stakeholder management requires the health care executive to go beyond merely avoiding illegalities. The reason is that the law and ethical behavior are only loosely related. Proactive responses to ethical issues are more likely to be ethical since they go beyond minimum legal requirements. The complication is that some legal activities may not be socially responsible (for example, transferring indigent patients to public hospitals). Thus, ethical responsibilities impose expectations for responses that exceed legal responsibilities.

Finally, organizations that wish to go beyond being merely ethical may assume "discretionary responsibilities" (Carroll, 1979). These are truly proactive kinds of actions that are highly desirable from a social viewpoint, although not expected or required. One example is the Corporate Angel Network (CAN), in which corporations use their airplanes to carry cancer victims and their families without charge to needed medical treatment far from their own communities (Bedeian, 1989, p. 598). Some hospital medical staffs provide voluntary health education information by telephone or through the media.

These activities are discretionary, go beyond mere compliance with the law, and benefit society as a whole as well as certain specific stakeholders in particular. The managerial issue to be considered is in what discretionary activities (if any) the health care organization should be involved, given limited resources. Resources used to benefit one stakeholder are not available to benefit others. Implicit in this decision is a decision regarding which stakeholders deserve discretionary resources.

A process for making ethical decisions needs to be approached from a stakeholder management viewpoint. The particular decision made and its outcome are often a function of *which* stakeholders are considered as key stakeholders to be consulted and considered in the decision-making process. Since the values and perceptions of various stakeholders may differ from one another as well as from those of the health care executive, the process of arriving at an ethical decision in the management of stakeholder inducements and contributions is problematical.

Stakeholder Management Ethical Guidelines. Health care executives are in a position to significantly shape the ethical climate of their organizations by the actions they take or do not take. The most important factor is top management leadership. Top management can influence the organization through its ability to set a highly visible personal example of sound ethical action and policy. What management does is more important than what it says. Other top management actions that will encourage a strong ethical climate include setting realistic goals, developing ethical codes, disciplining violators, providing procedures to report wrongdoing, creating and enhancing an ethics committee, and training managers in ethical concepts. Kaluzny and Shortell (1987) also suggest that top management examine the ethical implications of every program, service, structure, and procedure.

Laura Nash (1981) has developed a series of questions a manager might pose to help examine the ethics of a managerial decision. Several of these deal with stakeholder relations:

- How would you define the problem if you stood on the other side of the fence?
- To whom and to what do you give your loyalty as a person and a member of the corporation?
- Whom could your decision or action injure?
- Could you disclose without qualm your decision or action to your supervisor, your chief executive officer, the board of directors, your family, and society as a whole?

An even tougher question might be: How willing are you to discuss your decision on national television with Mike Wallace from "Sixty Minutes" next Sunday evening? If you would look forward to the national exposure because explaining your decision would enhance your organization's image, the decision is probably ethical.

The American College of Healthcare Executives (1988) has also developed a code of ethics for health care executives. Table 12 provides a summary of those ethical guidelines that specifically involve relationships with stakeholders. Traditionally, ethical issues often were considered in the purview of the patient, the patient's family, the physician, and the administrator. These guidelines implicitly recognize the diversity of stakeholders who are impacted by and therefore need to be involved in such decisions.

Implementation of the generic stakeholder strategies discussed in Chapter Four and various specific stakeholder strategies discussed throughout the book are fraught with ethical implications. For example, the monitoring of marginal stakeholders may be more or less ethical. The organization might only monitor a marginal stakeholder to protect itself from this stakeholder's demands and resist unwelcome proposals. Alternatively, it might monitor the marginal stakeholder to determine if the stakeholder's interests, concerns, needs, wants, goals, and priorities have changed in a way that will allow the orga-

**Table 12. American College of Health Care Executives Ethical
Guidelines Relevant to Stakeholder Management.**

Guideline	Stakeholders
Avoid exploitation of professional relationship for personal gain.	Other health care executives, physicians
Conduct both competitive and cooperative activities in ways that improve community health services.	Other health care organizations, local citizens
Respect customs and practices of patients, clients, and others served consistent with organization's philosophy.	Patients
Be truthful in all forms of professional and organizational communication.	Employees, patients, other institutions, media, physicians, third-party payers, government regulators
Avoid practicing or facilitating discrimination and institute safeguards to prevent discriminatory organization practices.	Employees, patients
Ensure existence of process that will advise patients of rights, opportunities, responsibilities, and risks regarding available health services.	Patients
Conduct all personal and professional relationships so those affected are ensured that management decisions are made in best interest of organization and individual served by it.	Employees, patients, general public
Accept no gifts or benefits offered with intention of influencing a management decision.	Suppliers
Work to ensure that all people have reasonable access to health care services.	Indigent patients, other local citizens, other health care organizations

Source: Material extracted from American College of Healthcare
Executives, 1988, pp. 1–8.

nization to *mutually* meet the stakeholder's goals as well as its own. The latter approach indicates a more ethical approach than the former.

Defending against the nonsupportive stakeholder (competitor) might also be done more or less ethically. The cutthroat competition sometimes seen in general industry has no place in the health care industry. Approaching market competition from this perspective is unethical because it leaves out the needs of the community, which may be best served with having more (rather than fewer) alternatives for a given service. Likewise, an ethical approach to an investigative media is best served by open and honest communication rather than merely trying to use the media to manipulate public opinion.

Collaboration with a mixed-blessing stakeholder could be done in a way that does not facilitate the long-term interests of that stakeholder. For example, involving physicians in joint ventures where the physicians might experience conflict-of-interest problems or lose money would not be an ethical approach to collaboration. Rather, the long-term needs of the stakeholder with which the organization is collaborating need to be understood and supported.

The major contribution of the stakeholder approach to ethical decision making in health care organizations is to recognize the importance of considering *all* relevant key stakeholders *before* sensitive decisions are made. Which stakeholders are considered and involved often determines what decisions get made. The following section will illustrate this.

Ethical Dilemma of Indigent Care. There are a large number of ethical issues that health care executives and health care professionals must deal with on a continual basis. Among the most significant of these are access to health services on the part of indigent patients, AIDS patients, and rural residents; the right to die for terminal and nonterminal patients; the use of animals in medical research; funding and quality of care for patients in public hospitals and those supported by Medicare and Medicaid; the impact of rising malpractice insurance on access to care; the relative expenditures for high-tech rather than preventive medicine; and various linkages between physician ownership of facilities and referral patterns.

One health care executive we interviewed criticized the medical community for performing extraordinary procedures on terminally ill patients: "In my opinion the number-one reason for the high cost of health care is physician greed. I see it all the time. These poor people who are terminally ill are not going to get better. Yet these physicians take them in and do all kinds of procedures. The physicians scope them and do fancy surgery on them; then the patient ends up dying. Then the physicians submit their bills and charge those big rates. Now that is inhumane. Why not make what time is left for the patient as comfortable as possible? Maybe they need to have some medications or IV supplements, but let them have some quality of life."

Since it is impossible to cover all of these ethical dilemmas here, we will examine only indigent care in some detail. The issue of indigent care affects all types of health institutions in all parts of the country. Thirty-seven million Americans were without health insurance in 1988 (Southwick, 1988). Most of these are either unemployed, are out of the labor force, or work for a marginal employer that does not offer health insurance. The number of uninsured could grow as medical tests to identify persons at risk for serious disease (such as AIDS) become more widespread. Insurers and employers are beginning to deny coverage or boost premium costs for people whom tests identify as candidates for major health problems.

Yet hospital margins are declining due to increasing pressure from the prospective payment system and other third-party payers. The demand for services continues to increase while the ability of the delivery system to absorb the costs of caring for the uninsured and the underinsured has diminished. Health organizations are increasing cost shifting from the uninsured to the insured patients. State and local funding for indigent care is woefully inadequate relative to the magnitude of the problem. Individuals lacking health insurance usually do not have the personal resources to pay their own medical bills.

The result is a rationing of health services that begins with the growing discrepancy in the quality of care and the range of services available to public hospitals as compared to major private institutions, to inner city and rural areas compared to more affluent communities, and to the uninsured compared to the insured. The challenge for the individual institution as well as for society as a whole is that all patients receive the most critically needed care while the institution remains financially viable.

The cause of this crisis is not a failure of the delivery system itself or its individual institutions. Rather, it grows out of the nation's inability to define what we expect of our health care system and what we are willing to pay through our taxes and insurance premiums to have those expectations met. The government has shifted the issue of rationing to the individual hospitals by underpaying them. Even though this is a societal problem that should be addressed through public policy, it has not been except in a very piecemeal fashion.

Several proposals have been made to deal with the indigent care problem. These include (Easterbrook, 1987)

• Requiring all employers to provide adequate insurance while making those not employed eligible for Medicaid
• Passing national legislation that makes it illegal for doctors or hospitals to refuse any emergency patient and for hospitals to transfer any indigent for other than medical reasons
• Including catastrophic insurance coverage as a mandatory component of public and private insurance

Obviously, none of these proposals has been enacted. As a consequence, each health care institution has had to deal with the problem at the local level. Some institutions have dealt with the problem by identifying intake sources of indigent patients (for example, emergency departments or outpatient services) and then "demarketing," or limiting access to, these services. Others have tried to differentiate access, convenience, and amenities for indigent patients versus insured patients. Still others have attempted to qualify the indigent for various types of funding.

One CEO explained his hospital's strategy for managing indigent patients as follows:

> Unless we have a financially viable organization, we cannot successfully treat anyone. What we have done is work with our medical staff so they will do more financial screening up front. We are also trying to get them to clear out their schedules, which are often backlogged with indigents, so that paying patients do not have to wait for months for service. We are now making indigents go through several hoops to try to qualify for funding before we provide the service. Since many of these patients are from rural areas outside this county, we try to get the county judges to agree to provide funding up front. Once the service has been delivered, there is no incentive for the patient to become qualified for funding or for rural county judges to agree to pay the bill. We have two different orientations toward convenience for those who can pay and those who cannot. Necessary care should be provided for everyone, and the quality of care should not be different between the two groups. But front-end screening for indigent is incredibly important to make sure they have exhausted all attempts to be funded by county governments, government programs, and other sources.

What would a key stakeholder map for the indigent care issue look like? In providing service to an indigent patient, the hospital administrator is influenced by legislative and judicial organizations, the funding they provide, and the threat of judicial sanction they might invoke. The threat of adverse publicity in the media must also be considered as policies regarding indigent care are developed and implemented. The indigent population in the area may also become activated as a nonsupportive stakeholder if the institution takes negative action regarding indigent care.

Private third-party payers (through cost shifting), government funding agencies (through cost shifting), and county
judges (through billed expenses) all have an economic interest
in the indigent care policy adopted by the institution. These
stakeholders would prefer to see a comprehensive economic
solution to the indigent care problem. However, lacking such
a solution, they prefer that the institution institute policies that
do not adversely affect their own financial condition. Ultimately, the taxpayers and their political representatives will make
the decisions regarding a more comprehensive solution and the
allocation of these costs among the various stakeholders. In the
meantime, individual institutions need to assess various approaches to reconciling their service mission, stakeholder pressure from indigents and their representatives, ethical concerns
versus cost-containment pressures from other stakeholders, and
long-term economic survival.

There are no absolute rules that a health care organization can use in responding to the indigent care decision. Balance is needed between the organization's long-term goal of
survival and the health care needs of the indigent community.
The benefit of the stakeholder approach to this issue is that all
key stakeholders are identified, and their particular stake is
considered as input into the decision. While this approach does
not guarantee higher quality decisions, it does increase the
probability that all viewpoints are considered.

The managers of stakeholders in health care organizations need to be sensitive to ethical issues and to avoid approaching stakeholder management from a cynical or manipulative perspective. This means health care executives should
view stakeholders from a long-term perspective and develop a
relationship based on mutual trust. The emphasis should be
on the *mutual* advantages of a long-term relationship.

Decisions regarding sensitive ethical issues need to be
made after the key stakeholders are identified in terms of their
stakes in the decision. The adoption of codes of ethics (like that
of the American College of Health Care Executives), use of
screening criteria for ethical decisions, and establishment of

ethics committees can also assist health care executives in ethically managing their stakeholders.

Future Stakeholders

As noted earlier, health care executives need to continually monitor their external and internal environments in order to identify new and emerging key stakeholders. Many stakeholders that were not identified as key stakeholders in Chapter Two were mentioned by health care executives as potential *future* key stakeholders. The following list provides a profile of these future stakeholders. Obviously, some of them are more relevant for certain organizations in certain locations. Moreover, we expect to see a greater future emphasis on documentation of cost and quality differences between providers, a stronger relationship between positive outcomes and reimbursement, more diversification, and more competitive pressures.

External Stakeholders	*Potential Impact*
Employers	Comparative performance data; potential joint ventures
Health-Care Coalitions	Comparative performance data; pressure for cost containment
Political Pressure Groups (e.g., AARP)	Comparative performance data; adverse publicity
Third-Party Payors	Restrict reimbursement to selected providers
Other Health Care Organizations	Political joint ventures
Local Community	Pressure to meet community needs
Economic Development Organizations	Facilitate growth in insured patients
Patients outside of local area	Enhance utilization
Clergy	Potential referrals

Educational counselors	Potential referrals
Internal Stakeholders	
Professional Employees	Commitment and productivity
Non-Professional Employees	Commitment and productivity

Employers, health care coalitions, and political pressure groups are all in the process of gathering more and more comparative performance data on individual institutions. These data evaluate relative costs and quality and can be used to help employers or others direct patients to the "better" facilities. Many third-party payers, such as insurance companies, are using such data to direct their enrollees to certain facilities for particular expensive procedures. The political pressure groups can also threaten the organization with adverse publicity. Both employers and other health care organizations offer potential joint venture partners.

An institution which focuses on local community needs can generate favorable publicity and a large amount of volunteer activity (Roberts, 1989). Otherwise, it may be subject to community pressure and adverse publicity. If the institution also works with local economic development agencies in the community it can boost its patient days in the long run (Solovy, 1988).

Hospitals are also beginning to look outside the immediate local area for new patients. Marketing of particular service programs to patients in rural areas can be done directly if there are no similar services in those areas. Such services can also be marketed indirectly through rural hospitals on the basis of reciprocal relations. The clergy and educational counselors are other potential future sources of patient referrals, particularly for children's hospitals and substance abuse hospitals.

Finally, professional or nonprofessional employees have much more to contribute potentially to the productivity of health care organizations than has yet been achieved. These internal stakeholders need to be more involved in their facility's management, as noted in Chapter Six.

Challenges for Researchers

As noted throughout the book, our research on stakeholder management in health care organizations has been exploratory, based on qualitative interview dates and very limited questionnaire results. Our analysis should be viewed as suggestive rather than definitive. There are many unresolved research issues, the resolution of which should help practicing health care executives better manage their stakeholders to achieve their strategic objectives.

Stronger conclusions for both theory and managerial practice could be drawn if large-scale, longitudinal, empirical studies were done on strategic stakeholder management in the health care industry as well as industry in general. Such studies would help us understand more clearly who the key stakeholders are, what their goals are, how to balance competing demands, how to solve particular stakeholder management problems, how to satisfy key stakeholders, and the impact of stakeholder satisfaction on other organizational outcomes.

The following list of questions provides an initial agenda for empirical research on health care stakeholders. Hypotheses could be developed for each of these questions based on the material reported in this book. Such hypotheses could be tested through field research based on both interview and questionnaires. In-depth panel interviews with health care executives could be used to develop a comprehensive set of effectiveness criteria with high face validity for particular types of health care organizations. This could be done by having panelists identify their most important external, interface, and internal stakeholders. The demands of each key stakeholder could be identified. Both the stakeholders and their demands could then be prioritized and compared to the organization's actual goals.

Stakeholder Identification and Demands

1. Who are the key stakeholders for different types of health care organizations? How do these vary by the business strategies being pursued?

2. What criteria of organizational effectiveness are applied to organizational outcomes by which key stakeholders? What weightings or priorities do these key stakeholders apply to each of these effectiveness criteria?

3. Do different subunits in the organization have different key stakeholders, and do the same key stakeholders apply different effectiveness criteria to different subunits?

4. How do the key stakeholders for particular types of health care organizations change over the organization's life cycle or in response to changing environmental pressures? Which stakeholders are becoming more or less important?

5. How do the goals and priorities of particular key stakeholders change over the organization's life cycle? Which are becoming more or less important?

6. How do otherwise similar organizations who identify different key stakeholders differ in terms of organizational outcomes such as profitability?

7. How well are the key stakeholder demands matched with the organization's goals?

Stakeholder Management and Satisfaction

8. Which generic stakeholder management strategies and specific tactics produce the highest degree of satisfaction with the organization on the part of each specific key stakeholder?

9. Does agreement between stakeholder demands and organizational goals facilitate stakeholder satisfaction?

10. Which generic and specific business strategies are associated with satisfaction or dissatisfaction of particular stakeholders?

11. How satisfied or dissatisfied are stakeholders in different types of health care organizations?

12. How is key stakeholder satisfaction associated with other measures of organizational effectiveness such as profitability and growth?

13. Is there a generally agreed-on comprehensive set of effectiveness criteria that key stakeholders apply to specific

types of health care organizations? If so, what are its components?

14. How does a change in the business strategy impact key stakeholders and their demands? How do changes in key stakeholders and their demands impact the business strategy of the organization?

Follow-up studies involving precise hypothesis testing on the dynamic nature of stakeholders and stakeholder demands as well as improvement in the reliability and validity of stakeholder demands will then be needed. The effectiveness measure of meeting key stakeholder demands could be correlated with hard measures of effectiveness such as profitability, growth, and resource acquisition to improve the validity of the stakeholder demands criteria. Research efforts could also be directed at the generalizability of stakeholders and their demands to all types of health care organizations. Finally, longitudinal studies of the dynamic nature of stakeholders and stakeholder demands and their reciprocal impact on business strategy are necessary. There is probably a dynamic interaction between key stakeholders and business strategists in the organization such that key stakeholders both influence and are influenced by the business strategy.

Putting It All Together

In the health care industry and industry in general the implementation of business strategy has been problematical. While strategy formulation has become more formalized, systematic, and sophisticated over the past decade, the resulting strategic plans often are hidden in file drawers. They do not drive the day-to-day activities of managers or other organizational participants. The meetings, telephone calls, and other management activities regularly occurring at the operational level are detached from any strategic considerations, and strategic goals are not reinforced. Strategic goals are either not attained or only partially attained.

The gap between the strategic level and the operational

level found in practice is also mirrored in the management literature. The strategic management and the organizational theory literature focuses more on the relationship between the organization and its external environment, while the organizational behavior and operations management literature focuses more on internal management processes. Consequently, there is no literature that focuses on the integration of the macro and micro perspectives of management.

We feel that management activity at the middle (meso) conceptual level has been neglected up to the present. In particular, we believe that the management of *key stakeholders* is crucial to attainment of the organization's strategic objectives. Stakeholders are those individuals and groups who have an interest in and are influenced by the organization. Since not all stakeholders are equally important to the organization or to the particular manager, each manager needs to focus on and strategically manage only *key* stakeholders. Which stakeholders are key depends on the nature of the decision (that is, the issue under consideration) and the value of a particular stakeholder's actual or potential contributions to the organization. Such contributions can be economic or noneconomic.

This book has extended existing stakeholder management theory and applied it to the health care industry. It has also provided much more detail about how a health care executive might apply the stakeholder approach to integrate her or his day-to-day activities with the organization's strategic objectives. The book draws on existing case studies, more than thirty in-depth interviews with health care executives, and a survey questionnaire to determine current practices and attitudes regarding the management of stakeholders.

We have also presented an analytical framework and detailed procedure for applying the stakeholder approach. Throughout the book we integrated theoretical and practical approaches to stakeholder management. Such an approach allows us to close the gap between macro and micro approaches to management theory. By discussing the special techniques and specific applications of stakeholder management, our book helps readers understand and put in practice those skills necessary for the effective strategic management of key stakeholders. By emphasizing the necessity for managing stakeholders ethically and for viewing stakeholder management as a dynamic process, this book also contributes to the professionalization of health care management.

We believe that stakeholder management *is* what health care managers *actually do*. They basically try to determine who is important on a particular issue at a particular point in time and then try to keep those stakeholders at least minimally satisfied with the inducements offered by the organization. In this way, they ensure that the necessary stakeholder contributions will continue to flow to the organization. To this point, stakeholder management has been done intuitively or picked up in the "school of hard knocks." There has not previously been a systematic approach developed in the literature concerning how to identify, assess, diagnose, and manage key stakeholders through various generic and specific stakeholder strategies and tactics tied to the organization's strategic objectives.

This book provides a new academic perspective on what health care management is and what health care executives do. It also closes the present gap between the macro and micro theories regarding managerial behavior. The arguments are intuitively compelling and are buttressed by numerous case studies, anecdotes, and quotations from health care executives. In particular, the research challenges discussed in this chapter might be used as a basis for future research on stakeholder management by empirically testing some of the relationships developed through qualitative evidence.

Chapters One and Two introduced the reader to the concepts applicable to strategic stakeholder management in health care organizations. In Chapter One concepts such as stakeholder, key stakeholder, different levels of strategy, inducements, contributions, disinducements, discontributions, and the strategic stakeholder management process were defined and illustrated. The increasing number, significance, and lack of supportiveness of health care stakeholders were also presented along with case studies of the effects of stakeholder management. Chapter Two further examined the theoretical under-

pinnings of strategic stakeholder management by defining, assessing, and illustrating the middle (meso) level of analysis (not
middle management), where stakeholder management integrates the strategic and operational activities of managers.
Stakeholder demands and pressures make the macro environment "real" to managers who have to interact with real people
who represent these stakeholders.

Chapters Three through Five described the generic processes involved in managing stakeholders. Chapter Three described the processes of assessing organizational stakeholders
and concluded with a toolkit of forms for assisting managers
to implement these processes. Chapter Four described the four
general stakeholder management strategies (involve, collaborate with, defend against, and monitor) applicable to supportive, mixed-blessing, nonsupportive, and marginal stakeholders. It also described an overarching strategy for moving
stakeholders from less supportive to more supportive categories. A case study and assignment of managerial responsibility
for various stakeholders are discussed. Chapter Five described
the generic process of negotiation with various types of stakeholders to achieve at least minimal levels of positive outcomes
and positive relations with stakeholders. Chapters Three through
Five also provided toolkits for practitioners to allow them to
apply the concepts to their own organizations.

Chapters Six through Nine provided detailed discussion
concerning the various strategies, illustrating how to apply the
generic strategies for managing particular stakeholders. Chapter Six discussed a wide variety of specific strategies for managing physician stakeholders, which require different degrees
of commitment of time and resources on the part of both physicians and hospitals. The physician perspective is also presented, since we believe that it is important for a manager to
understand the stakeholder's perspective to effectively manage
the stakeholder. Chapter Seven elaborated on one type of hospital-physician collaboration—the joint venture. The subtleties
of achieving both financial and collaborative success in joint
ventures were illustrated. Chapter Eight discussed what health
care executives can do to more effectively involve their own

internal stakeholders in achieving the organization's strategic objectives. Steps in implementing this involvement strategy were outlined and detailed. Finally, this chapter summarized the book's line of argument and addressed challenges facing both health care executives and health care management scholars.

Strategic stakeholder management, as outlined and detailed in this book, provides a new theoretical and practical perspective that we believe advances the field by integrating strategic and operational concerns. It also provides systematic guidelines to assist health care executives to do a better job of what they are already doing.

All of the health care executives interviewed for this book agreed that the management of stakeholders is the essence of what they do daily on their jobs. They agreed that this is the essence of health care management. Moreover, most claimed that they were already doing the process of stakeholder management intuitively since there is no book or manual that attempts to describe it. Nor is it taught in graduate programs or continuing education programs for health care executives. In addition to interaction, most learn it through observation, mentoring by more-senior executives, and the "school of hard knocks."

What has been missing in the literature until this time is a detailed, systematic process for managing stakeholders in general industry or in the health care industry. This is the unique contribution of this book, which details the process for managing stakeholders strategically. The following steps provide a convenient summary:

- Formulate a business strategy consistent with the organization's mission and goals.
- Identify all external, interface, and internal stakeholders relevant for implementation of business strategy.
- Assess each stakeholder in terms of core values, power sources, and power relative to the organization.
- Categorize each stakeholder as either key or marginal in general and in relation to particular decisions based on the corporate and business strategies being pursued.

- Diagnose each stakeholder in terms of potential for threat and potential for cooperation.
- On the basis of the above diagnosis, classify each key stakeholder as supportive, mixed blessing, or nonsupportive.
- Formulate generic stakeholder management strategies: involve the supportive stakeholder, collaborate with the mixed-blessing stakeholder, defend against the nonsupportive stakeholder, and monitor the marginal stakeholder.
- Implement these generic strategies by developing specific implementation tactics and programs for each.
- Determine what changes will be made if the targeted stakeholders fail to respond as desired.
- Determine what other employees as internal stakeholders should be involved in the implementation process.
- Determine what contingency approach will be used if the implementation process does not work as planned.
- Evaluate the success of both the corporate or business strategy being pursued and the management of key stakeholders.
- Modify the business strategy or stakeholder management strategy and tactics based on this evaluation.
- Continually monitor the environment to determine whether new strategies or new stakeholders need to be pursued.
- Repeat the process described above for all new stakeholders.

The detailed guidelines for implementing this process are shown in Chapters Three, Four, and Five. In particular, the reader can use the various toolkits provided in those chapters to identify and assess stakeholder values, diagnose and assess stakeholder power, and formulate and implement stakeholder management strategies and tactics. At each stage, ethical considerations should be an *explicit* part of both the business strategy formulation and implementations *and* the stakeholder management process.

References

Albrecht, K., and Zemke, R. *Service America.* Homewood, Ill.: Dow Jones–Irwin, 1985.

Alexander, J. A., and Morrisey, M. A. "Hospital-Physician Integration and Hospital Costs." *Inquiry,* Fall 1988, *25* (4), 388–401.

Alexander, J. A., Morrisey, M. A., and Shortell, J. M. "Effects of Competition, Regulation, and Corporatization on Hospital-Physician Relationships." *Journal of Health and Social Behavior,* 1986, *27* (3), 220–235.

American College of Healthcare Executives. *Code of Ethics.* Chicago: American College of Healthcare Executives, 1988.

Autrey, P., and Thomas, D. "Competitive Strategy in the Hospital Industry." *Health Care Management Review,* 1986, *11* (1), 7–14.

Bacharach, S. B., and Lawler, E. J. "Constituent-Representation Dimension of Bargaining." In S. B. Bacharach and E. J. Lawler (eds.), *Power and Politics in Organizations: The Social Psychology of Conflict, Coalitions, and Bargaining.* San Francisco: Jossey-Bass, 1980.

Baliga, B. R., and Johnson, B. "Analysis of an Industry in Transition." *Health Care Strategic Management,* 1986, *4* (12), 5–15.

Barber, D. "Health Care Firm Banks on a New Start." *The Birmingham News,* Nov. 8, 1987, pp. D1, D6.

Barlow, J. "Animal Rights Group Blasts Tech Research." *Lubbock Avalanche Journal,* Sept. 21, 1989, sec. C, p. 2.

Barnard, C. *The Functions of the Executive.* Cambridge, Mass.: Harvard University Press, 1938.

Barwick, M. R., and Alexander, R. A. "A Review of Quality Circles and the Existence of Positive-Findings Bias." *Personnel Psychology,* 1987, *40* (3), 579–591.

Beam, E. "National Healthcare's Ailments Mount: Shareholders Suit, Resignations Are Symptoms." *Wall Street Journal,* Sept. 4, 1987, pp. 2–3.

Bedeian, A. G. *Management.* Chicago: Dayden Press, 1989.

Bettner, M., and Collins, F. "Physicians and Administrators: Inducing Collaboration." *Hospital and Health Services Administration,* May 1987, *32,* 151–160.

Blair, J. D., and Savage, G. T. "Stakeholder Negotiation Strategies for Hospitals." Paper presented at annual meeting of the Health Care Administration Division of the Academy of Management, New Orleans, La., Aug. 9–12, 1987.

Blair, J. D., Savage, G. T., and Whitehead, C. "A Strategic Approach for Negotiating with Hospital Stakeholders." *Health Care Management Review,* 1989, *14* (1), 13–23.

Blair, J. D., Slaton, C. R., and Savage, G. T. "Hospital-Physician Joint Ventures: A Strategic Approach for Both Dimensions of Success." *Hospital and Health Services Administration,* Spring 1990, *35* (1), 3–26.

Blair, J. D., and Whitehead, C. J. "Can Quality Circles Survive in the United States?" *Business Horizons,* Sept./Oct. 1984, 17–23.

Blair, J. D., and Whitehead, C. J. "Too Many on the Seasaw: Stakeholder Diagnosis and Management for Hospitals." *Hospitals and Health Services Administration,* Summer 1988, *33* (2), 153–166.

Blau, P. M. *Exchange and Power in Social Life.* New York: Wiley, 1964.

Boland, P. (ed.). *The New Health Care Market: A Guide to PPOs for Purchasers, Payors and Providers.* Homewood, Ill.: Dow Jones–Irwin, 1985.

Bourgeois, L. J., III. "Strategy and Environment: A Conceptual Integration." *Academy of Management Review,* 1980, *5* (1), 25–39.

Bradford, D. L., and Cohen, A. R. *Managing for Excellence.* New York: Wiley, 1984.

Brenner, S. N., and Molander, E. A. "Is the Ethics of Business Changing?" *Harvard Business Review,* Jan./Feb. 1977, *56,* 57–71.

Brice and Mankoff. "The 'Safe Harbor' Rules." *Special Alert to Providers and Investors in Health Care Services.* Dallas, Tex.: Brice & Mankoff Attorneys and Counselors at Law, Sept. 13, 1988, pp. 3–6.

Brief, A., Aldag, R., VanSell, M., and Melone, N. "Anticipatory Socialization and Role Stress Among Registered Nurses." *Journal of Health and Social Behavior,* June 1979, *20* (2), 161–166.

Burke, G. C. "Understanding the Dynamic Role of the Hospital Executive: The View from the Top Is Better." *Hospital and Health Services Administration,* Spring 1989, *34* (1), 99–112.

Business Roundtable Statement on Corporate Responsibility. New York: The Business Roundtable, 1981.

Carroll, A. B. "Managerial Ethics: A Post-Watergate View." *Business Horizons,* April 1975, *18* (2), 75–80.

Carroll, A. B. "A Three-Dimensional Conceptual Model of Corporate Social Performance." *Academy of Management Review,* Oct. 1979, *4,* 492–504.

Carroll, A. B. *Business and Society: Ethics and Stakeholder Management.* Cincinnati, Ohio: South-Western, 1989.

Carswell, H. "Researchers Report Ongoing Progress in MR Angiography." *Diagnostic Imaging,* July 1988, *10* (7), 25–27.

Center for Nursing. *Restructuring the Work Load: Methods and Models to Address the Nursing Shortage.* Chicago: American Hospital Association, 1989.

Cerne, F. "CEO Builds Employee Morale to Improve Finances." *Hospitals,* June 5, 1988a, *62* (11), 110.

Cerne, F. "Collaborative Practice Benefits Nurses, Patients." *Hospitals,* Feb. 5, 1988b, *62* (3), 78.

Cherskov, M. "Clinical Integration Elusive but Possible." *Hospitals*, Jan. 5, 1987, *61* (1), 40.

Cleverley, W. O., and Stetson, R. C. "In Search of Excellence: Fact or Fiction." *Hospital and Health Services Administration,* Nov./Dec. 1985, *30* (4), 26–47.

Coddington, C. D., and Moore, K. D. *Market-Driven Strategies in Health Care.* San Francisco: Jossey-Bass, 1987.

Coile, C. C., Jr. *The New Medicine.* Rockville, Md.: Aspen, 1990.

Committee to Study the Role of Allied Health Personnel. *Allied Health Services: Avoiding Crises.* Washington, D.C.: Institute of Medicine, National Academy of Sciences, 1989.

Cornell, L. "Quality Circles: A New Cure for Hospital Dysfunctions?" *Hospital and Health Services Administration.* Sept./Oct. 1984, *29* (4), 88–93.

Counte, M. A., Barhyte, D. Y., and Christman, L. P. "Participative Management Among Staff Nurses." *Hospital and Health Services Administration,* Feb. 1987, *32* (1), 97–108.

Dalston, J. W. "Hermann Trauma Patient Rules." *Houston Post,* Oct. 1, 1989, pp. E1, E4.

Deming, E. *Out of Crisis.* Cambridge, Mass.: MIT Press, 1986.

Dennison, D. "Bringing Corporate Culture to the Bottom Line." *Organizational Dynamics,* 1984, *13* (2), 4–22.

Derr, C. B. "Managing Organizational Conflict: Collaboration, Bargaining, and Power Approaches." *California Management Review,* 1978, *21*, 76–82.

Droste, T. "Physician Marketing Pays Off in Admissions." *Hospitals,* Oct. 5, 1987, *61* (19), 48.

Droste, T. "Practice Enhancement: What MDs Want." *Hospitals,* Mar. 20, 1988, *62* (6), 44.

Dunlop, J. T. *Dispute Resolution: Negotiation and Consensus Building.* Dover, Mass.: Auburn House, 1984.

Easterbrook, G. "The Revolution in Medicine." *Newsweek,* Jan. 26, 1987, pp. 40–74.

Eudes, J. A., Divis, K. L., Vaughan, D. G., and Fottler, M. D. "Marketing Physician Services in an Academic Medical Center." *Health Care Management Review,* 1987, *12* (1), 37–45.

Fahey, L., and Christensen, K. H. "Evaluating the Research on

Strategy Content." *Yearly Review of Management,* Summer 1986, *12* (2), 167–184.

Fahey, L., and Narayanan, V. K. *Macroenvironmental Analysis for Strategic Management.* St. Paul, Minn.: West Publishing, 1986.

Filley, A. C. "Some Normative Issues in Conflict Management." *California Management Review,* 1978, *21,* 61–65.

Fisher, R., and Ury, W. *Getting to Yes: Negotiating Agreements Without Giving In.* Boston: Houghton Mifflin, 1981.

Fitzgerald, P. E., and Wahl, L. E. "Media Relations: Clues for Improvement." *Hospital and Health Services Administration,* Feb. 1987, *32* (1), 39–47.

Fottler, M. D. "Improving Health Care Planning: Some Lessons from Immunization." *Long Range Planning,* Oct. 1984, *17,* 88–95.

Fottler, M. D. "Health Care Organizational Performance: Present and Future Research." In J. D. Blair and J. G. Hunt (eds.), *1987 Yearly Review of Management* of the *Journal of Management,* Summer 1987, *13* (2), 179–203.

Fottler, M. D. "Strategic Human Resources Management." In N. Metzger (ed.), *Handbook of Health Care Human Resources Management.* Rockville, Md.: Aspen, 1990, 21–26.

Fottler, M. D., Hernandez, S. R., and Joiner, C. L. (eds.). *Strategic Management of Human Resources in Health Services Organizations.* New York: Wiley, 1988.

Fottler, M. D., and Maloney, W. F. "Guidelines to Productivity Bargaining in the Health Care Industry." *Health Care Management Review,* 1979, *3,* 59–70.

Fottler, M. D., Phillips, R. L., Blair, J. D., and Duran, C. A. "Achieving Competitive Advantage Through Strategic Human Resources Management." *Hospital and Health Services Administration,* forthcoming.

Fottler, M. D., Slovensky, D., and Rogers, S. J. "Public Release of Hospital-Specific Death Rates: Proactive Responses for Health Care Executives." *Hospital and Health Services Administration,* Aug. 1987, *32,* 343–356.

Fottler, M. D., and others. "Who Matters to Hospitals and Why? Assessing Key Stakeholders." *Hospital and Health Services Administration,* Winter 1989, *34* (4), 525–546.

Fredrickson, J. W. "The Comprehensiveness of Strategic Decision Processes: Extension Observations, Future Directions." *Academy of Management Journal*, Sept. 1984, *27*, 692–710.

Freeman, R. E. *Strategic Management: A Stakeholder Approach.* Marshfield, Mass.: Pitman, 1984.

Friedman, M. *Capitalism and Freedom.* Chicago: University of Chicago Press, 1962.

Gay, E. G., Kronenfeld, J., Baker, J. L., and Amidon, R. L. "An Appraisal of Organizational Response to Fiscally Constraining Regulation: The Case of Hospitals and DRGs." *Journal of Health and Social Behavior*, 1989, *30* (1), 41–55.

Grayson, M. A. "Survey Spots the Tight Turns in MD-CEO Relations." *Hospitals*, Feb. 5, 1988, *62* (3), 48–53.

Greenberger, D., Strasser, S., Lewicke, R. J., and Bateman, T. S. "Perception, Motivation, and Negotiation." In S. M. Shortell, A. D. Kaluzny, and Associates (eds.), *Health Care Management: A Text in Organization Theory and Behavior*, no. 3. New York: Wiley, 1988.

Greer, A. L. "Medical Technology and Professional Dominance Theory." *Social Science and Medicine*, 1984, *18* (10), 185–235.

Greer, A. L. "Medical Conservatism and Technological Acquisitiveness: The Paradox of Hospital Technology Adoptions." *Research in the Sociology of Health Care*, 1986, *4*, 185–235.

Griffith, J. R. *The Well Managed Community Hospital.* Ann Arbor, Mich.: Health Administration Press, 1987.

Hage, J. *Theories of Organizations: Form, Process, and Transformations.* New York: Wiley Interscience, 1980.

Hanlon, M. D., and Gladstein, D. L. "Improving the Quality of Work Life in Hospitals." *Hospital and Health Services Administration*, Sept./Oct. 1984, *29* (3), 94–107.

Herkimer, A. G. "Quality Circles: New Wave or Fad?" *Healthcare Financial Management*, 1984, *38*, 34–41.

Hermann Hospital. "To Every Citizen Concerned About Trauma Care in Houston." *Houston Post*, Oct. 1, 1989, advertisement, A19.

Holthaus, D. "HHS Outlines 'Safe Harbor' Business Practices." *Hospitals*, Oct. 5, 1988a, *62* (17), 53.

Hrebiniak, L. B., and Joyce, W. F. *Implementing Strategy.* New York: Macmillan, 1984.

Hurka, J. J. "Need Satisfaction Among Health Care Managers." *Hospital and Health Services Administration,* Summer 1980, *25* (2), 43–45.

Jensen, J. "Hospital CEOs: They Would Rather Fight than Switch." *Healthcare Executive,* Jan./Feb. 1989a, *4* (1), 20–21.

Jensen, J. "Programs to Support Physician Practices at 86 Percent of Hospitals." *Modern Healthcare,* June 30, 1989b, *19* (12), 36.

Johnson, E., and Johnson, R. *Hospitals Under Fire: Strategies for Survival.* Rockville, Md.: Aspen, 1986.

Johnston, R. "Negotiation Strategies: Different Strokes for Different Folks." In R. Lewicki and J. Litterer (eds.), *Negotiation: Readings, Exercises, and Cases.* Homewood, Ill.: Irwin, 1985.

Joint Commission for the Accreditation of Health Care Organizations. *Accreditation Manual for Health Care Organizations.* (1989 ed.) Chicago: Joint Commission for the Accreditation of Health Care Organizations, 1989.

Kahn, R. L., and others. *Organizational Stress: Studies in Role Conflict and Ambiguity.* New York: Wiley, 1964.

Kaluzny, A. D. "Revitalizing Decision-Making at the Middle Management Level." *Hospital and Health Services Administration,* Spring 1989, *34* (1), 39–51.

Kaluzny, A. D., and Shortell, S. M. "Creating and Managing Our Ethical Future." *Healthcare Executive,* Sept./Oct. 1987, *2* (5), 29–32.

Katz, D., and Kahn, R. L. The Social Psychology of Organizations. New York: Wiley, 1966.

Kaufman, N. "Rx for Imaging Center Turnaround Can Make a Champ out of a Loser." *Diagnostic Imaging,* July 1988, *10* (7), 77–79.

Keele, R. L., Buckner, K., and Bushnell, S. "Identifying Health Care Stakeholders: A Key to Strategic Implementation." *Health Care Strategic Management,* 1987, *5* (9), 4–10.

Khandwalla, P. N. "Effect of Competition on the Structure of

Top Management Control." *Academy of Management Journal,* 1973, *16,* 285–310.

Korukonda, A. R., and Blair, J. D. "Resource Dependence and Stakeholder Management: Strategies for Managers of Today's Health Care Organizations." *Proceedings of the Southern Management Association,* Nov. 1986, pp. 97–99.

Koska, M. T. "Low Cost Strategies Aid Physician Bonding." *Hospitals,* May 5, 1988, *62* (9), 60.

Kotter, J. P. "Managing External Dependence." *Academy of Management Review,* 1979, *4* (1), 87–92.

Kravetz, D. J. *The Human Resources Revolution: Implementing Progressive Management Practices for Bottom-Line Success.* San Francisco: Jossey-Bass, 1988.

Larkin, N. "Communication Can Prevent Med Staff Conflict." *Hospitals,* Mar. 20, 1988, *62* (7), 109.

Lawler, E. E., III. *High-Involvement Management: Participative Strategies for Improving Organizational Performance.* San Francisco: Jossey-Bass, 1986.

Lawler, E. E., III. "Choosing an Involvement Strategy." *Academy of Management Executive,* 1988, *2* (3), 197–204.

Lawler, E. E., III, and Mohrman, S. A. "Quality Circles After the Fact." *Harvard Business Review,* Jan./Feb. 1985, *63* (1), 65–70.

Lawler, E. E., III, Renwick, P. A., and Bullock, R. J. "Employee Influence on Decisions: An Analysis." *Journal of Occupational Behavior,* 1981, *2* (2), 115–123.

Lax, D. A., and Sebenius, J. K. *The Manager as Negotiator: Bargaining for Cooperation and Competitive Gain.* New York: Free Press, 1986.

Lindblom, C. E. "The Science of Muddling Through." *Public Administration Review,* Spring 1959, *19* (2), 79–88.

Longest, B. B., Jr. "Interorganizational Linkages in the Health Sector." *Health Care Management Review,* Winter 1990, *15* (1), 17–28.

Luke, R. D., and Begun, J. W. "Strategic Orientations of Small Multihospital Systems." *Health Services Research,* Dec. 1988, *23* (5), 596–618.

Luthans, F., Hodgetts, R. M., and Rosenkrantz, S. *Real Managers.* Cambridge, Mass.: Ballinger, 1988.

Lutz, S. "Chain Posts Record Loss in Fiscal '89." *Modern Healthcare,* Oct. 6, 1989, *19* (40), 14.

McColl, C. M. "Managers and Staff Improve Quality of Working Life." *Dimensions,* Feb. 1987, pp. 37–39.

McKinney, M. M. "The Newest Miracle Drug: Quality Circles in Hospitals." *Hospitals and Health Services Administration,* Sept./Oct. 1984, *29* (4), 74–87.

MacStravic, S. "A Customer Relations Strategy for Health Care Employee Relations." *Hospital and Health Services Administration,* Fall 1989, *34* (3), 397–461.

Mancino, D. M. "Hospital-Physician Joint Ventures: Some Crucial Considerations." *Hospital Progress,* 1984, *65,* 30–35.

March, J., and Simon, H. *Organizations.* New York: Wiley, 1958.

Mason, R. O., and Mitroff, I. I. *Challenging Strategic Planning Assumptions.* New York: Wiley, 1981.

Merton, R. K. *Social Theory and Social Structure.* (Rev. ed.). New York: Free Press, 1957.

Merz, M. "Preferred Provider Organizations: The New Health Care Partnerships." *Hospital and Health Services Administration,* 1986, *31,* 32–42.

Miles, R. E., and Snow, C. C. *Organizational Strategy, Structure, and Process.* New York: McGraw-Hill, 1978.

Miles, R. H. *Macro Organizational Behavior.* Santa Monica, Calif.: Goodyear, 1980.

Miller, D., and Friesen, P. H. "Archetypes of Strategy Formulation." *Management Science,* 1978, *24,* 921–933.

Mintzberg, H. *Power in and Around Organizations.* Englewood Cliffs, N.J.: Prentice-Hall, 1983.

Mintzberg, H. "The Strategy Concept I: Five Ps for Strategy." *California Management Review,* Fall 1988a, *30* (1), 11–24.

Mintzberg, H. "The Strategy Concept II: Another Look at Why Organizations Need Strategies." *California Management Review,* Fall 1988b, *30* (1), 25–32.

Morlock, L. L., Alexander, J. A., and Hunter, H. M. "Formal Relationships Among Governing Boards, CEOs, and Medical Staffs in Independent and System Hospitals." *Medical Care,* 1985, *23* (4), 1193–1213.

Morlock, L. L., Nathanson, C. A., and Alexander, J. A. "Authority, Power, and Influence." In Shortell, J. M. and Kaluzny, A. D. (eds.) *Health Care Management: A Text in Organization Theory and Behavior.* New York: John Wiley and Sons, 1988, 265–300.

Morrisey, G. L., Below, P. J., and Acomb, B. L. *The Executive Guide to Operational Planning.* San Francisco: Jossey-Bass, 1987.

Morrisey, M. A., and Brooks, D. C. "Hospital-Physician Joint Ventures: Who's Doing What?" *Hospitals,* May 1, 1985a, *59* (9), 74, 76, 78.

Morrisey, M. A., and Brooks, D. C. "Physician Influence in Hospitals: An Update." *Hospitals,* Sept. 1, 1985b, *59* (17), 80–89.

Morrisey, M. A., Shortell, S. M., and Noie, N. E. "A Survey of Hospital Medical Staffs—Part 2." *Hospitals,* 1983, *57,* 91–94.

Murray, E. A. "Strategic Choice as a Negotiated Outcome." *Management Science,* May 1978, *24* (9), 960–972.

Nash, L. L. "Ethics Without the Sermon." *Harvard Business Review,* Nov./Dec. 1981, *59,* 79–90.

Nigosian, G. J. "Board Operating Practice Subject of AHA Survey." *Hospitals,* Nov. 16, 1980, *54* (22), 81–85.

Osborn, S. "A Quality Circle Investigation." *Nursing Times,* Feb. 1987, *83* (7), 73–76.

Pearce, R. B. "Investigators Push for Wider Clinical Acceptance of MRI!" *Diagnostic Imaging,* May 1988, *10* (5), 130–145.

Perry, L. "Physician Ownership May Give Hospitals a Shot in the Arm." *Modern Healthcare,* June 30, 1989, *19* (12), 25–34.

Peters, T. *Thriving on Chaos.* New York: Knopf, 1987.

Peterson, K. *The Strategic Approach to Quality Service in Healthcare.* Rockville, Md.: Aspen, 1988.

Pfeffer, J., and Salancik, G. *The External Control of Organizations: A Resource Dependence Perspective.* New York: Harper & Row, 1978.

Phillips, R. L., and others. "Quality Circles in Healthcare Organizations: Pitfalls and Promises." In N. Metzger (ed.),

Handbook of Health Care Human Resources Management, no. 17. (2nd ed.) Rockville, Md.: Aspen, 1990, 137–146.

Porter, M. E. *Competitive Strategy.* New York: Free Press, 1980.

Porter, M. E. *Competitive Advantage: Creating and Sustaining Superior Performance.* New York: Free Press, 1985.

Powills, S. "Hospital-Physician Link Generates $4 Million." *Hospitals,* June 20, 1987, *61* (14), 56.

Powills, S. "Nurses: A Sound Investment for Financial Stability." *Hospitals,* May 5, 1988, *62* (9), 46–50.

"Pressure to Compromise Personal Ethics." *Business Week,* Jan. 31, 1977, p. 107.

Pruitt, D. G. "Strategic Choice in Negotiation." *American Behavioral Scientist,* 1983, *27,* 167–194.

Quick, J. C., Dalton, J., and Nelson, D. L. "Health Administration Can Be Stressful but Not Necessarily Distressful." *Hospital and Health Services Administration,* Sept./Oct. 1985, *30* (3), 101–129.

Quinn, J. B. *Strategies for Change: Logical Incrementalism.* Homewood, Ill.: Irwin, 1980.

Raiffa, H. *The Art and Science of Negotiation.* Cambridge, Mass.: Harvard University Press, 1982.

Roberts, C. C. "Copley Hospital's Commitment to Its Community." *Healthcare Executive,* July/Aug. 1989, *4* (4), 24–25.

Robinson, J. C., and Luft, H. S. "Competition and the Cost of Hospital Care, 1972–1982." *Journal of the American Medical Association,* June 19, 1987, *257* (22), 3241–3245.

Robinson, J. C., Luft, H. S., McPhee, J. J., and Hunt, S. S. "Hospital Competition and Surgical Length of Stay." *Journal of the American Medical Association,* Feb. 5, 1988, *259* (5), 696–700.

Robinson, M. L. "Rural Providers Ask: What's a Hospital?" *Hospitals,* Dec. 5, 1987, *61* (23), 48–52.

Roemer, M. I., and Friedman, J. W. *Doctors in Hospitals.* Baltimore, Md.: Johns Hopkins University Press, 1971.

Rosenfield, R. H. "Refocusing the Hospital/Physician Relationship." *Healthcare Executive,* 1988, *3* (5), 23–25.

Rosenfield, R. H., Mancino, D. M., and Miller, J. N. "Health Care Joint Ventures." In L. F. Wolper and J. J. Pena (eds.),

Health Care Administration Principles and Practices. Rockville, Md.: Aspen, 1987, 197–213.

Sandrick, K. "Multis Putting More Effort into MD Relationships." *Hospitals,* Mar. 5, 1988, *62* (5), 70–71.

Savage, G. T., and Blair, J. D. "The Importance of Relationships in the Hospital Negotiation Strategies." *Hospital and Health Services Administration,* Summer 1989, *34* (2), 231–253.

Savage, G. T., Blair, J. D., and Sorenson, R. L. "Consider Both Relationships and Substance When Negotiating Strategically." *Academy of Management Executive,* Feb. 1989, *3* (1), 37–48.

Schuster, M. H. *Union-Management Cooperation.* Kalamazoo, Mich. Upjohn Institute, 1984.

Shahoda, T. "Before You Buy, Take Time to Involve Medical Staff." *Hospitals,* Feb. 20, 1987, *61* (7), 76.

Sheldon, A., and Windham, S. *Competitive Strategy for Health Care Organizations.* Homewood, Ill.: Dow Jones–Irwin, 1984.

Shellenbarger, S. "As HMO Premiums Soar, Employers Sour on the Plans and Check Out Alternatives." *Wall Street Journal,* Feb. 27, 1990, pp. B1, B4.

Shorr, A. S. "The Physician/Hospital Joint Venture: Developing a Win/Win Strategy for Success. The First Step: Developing the Environment." *Health Care Strategic Management,* Feb. 1987a, pp. 4–8.

Shorr, A. S. "The Physician/Hospital Joint Venture: Developing a Win/Win Strategy for Success. Part II: Joint Venture Strategies and Considerations." *Health Care Strategic Management,* May 1987b, pp. 5–10.

Shorr, A. S. "The Physician/Hospital Joint Venture: Developing a Win/Win Strategy for Success. Part III: Structuring and Negotiating the Deal." *Health Care Strategic Management,* Aug. 1987c, pp. 4–9.

Shortell, S. M. "Theory Z: Implications and Relevance for Health Care Management." *Health Care Management Review,* 1982, 7, 7–21.

Shortell, S. M., Morrison, E. M., and Friedman, B. *Strategic Choices for America's Hospitals: Managing Change in Turbulent Times.* San Francisco: Jossey-Bass, 1990.

Shortell, S. M., Morrison, E. M., and Robbins, S. "Strategy Making in Health Care Organizations: A Framework and Agenda for Research." *Medical Care Review,* Fall 1985, *42* (2), 219–267.

Shortell, S. M., Wickizer, T. M., and Wheeler, J. R. *Hospital-Physician Joint Ventures: Results and Lessons from a National Demonstration in Primary Care.* Ann Arbor, Mich.: Health Administration Press, 1984.

Simon, H. *Administrative Behavior.* (2nd ed.). New York: Macmillan, 1957.

Simon, H. Smithberg, D., and Thompson, V. *Public Administration.* New York: Knopf, 1950.

Smith, H. L., and Reid, R. *Competitive Hospitals.* Rockville, Md.: Aspen, 1986.

Smith, H. L., and Fottler, M. D. *Prospective Payment: Managing for Operational Effectiveness.* Rockville, Md: Aspen, 1985.

Snook, D., and Kaye, E. *A Guide to Health Care Joint Ventures.* Rockville, Md.: Aspen, 1986.

Solovy, A. T. "Economic Development Means Patient Days." *Hospitals,* March 15, 1988, *62* (5), 37–38.

Southwick, K. "Report: Medical Testing May Swell Ranks of Uninsured." *Healthweek,* Aug. 22, 1988, *2* (17), 13.

Steel, R. P., Mento, A. J., Dilla, B. L., and Lloyd, R. F. "Factors Influencing the Success and Failure of Two Quality Circle Programs." *Journal of Management,* 1985, *11* (1), 99–119.

Strader, M. K. "Adapting Theory Two to Nursing Management." *Nursing Management,* Apr. 1987, *18* (4), 61–64.

Thibault, J., and Kelley, H. *The Social Psychology of Groups.* New York: Wiley, 1959.

Tokarski, C. "Physician Ownership Exceptions Approach." *Modern Healthcare,* July 7, 1989, *19* (13), 22.

Topping, S., and Fottler, M. D. "Improved Stakeholder Management: The Key to Revitalizing the HMO Movement?" *Medical Care Review,* forthcoming.

Vaughan, D. G., and Bamberg, R. *Hospital Utilization of Multiskilled Health Practitioners: A National Perspective.* Birmingham, Ala.: The National Multiskilled Health Practitioners

Clearinghouse, School of Health Related Professions, University of Alabama, Birmingham, 1989.

Walton, R. E. "From Control to Commitment in the Workplace." *Harvard Business Review,* 1985, *63* (2), 76–84.

Walton, R. E., and McKersie, R. B. *A Behavioral Theory of Labor Negotiations: An Analysis of a Social Interaction System.* New York: McGraw-Hill, 1965.

Weick, K. *The Social Psychology of Organizing.* Reading, Mass.: Addison-Wesley, 1979.

Weil, P., Williams, A., and Carver, M. "Hospital CEO Turnover: National Trends and Variations (1981–1987)." *Healthcare Executive,* Jan./Feb. 1989, *4* (1), 42–45.

Weiner, S. L. and others. "Economic Incentives and Organizational Realities: Managing Hospitals Under DRGs." *Milbank Quarterly,* 1987, *65* (4), 463–487.

Wheelen, T. L., and Hunger, J. D. *Strategic Management and Business Policy.* Reading, Mass.: Addison-Wesley, 1989.

White, D., and Wisdom, B. "Stress and the Hospital Administrator." *Hospital and Health Services Administration,* Sept./Oct. 1985, *30* (3), 112–119.

Whitehead, C. J., and others. "Stakeholder Supportiveness and Strategic Vulnerability: Implications for Competitive Strategy in the HMO Industry." *Health Care Management Review,* Summer 1989, *14* (3), 65–76.

Williams, K. "The Role of the Medical Director." *Hospital Progress,* June 1978, *59,* 52–57.

Wilson, D. J. "Ben Taub to Carry Load of City's Trauma Victims." *Houston Post,* Oct. 1, 1989, pp. A1, A20.

Winslow, R. "Medical Clash: Expansion of Hospitals into New Territories Draws Local Staffs' Ire." *Wall Street Journal,* Aug. 18, 1989, *84* (34), p. A1.

Zemke, R. *The Service Edge: 101 Companies That Profit from Customer Care.* New York: New American Library, 1989.

Zwanziger, J. "A Dangerous Concentration in Hospital Markets." *Wall Street Journal,* June 19, 1989, p. A10.

Index